# Conte[

C000254680

onlydo.online

URBAN BUSINESS SOLUTIONS

CLEARWATER

**Dedicated to Dear J.**

# Slide Tackles
# &
# Boardroom Battles

# David Mackinnon
**EDITED BY ALISTAIR AIRD**

**FOREWORD BY JOHN GREIG CBE**

First Edition.
First published 2023

Published by:
Morgan Lawrence Publishing Services Limited
Ridge House Annexe
16 Main Ridge West
Boston
Lincolnshire
PE21 6QQ
www.morganlawrence.co.uk
email: info@morganlawrence.co.uk
Company number: 12910264

©David Mackinnon, 2023
ISBN: 9781739296940

A CIP catalogue record is available for this book from the
British Library.

Photographs are courtesy of:
Trinity Mirror / Mirrorpix / Alamy Stock Photo, Bob Thomas,
Getty Images, SNS Group.

Cover design by LCgrapix. Cover photos by Trinity Mirror /
Mirrorpix / Alamy Stock Photo, Bob Thomas, SNS Group.

Every effort has been made to trace the copyright. Any
oversight will be rectified in future editions at the earliest
opportunity by the publisher.

Printed and bound in Bulgaria
by Pulsio Print.

# FOREWORD
## BY JOHN GREIG CBE

IN THE SUMMER of 1982, I needed a right full-back. Sandy Jardine, a world-class player who was a very good friend and colleague of mine, had always had an ambition to play for Hearts, so I allowed him to sign for them.

To replace Sandy, I went for David Mackinnon, a player who always impressed me when he played against Rangers for Partick Thistle. In David I saw a very humble, honest professional who would give you 90 minutes and more in every game. And he had one attribute that Sandy didn't have; he could tackle.

David was a quiet lad in the dressing room, but he mixed very well with the group. He was accepted by them because he was like Tam Forsyth, he gave you 100 per cent in every game. The other players appreciated that.

When David joined, I was trying to rebuild the team. We had a lot of older players in the squad, so I was trying to bring in some younger players. David was an experienced professional and he gave me everything that I asked of him and more. He was a very physical player, but the fact that he was only ordered off once in his career shows how good he was at tackling. To have that kind of disciplinary record in the position he played illustrates that David had good timing and tackled legally for the most part.

I lost track of a lot of players like David after I left Rangers, but I always kept an eye on his career. He was a pleasure to work with and I wish him all the very best with his book, *Slide Tackles and Boardroom Battles*.

# PROLOGUE

*February 2022*

IT WAS A wintry night in Edinburgh. I was chatting with two of my colleagues after a business meeting, and as we exited the venue, we reached a set of concrete stairs. The snow and sleet had made the stairs treacherous and I slipped. From that moment on, I recall nothing. The memories are much more lucid for my unfortunate colleagues, though, and they have since recounted how they watched me fall down 12 concrete steps and batter my head off a bottom lintel.

Fortunately, luck was on my side. During the COVID pandemic, much was reported about the time that it was taking ambulances to arrive at emergencies. But someone was looking after me. As blood spurted out from a ruptured artery to my brain, two ambulances arrived within 10 minutes of me falling.

Unconscious, I was rushed to hospital where the amazing staff in casualty at the Edinburgh Royal Infirmary fought to save my life as I bled out. I found out later that a vascular surgeon was on site and was able to suture the artery, further evidence that someone was looking after me.

As I recovered, I was very fortunate to have the support of my wife in dealing with this latest challenge. Times were very tough for around two months when the trauma of a head injury and a lesion on my brain created some unusual episodes, including severe anxiety, concussion and headaches. I also required therapy as I couldn't fathom out why I had been saved whilst others such, as Neale Cooper, the former footballer who had a similar experience, sadly didn't make it.

Once again, though, I had the support of a wonderful doctor at Inverclyde Royal Infirmary and gradually I've managed to get back to some normality in my job as Managing Director at ZLX, tax credit experts, supported by the staff and the company.

I also had an ally from an unlikely source – the PR man for the likes of Johnny Depp and Mike Ashley, Keith Bishop. Keith is the head of KB Associates, the top public relations agency in London. I'd been introduced to 'The Bish' by a friend, Ray Jones, on a business trip to London. Bish had gone through a similar experience a year before me when he fell down stairs at an English Premiership game.

Keith phoned on a regular basis to check up on me and offer advice on my latest headache or lapse in concentration. His re-assurance was instrumental in a quicker recovery and I thank him for that.

The accident gave me time to contemplate the past, the present, the future and what I wanted to do with whatever time I had left. I thought about my career, both in and out of the boardroom, and the players, managers, and teams that I'd played with and been an executive for. During my time recuperating, I spent 10 long weeks flitting from bed to the sofa and decided I was at last ready to get my experiences down on paper.

# CHAPTER 1
# THE RED BALLOON CHALLENGES

*February 2022 - Recovery*

THE SCARS ON my head are throbbing. My hair is heavily matted by the congealed blood and glue. I manage, with assistance, to get to the shower, but as the water cascades over me, the base turns a shade of red that is reminiscent of Ribena as blood is infused into the hot water. It's fair to say that I'm feeling sorry for myself.

During my career in football and business, I've overcome worse, but as I dry and return to bed, I recognise that a big challenge lies ahead.

Just like life, football is festooned with challenges. Each of them is thrown to test and teach us to ensure that we deal with the next challenge that will inevitably come our way. I'm no different from anyone and I'm amazed that somewhere from deep within, I've managed to reach my mid-60s feeling blessed to have had the life that I've had.

It is well-documented that early life experiences shape our adult thinking and help us as we deal with the twists and turns of life. That was most certainly the case for me, and from the day my late mother came home from hospital after my brother Alan was born, I have experienced many challenges. Some of them have been life threatening, while others have had a detrimental and damaging effect on my mental health. These early experiences are woven into our DNA and there is no doubt that they have an effect that lasts a lifetime. However, I have been able to rationalise challenges in my later life and realised that you can make changes to a pattern for the better. Touch wood, I've managed to survive!

My first challenge started early. I was born on 23 May 1956, three years and six months prior to my brother Alan. I had an idyllic first three years, before a barbaric procedure, prevalent in the 1950s, erased many parts of the loving mother that I knew. It's hard to fathom in this day and age, but as my mother developed post-natal depression following Alan's birth, she was taken into a psychiatric hospital where a dose of electric shock treatment was administered.

I was three and a half, but the memory of my mother being brought back into our house by my father has been embedded indelibly into my psyche to this day. The happy, caring mother that I'd known since I was old enough to understand was a poor soul, whose eyes had changed from sparkling, vibrant and loving to dark, soulless, and haunted.

The knock-on effect of this led to a life where only fleetingly the old character re-appeared, and every four years or so, another stay in the psychiatric ward was required.

For a young boy it was devastating, but my father, not without his own challenges in life, managed to keep the family together against what at times seemed unfavourable odds. Mercifully, I was able to overcome this early challenge and protect not only myself but my brother too.

This particular challenge constantly threw up numerous sub-challenges. I remember vividly being sent to primary school by my mother who was having a good day. I must have been around eight or nine at the time, kisses and cuddles were exchanged and I remember skipping to school feeling loved. It was great and I hoped that the 'good' mother was back.

But as I returned at 3 p.m. to our third floor flat in a typical west of Scotland sandstone tenement building, I quickly realised that the 'dark' mother had returned. I ran up the flights of stairs with a sense of anticipation of more cuddles and banged on the door. After a period of five minutes, my mother slowly opened the door and I could see instantly her mood, and her eyes, were dark. "Yes, little boy, what do you want at this door?"

I tried to push past her into the hallway, but my mother's left arm blocked my entrance. "It's me, Mum," I said, "It's David."

My mother stared deep into my soul and said, "David? There's no David stays in this house," before slamming the door in my face.

It felt like a dagger to my heart and I banged on the door shouting, "Mum, it's me, your son David."

From behind the door, she hollered, "Go away wee boy or I'll get the police."

With my attempts to gain entry by now forlorn, I retreated to the coal bunker on the half-landing and sat looking out into the backyard, trying to fathom what I'd done to upset my mother.

As darkness fell and the tenement lights came on, my father arrived home from his job as an engineer at a local firm.

He looked at me and said, "Is Mum not well again, Davie?"

"Yes, Dad," I replied. "She said there's not a David in our house."

My dad gave me a cuddle and a tobacco-soaked white milk sweet from his jacket pocket. I recall it had a horrible taste and that was one of the reasons why I have never smoked in my life.

My dad went up the stairs to the door of our house. He pulled out his bunch of keys, unlocked the door, and went inside.

I remained on the bunker for what seemed like a couple of hours until I heard footsteps on the landing. It was my Aunt Ella who was a senior nurse. She was a lovely woman who immediately made me feel calm as she cuddled me and looked into my eyes. She said, "I've spoken to the hospital, Davie, we'll get your mum in and make her better. Are you OK?"

I told her that I was and she left me and chapped the door lightly. My dad answered and they embraced and spoke to each other in Gaelic.

Half an hour later two ambulance men appeared and went into the house. A short time later they emerged holding my mum between them. She was crying and sobbed, "I'm sorry Davie. Mum's not well but I'm going to get better."

I understand many poor souls were given the same electric shock treatment in that era and I suspect that there are many people of my vintage out there who have experienced the same challenges that shaped their lives and relationships in many ways.

This circle of events happened many times during my formative years, and I managed to adapt and see the signs early, which was very helpful. As an adult, I became proactive rather than reactive when it came to getting my mother the treatment that she required to overcome, as best she could, the trauma that had been delivered to her by a system that appeared to have no compassion. I fought tooth and nail for my mother and family to ensure that she got the treatment she not only needed but deserved. But to do that there were still barriers to overcome.

On one occasion, I remember calling my mother's GP and advising him that she was at the start of the path towards that spiral of decline; I asked if they could provide the necessary support to have her admitted into the Dykebar Psychiatric Hospital for the treatment she needed.

Remarkably, rather than offer support, the doctor questioned me. He said, "Do you have a medical background?"

"No" was my terse reply, but I told him that I knew the signs when my mother's health was starting to deteriorate. After all, my family had lived with it for over 20 years.

"I'm sorry," said the doctor curtly. "If we were to respond to every *expert*, the NHS would be overrun."

I pleaded, "You're her doctor, you should know her history, and you should at least come and see her."

But he didn't come. Instead, he merely apologised again and put the phone down.

However, this particular GP hadn't accounted for my tenacity. My mother had written some disturbing letters about her previous time in Dykebar, so I decided to collect them and go to the doctor's surgery. Even being advised when I arrived that I couldn't see him unless I had an appointment didn't deter me. I simply asked for an appointment and was told to come back the next day at 10.30 a.m.

The next day I waited patiently in reception and was soon called into the doctor's office. As I entered, he asked what was wrong with me – he hadn't recognised the connection – so I took the letters from my coat pocket and put them on his desk. "I called you yesterday about my mother," I said. "These may be of help to you."

He opened the first letter and started reading. After a couple of minutes, he clicked his intercom. "Please can you get me the admissions doctor at Dykebar."

Within the hour my mother was admitted to hospital and the next in a long line of routes to recovery had started.

My mother and father were good people who provided wonderful support to our family, particularly when my mother was in remission. They tried hard during the difficult times that they were living in. Back then, mental health and the trauma that it inflicted was not acknowledged by society or supported fully by the medical fraternity. To a certain extent they had no option but to offer the stiff upper lip approach and to simply get on with it.

I carried a lot of things around for many years. During my football career, I didn't enjoy any success fully as I had this feeling that the bad times were just around the corner. It certainly affected my confidence at times, but I didn't fully appreciate how much until I engaged in some therapy following that near death fall in February 2022.

*****

My first real football challenge came when I made a huge mistake in leaving Arsenal. I joined the Gunners in 1972, but by the summer of 1976, I still hadn't made any real inroads into the first XI.

I was still under contract, and although I was yet to make a league appearance for the club, the manager Bertie Mee, a rather unique and unusual football boss and not typical of a top team leader, had told me that season 1976/77 was the one in which I would make the breakthrough.

I'd been in the first team squad on two occasions for games against Leicester City at Filbert Street and Chelsea at Stamford Bridge, but, unfortunately, there was only one substitute in those days, so my inclusion was as the 13th man. I was still grateful for the opportunity, as being involved did give me an insight into the preparation and focus required on match day, although in essence my roles and responsibilities were helping our kitman, Tony, with the kit and boots.

Player welfare was a totally different proposition at that time. Apprentices travelling from all around the country into the busy London metropolis were often left to their own devices.

I remember the first time that I arrived in London after I signed for Arsenal. I had to criss-cross the city's complicated transport network to get to my digs in Bounds Green. I had a map, but very little else when it came to knowledge of London. I was also dragging a huge suitcase – they didn't have wheels in those days – and I was lucky that I didn't run into the sort of unsavoury individuals that young boys and girls often fell foul of in the 1970s and 1980s.

On that subject, I met a young guy from Glasgow a year later. He had come to London with the best of intentions, but was dragged into various nefarious activities by a 'friendly' con man offering sustenance and a place to live. This particular kid was distributing flyers for a 'good time' at one of the Soho strip clubs and I often wonder what happened to him.

Leaving home at 16 years of age to travel 400 miles to a new environment was very difficult for me and others in the same position. Barely through puberty we had to manage the transition to adulthood on our own, whilst striving for full fitness – mentally and physically – within a hugely competitive and, at times, aggressive environment. Homesickness was a common feature for us all, and some, including the hugely talented Liam Brady, decided to go back home. He later returned to become one of Arsenal's greats.

My absence also had an impact on my family. I know that my younger brother, Alan, had a painful time adjusting, and my father also indicated that from time to time my mother's mental health suffered when I was away too. My brother was emerging as a talented player in his own right and after a successful trial, Wolverhampton Wanderers offered him a contract as an apprentice professional.

My father though, anxious not to put further pressure on my mother's mental health, with another son leaving the nest, decided not to support this move and the deal dissipated. I didn't find out about this until years later.

Alan did pursue a semi-professional route to complement his work as an industrial chemist with the likes of Dumbarton F.C. and several high-ranking junior sides; but I know that this had a devastating effect on him and into his 60s, he has still to let that particular red balloon challenge sail into the sky.

I am incredibly proud to say that I played in the same company as so many footballers who became household names.

A few of them went on to have hugely successful careers and to get so many top players coming through the club's youth system was incredible. Among them were the likes of, Liam Brady, Frank Stapleton, David O'Leary, John Devine, Graham Rix, Wilf Rostron, John Mathews, Trevor Ross, Richie Powling and David Price.

So, why would David Mackinnon have the audacity to leave a club that had such a productive youth policy? It's a question that I asked myself on a daily basis until a couple of years ago, when my lovely and astute wife told me that I'd held on to this for too long; it was time to "let the red balloon go."

'Letting the red balloon go' is a mental discard of something that you want rid of. I remember the day that I let my 'red balloon' sail high into the air and the weight of half a century of carrying it around suddenly disappeared into a metaphoric sky. I'll always be thankful to my wife for that.

We all make mistakes, but the learning comes in how you recover from them. Everything happens for a reason in my book and you always have a choice. My choice at that time was to tell the Arsenal manager, Bertie Mee, that I wanted to leave London and join Dundee in an attempt to find solace. I've lost count of the number of times that I rued that decision.

*****

I met some incredible people at Arsenal and in my time there I made so many memories, some of them good, some of them not so good. I'll expand upon the latter when I look at man-management later.

When I was with Arsenal, I played around the world. In February 1975 we played in a tournament in Iran. The event was organised by the Shah of Iran in honour of his son, who was an Arsenal supporter. After coming through knock-out stages held in Shiraz, Ahwaz, and Tehran, we were beaten on penalties in the semi-finals.

A year earlier we played in a tournament in Laupheim in West Germany, but this was the first proper cultural experience for us. The games around the country had attendances in excess of 30,000 and this provided an opportunity to play in front of partisan fans, all of which eliminated the fear factor which all young players have of playing in front of big attendances.

As the tournament progressed, we started to really gel as a team on the pitch, while off it, we were guided towards the cultural and social aspects of the country. The people were fantastic and our guide ensured that we were always engrossed by what we were seeing.

There were a couple of moments from that tour that I remember clearly. Iran at that time had a problem with stray dogs attacking people and livestock. This, we were told, was caused by families releasing domestic pets out into the countryside due to a lack of money to feed them. This situation had been going on for years and significant feral packs had formed throughout the country.

The Iranians referred to these packs as 'Joob' dogs and their existence and sporadic information on attacks by packs became a source of scare tactics at team excursions. "Better watch you don't get attacked by Joob dogs," became the mantra for any player going out of the hotel, or into bushes to collect balls at training venues.

It became an urban myth until the day that we went by bus from our base in Shiraz to the historical site of Persepolis. The journey took around an hour, traversing through dry country roads and villages with the constant sound of our guide giving a history lesson on each turn.

As we approached one village, the guide, knowing of our obsession with Joob dogs, announced that he'd heard that the villagers had secured a government bounty to kill one of the packs and that they had displayed them for collection and payment by government officials.

There was a stir on the bus as the players moved to the windows. As we drove through the village, dogs of various sizes and breeds were hanging by ropes from poles. It was horrendous and caused a great deal of distress. It took the lads a long time to get over it too. Despite the modern facade promoted by Iran, we knew then that it was still in the dark ages as the killing of domestic dogs was the badge of a barbaric country. When the Shah's empire fell five years later and the revolutionists took control, I knew that the country would be lost to fundamentalism.

I also played in Iraq, a country under the same conditions as Iran. That was in 1985 when I was with Rangers and I sadly witnessed a similar disregard for life. Thus, playing football in both Iran and Iraq are on my CV. I'll discuss later the reasons why the Rangers manager, the indomitable Jock Wallace, decided to take us into a war zone when he did.

*****

In addition to travelling far and wide, I was very keen to see a lot of football to develop my understanding of the game while I was at Arsenal. I could always get tickets courtesy of club officials, like Ken Friar and George Male, and I attended countless matches involving West Ham United, Tottenham Hotspur, and Chelsea. I went to games held at the iconic Wembley Stadium too.

I witnessed some wonderful players in the game in the 1970s and I marvelled at some of the household names that I saw on those midweek journeys through the London transport system. England at that time had a host of top players and I was fortunate enough to be present at some historic games at Wembley too.

There are two that stand out. The first was in October 1973 when England faced Poland in a qualifying match for the 1974 World Cup. The visiting goalkeeper was a chap called Jan Tomaszewski. Prior to the match Brain Clough had called him "a circus clown in gloves." But he heroically kept out the best that England could muster, the 1-1 draw saw Poland edge out England for a place in the finals in West Germany. Scotland, as was habitual in those days, qualified.

I was also at Wembley two years later, when Malcolm Macdonald scored all five goals against Cyprus in a qualifier for the 1976 European Championships. The experience of witnessing accomplished players like 'Supermac' was uplifting and I remember after games going back into training with a more rounded approach of how to play the game.

I also became a draw for school friends from back home. Several came down to watch games and training and on one occasion, one friend, who shall remain nameless, created a story of his own.

I received a phone call from him at the beginning of May 1975 asking if I could keep him one of the tickets that I was allocated as a player for the England v Scotland game at Wembley. The game was generally the culmination of the Home International series which also included Northern Ireland and Wales.

I duly received my tickets and arranged to meet him at Euston Station on the Friday before the game. As he arrived, I noticed that the only accompaniment to his double denim jeans and jacket was a small plastic bag. "You're travelling light," I said as he passed through the ticket barrier.

"Aye," he said as he pulled open the bag. "Just my Scotland flag and a toothbrush," he said proudly. "I'm sure you'll have spare pants?" he asked.

"That'll be right, you're on your own," was my terse reply.

We travelled back to my digs where he had kindly been allocated an area of floor in the dining room. That night we went into the West End and met up with the throng of Scotland supporters.

He was a bit the worse for wear in the morning but sobered up as we travelled across to Wembley. The game was of the usual competitive variety, but England were superior in every department and thrashed Scotland 5-1.

"I'll need to drown my sorrows tonight," he said as we travelled back into Central London. We were together until around 9 p.m. at which point he went to the toilet and never came back!

As I returned alone to my digs, I left the door on the latch hoping that he'd make his way back. There were no mobile phones in those days, so his return was in the lap of the Gods.

I woke up the next morning to find him in my bed, albeit with his head at the bottom and his feet in my face.

"Oi, wake up," I said. "Your train is at one o'clock."

He was naked but as he stirred, I became aware of a terrible smell in the room.

His jeans were lying on the floor and the smell was emanating from within them. I lifted them up and he'd defecated in his pants, which were lodged and spread inside his jeans. The smell was disgusting.

He moved to his feet and grabbed the jeans and went to the bathroom. Just 10 minutes later he arrived back in the room with the jeans on. "I've put my pants in the bin and I'm going commando," he laughed. "You got a pair of pants I can take?"

I reiterated my reply of the previous day, cleaned up my room and left the digs to travel back to Euston. As we arrived, there was a market set up outside. "Get yourself a new pair of jeans," I said. "You're stinking".

We found a stall selling denims and he started picking up different jeans, "I only wear Levis," he said, "They've no' got any."

"Just take these," I said as I pointed to some denims on a table. The guy put them in a bag and my schoolmate paid for them.

"I'll put them on when I get on to the train." He smiled as he made his way on to the platform which was festooned with Scotland fans singing despite the hammering of the previous day.

As he stepped on to the train, I said, "Give me a phone at the digs once you're home, ok?"

"Aye, nae bother," he replied and he was off.

Around 8 p.m., the phone rang in the digs and the landlady said, "That's your mate on the phone, David, he got home safely."

I walked into the hall and lifted the receiver. "Hello, so you got home alright?" I asked.

"Aye just in, but I had a nightmare. I was in a carriage wi' boys fae Paisley and the heating was on. The smell was terrible, and they told me to get out. I went to the toilet and pulled off my jeans and threw them out the window."

He paused for a second. "I then went into the bag for the jeans, and it was a fucking denim jacket! He sold me a denim jacket instead of jeans!"

"I had tae tie my jacket aroon ma waist tae hide ma willie."

*****

The Gunners had just won the First Division championship (the predecessor of the Premiership) and the FA Cup to complete the double in season 1970/71. I joined them in the summer of 1972, and in the previous season, they had lost out to Leeds United in the FA Cup Final and finished fifth in the league, six points behind champions Derby County. I had to pinch myself several times on the first day of pre-season training when the likes of Charlie George, Bob Wilson, George Graham, Frank McLintock, Pat Rice, Peter Marinello, John Radford, Ray Kennedy, and Bob McNab treated me like I was a seasoned pro.

They were all wonderful men and bona fide legends of Arsenal Football Club.

Their help gave me a tremendous grounding in the art of how to play the game with a professional head on, and I quickly became competent in training and games.

But there was one peculiar training concept in particular that gave me a real understanding of positional play and how to create space and influence games. On the face of it, the idea of playing a game without a ball seems bizarre, but every so often Steve Burtenshaw, our coach, would announce a game, first team against reserves, on the showcase pitch where we trained at London Colney.

We would be lined up in our positions and Steve's whistle would announce 'kick off'. He would do a running commentary of where the imaginary ball was, and stop the game periodically, for the players to adjust their position to the 'ball' location.

The *game* lasted for around an hour and from my perspective it was a great learning experience. After a few weeks raising your thought process to fully understand positional play, the *games* became very competitive with tackles flying in.

We usually had groups of fans allowed in to witness training, but on days when the 'no ball' games took place, a large sign was placed at the entrance stating *Closed session today.* I can only imagine this was to deter fans from witnessing the ball-free game as they may well have thought the management team had gone mad.

As with all team training sessions, there are always a few players who try and inject some humour. About six games into this training exercise, I remember wee Geordie Armstrong, a nippy winger, and a really decent man, running into the box with the imaginary ball tied to his feet, before being upended by one of the centre halves. He went down and Steve pointed to the penalty spot. It was becoming surreal but the team spirit amongst the squad was top notch and we stood around the penalty box as if it was a real game. Alan Ball put the 'ball' on the spot and Geoff Barnett, the reserve keeper, came out and picked up the imaginary ball before placing it back on the spot in an effort to psyche out the wee man. Bally laughed, re-spotted the 'ball' and promptly sent Geoff the wrong way!

Steve then blew for full-time and I remember feeling part of something as we made our way back to the changing rooms, with amazing banter rattling about.

I've relayed the story to a few of my team-mates and managers at other clubs; it appears that the 'no ball' concept was nothing new for the players who'd played in England as they had experienced something similar at their clubs.

I've often wondered what would be made of an Old Firm no ball game. The thought makes me laugh as I still think there would be a few bookings and red cards even without a ball!

My early games for Arsenal came in the South-East Counties league. One of the first league matches that I played in was a 9-0 win over Reading in August 1972. There was a bit of a collector's item in that match too, a goal from D. Mackinnon! That wasn't the last high-scoring game that season either. There was a 5-5 draw against Millwall and a 7-1 win away from home against Luton Town too.

We would finish as runners-up in the league that season, three points behind our great London rivals Tottenham Hotspur. I was a regular in the team – I think I played in something like 27 of the 32 league matches – and it was a magnificent experience playing against the likes of Glenn Hoddle at Spurs, Ray Wilkins at Chelsea, and George Burley at Ipswich Town.

Those games provided a stern test, one that gave you an insight into how high the standards were at that time. Each team was filled with ambitious young bucks like me who were trying to make an impression so that they could knock on the door of the reserves, then make inroads towards the first team. That made for a competitive environment, something I relished.

I recall one game against a Leyton Orient side featuring the precocious talents of the late Laurie Cunningham. Laurie was a speedy winger, who went on to play at West Bromwich Albion, Real Madrid, and Manchester United among others. Sadly, he was killed in a car crash in Madrid, at only 33 years of age, such a tragic loss.

There was a lot of talent in our team too and it was easy to fit in. Adopting a 'give and go' philosophy, my role was to win the ball and play it to the likes of Liam Brady and Graham Rix to work their magic. As I progressed into the reserves it was the same arrangement, although I didn't really become a regular at that level until season 1974/75.

Our second XI contained guys like me who had graduated from the youth team, and we were joined by guys from that great Double winning team from 1970/71. They were either returning from injury, or out of favour with the manager. Playing alongside these experienced professionals was something else that helped with my development as a player.

Among those experienced pros were Pat Rice and Alan Ball, both of whom seemed to single me out for extra support and guidance. At that time, I was flitting between right full-back and centre midfield, and now I had two players who excelled in those positions taking me under their wing.

Pat had joined Arsenal as an apprentice in December 1964. He made his first-team debut at the age of 18 in a League Cup tie against Burnley, and he became a regular at right back in season 1970/71 – that fabled Double-winning campaign – when Peter Storey was moved into midfield.

He was an excellent full-back and a lovely man. He used to take me for some extra coaching in the afternoon. His tuition was always clear and concise, so it was no surprise when he became club captain in 1977 and then assistant manager at the club during the successful years under Arsene Wenger.

It was Pat who taught me arguably the most important pieces of defensive discipline for a full-back, one that I would use throughout my career.

George Best was a hero of mine when I was growing up. I'd seen him in the flesh many times at Highbury and although his skill impressed me, what stood out was his courage. He would get battered from pillar to post, but time after time he would get up and go again.

Pat was a direct opponent when Arsenal faced Manchester United and was also a teammate at international level with Northern Ireland. He, therefore, knew George and how he played better than most, and he would take me on the Highbury pitch after training and say, "I'm Bestie, how do you play me?"

Pat would move his body from side to side with the ball stationary. "See, he moves his body, and the ball never moves, so keep your eye on the ball and you'll get a touch."

We would then practice this strategy of crouching down and keeping your eye on the ball. I perfected the technique and in reserve games I was able to take the ball cleanly from players, although admittedly they were not of Bestie's calibre. That brought me to the attention of the manager, Bertie Mee, and he used to take me aside and say, "You're next in my team, son, keep it going." Little did he know that my progression was owed to the man whose place he wanted me to take.

The other great influence on me was Alan Ball. A World Cup winner in 1966, Bally arrived at Highbury for what was then a British record transfer fee of £220,000 in December 1971. He was the epitome of perpetual motion. Although he was disliked by the majority of Scottish fans, I loved him. He was a wonderful man who gave me another lesson which I used throughout my career. "Right, son," Bally would say in the famous high-pitched voice. "You can run and tackle so what I want you to do is run and tackle in the first minute and run and tackle in the last minute."

"Why's that, Bally?" I'd ask.

"Because, son, people at the game – fans, managers, scouts – remember the start and finish of a game so if Mackinnon's the guy that catches their eye in the first and last minute then you're the man."

That was another valuable lesson, and one I used throughout my career.

Bally was an exceptional human being and he knew how to look after young players. I was honoured to be taken under his wing, and I have countless great memories of our time together. But there are two occasions that stick out more than most.

The first was after a reserve game at Highbury when my room-mate, Frank Stapleton, and I excelled in the exceptional company of legends, such as Bally, Peter Simpson, Frank McLintock, John Radford and Charlie George. In Bally's opinion, Frank and I were the star men. I was at right back and that day I executed Pat Rice's 'keep the eye on the ball' tactic to perfection, A clean tackle when the winger made his first dart into the penalty area drew applause from the Highbury crowd, which numbered around 5,000, not uncommon for second XI fixtures at that time.

I recall coming up against Tommy Hutchison of Coventry City, too. Tommy was an exceptional winger whose signature move was coming up to the full-back, moving his hips before pushing the ball past into the crossing area. As he moved those hips, I only had eyes for the ball. I heard Pat's dulcet Irish tones in my ears – "watch the ball" – as Tommy shifted his weight onto his right side. I knew the next move was to move past into the space and my time had come to slide in and not only win the ball but to keep possession. Tommy looked shocked but in a second, I dragged the ball forward and passed to Bally who was, as always, available.

Later as I returned to the digs for the evening, the doorbell rang. I was surprised to find Bally on the doorstep. "The guys wanted to thank you for your contribution today," he said as he swept his arm to the street where Frank McLintock's Jaguar was parked. Frank and John Radford were waving out the window. "C'mon," said Bally. "We're taking you to Catford dogs, bring all the money you've got." I rummaged around and mustered what I had. It wasn't much – by a Saturday night usually all I had left of my wages was a fiver!

I grabbed my jacket and jumped into Frank's car and within the hour we were at the Catford greyhound racing track. "Right," says Bally. "I've spoken to the trainer with a dog in the first race and he's going for it. Dog number 10 at 10- 1, give us all you've got." I handed over my fiver and I remember thinking that was me cleaned out even before the second race on the card.

The traps snapped up and dog 10 won by several lengths. I was jumping up and down. *Ya beauty*, I thought. *That's £50 plus my stake.*

Bally disappeared to collect the winnings, which I was already thinking of spending by taking a trip to the fashion boutiques on Carnaby Street.

Bally returned five minutes later. "Right put out your hand," he said before he started counting out loud, "10, 20, 30, 40, 50, 60 . . ." I shook my head in disbelief: I had never seen so much money. But Bally wasn't finished, stopping only when he got to 105.

I recall blurting out, "But, Bally, I only gave you a fiver."

Frank, John, and Bally started laughing and Bally shrieked, "We know what your wages are, so we thought we'd add a fiver to your stake as it was a dead cert. You deserve it after the performance you gave to the team today."

Princes amongst men! It could have turned me into a seasoned gambler at that point, but instead, I was simply an awe-struck young player in the presence of a trio of true legends.

The second Bally story started at the Arsenal Christmas party. I think it was in 1975. The club had booked an Italian restaurant for all the players. After training at London Colney, we had returned to Highbury to be given our 20lb Norfolk turkeys, which were dispensed in a brown hessian bag. I was going home to Scotland on the late train as the reserve fixtures had been cancelled for the festive season. En-route to the restaurant I'd gone to the left luggage lockers at Euston to leave my turkey and my travel case for collection later.

At the lunch I sat between Bally and Frank McLintock and Bally said we'd been invited to the BBC studios at White City, as they were recording the Christmas *Top of the Pops*. When the lunch finished, we grabbed a taxi to Television Centre where Bally, with me in tow, was ushered into the studio. All the big acts were there and they all wanted to chat to Bally. I hung about like a bad smell, but I was sticking with it. I had long hair, flares and a hooped tank top on so I fitted the mid-seventies audience profile. As Bally went away to speak to someone, I was suddenly ushered to the dance floor where a song was playing. As was my wont I shuffled into my best dance mode and moved around the audience. The music stopped and Bally re-appeared before I wished him a Merry Christmas and left for my train.

I arrived in Glasgow Central and got the bus from St Enoch's to my family home in Renfrew with the turkey still intact in the bag. I gave the bird to my mother, and she pulled it out of the bag and sat it on top of the small blue and white enamel cooker. It was one of those four ring hobs with a tiny oven and my dad had to be summoned to stuff the large bird onto a tray before pushing it inside. "This is going to have to be on all night to make sure it's cooked," said my mother in a posh voice. This was one of her better days.

The oven was duly switched on and we retired to the living room.

The turkey was left to cook overnight, but when I woke up on Christmas morning, I went into the kitchen and nearly crashed into the table. The linoleum floor was flooded with grease which had emanated from the cooker. I think Christopher Dean would have admired my poise as I managed to avoid injury as I skated across the slippery surface.

My mother arrived and gracefully glided over to the oven and switched it off. She was an accomplished skater and I shouted, "A perfect 10 for Margaret Mackinnon".

My father arrived and said, "Wait till it cools and I'll get a shovel to stick the grease in the bin."

Later as the grease found its way into the communal bin, I asked my mother if I could put on *Top of the Pops*. We all sat in the living room with our eyes transfixed on the 15-inch Grundig TV we had courtesy of Glen's TV rentals. My mother started singing before stopping mid-song to shriek, "Oh son, that boy dancing looks like you."

A casual smile ran across my face, "It is me, Mum," That was one of our most memorable Christmases.

Bally also tried to talk me out of going to Dundee. I played in an end of season tournament in Holland in May 1975 for the youth team. We played games in Haarlem and Deventer, and thanks to Bally's 'perpetual motion' advice, I had played very well in midfield throughout the tournament.

In the final we defeated Dundee 1-0, and after the match both teams attended a reception. It was there that I was approached by the Dundee manager, Davie White. Davie, who had also managed Rangers for a couple of years, took me aside and said he wanted me join Dundee on loan. He dangled the carrot of guaranteed first-team football too.

I went on loan to Dens Park for a month, but when I came back to London, my first-team chances hadn't changed. *Decision time, David*, I said to myself – boy did I rue the one that I made!

In March of 1976, I decided to go and speak to Bertie Mee. He had previously told me I'd get some opportunities to play league football for Arsenal, and I asked him why that hadn't happened. I also asked if I had a first-team future, as at the age of 20, I wanted to take that next step and play for the top team. At that time, Arsenal were languishing near the bottom of the First Division, and Bertie felt that it wasn't the right time to pitch me in. He did, however, assure me that I'd get a chance once the team was in a better league position.

To this day I don't know why I didn't take Bertie at his word, accept the situation, and get on with it. Instead, I elected to say, "Well, if you can't guarantee me a first-team place then release me from my contract and I'll sign for Dundee." I regretted those words for years afterwards.

In actual fact, though, my head had been turned. Dundee offered me an incredible signing on fee and a sizeable contribution to a new house. On reflection now, those financial incentives were at the forefront of my mind when I spoke to Bertie about my future at Arsenal.

I remember the look of shock on Bertie's face as I stormed out of his office. I went back into the marble dressing rooms in the bowels of Highbury, and Bally was there. He was aware that I had been summoned to the manager's office and was waiting for me.

"How did you get on?" he asked.

I replied, "I'm leaving, Bally. He couldn't guarantee me first-team football, so I've told him to rip up my contract. I'm going to Dundee."

Bally's face mirrored that of Bertie's. "You're making the biggest mistake of your career, young man. Get back up those stairs and apologise. I'll come up with you if you want?"

"Naw Bally, there's no going back," I retorted.

At that point, I shook his hand and went to collect my boots. As I went into the boot-room, I saw Bally run up the stairs to the laundry room. As I was walking out, Bally appeared by my side. He had a jersey in his hand and handed it to me. It was a number 8 shirt that he had worn. "Reconsider," he pleaded. I was on the verge of walking away from one of the biggest clubs in English football with the club captain and World Cup winner, Alan Ball, suggesting that I stay put. I still can't fathom why at that point I simply shook my head and left the building.

*****

I often reflect back on some surreal memories from my time at Arsenal. I remember one day I that arrived at our training ground, and our assistant manager, Bobby Campbell, called me into his changing room. "Ricey's got a cold so get yourself into the first-team dressing room, young man. You're playing in the friendly against Luton this morning. This is a big chance for you, so don't fuck it up."

A mixture of joy and nerves started to course through my body, and I started to smile. Admittedly, it was a friendly played behind closed doors at London Colney, but that didn't matter to me; I had waited a long time for this moment.

I went into the dressing room and Bally was the first one to shake me by the hand. He said, "Big chance Dave, do you want to wear the boots you've been breaking in for me?"

Now Alan Ball was an iconic figure, and he was recognised for wearing white boots. As often happened, the stars don't like to have the pain of breaking in new boots, so they get apprentices or reserves to do the needful. Bally had chosen me to break in his boots in training, and I had done so for over a year. Bally always complemented me on how well I stretched his new boots to allow him to use them on match day, so not at any point in that year did I have the desire or courage to tell him that my feet were a size bigger than his.

But as I prepared to face Luton, I respectfully declined his offer saying, "No, Bally, I'll wear my own, thanks. There's only one pair of white boots in this team."

With a pair of black size eights on my feet, I took up my position at right back. I can't remember much about the game other than we won it quite comfortably, 4-1, I think.

One memory that I have retained is the contribution made that day by the Luton Town chairman, Eric Morecambe, one half of the legendary comedy duo, Morecambe and Wise.

There were no linesman and the referee asked if each team could provide someone to run the line.

I think our youth coach, Ian Crawford, stepped in for us, and Eric, resplendent in a sheepskin coat and deerstalker hat, reciprocated for Luton. He also ran the line with a pipe glued to his mouth.

As the game moved into the second half, I stepped out to leave the Luton left winger yards offside. Eric, running the line beside me, shouted, "Onside referee, play on."

The winger crossed the ball into the box and their centre forward scored a consolation goal. The Scottish will to win mentality kicked in and I shouted at the referee. "He was a mile offside, ref, the linesman's having a laugh."

Eric stopped and shouted over to me. "I make people laugh

young man; I don't laugh at others. Well onside." He smiled and walked back to the centre line and the game kicked off.

After the game, Eric came over to me and shook my hand. "A mile offside, young man, but we need all the support we can get." He laughed and walked away.

The appearance at least afforded me the luxury of being first in the bath. Believe it or not, we didn't have showers after training but filled steel baths to bathe in. There was a system of hierarchy where the baths were filled with water by the apprentices, then used by a first-team player, followed by the reserves, before lastly, the apprentices were allowed to bathe.

After many sessions of being last and bathing in discoloured, brown water, I found myself wallowing in a crystal-clear, clean bath for the first time as an Arsenal player.

This practice of communal bathing was prevalent at all teams that I played for during my 20-year career. Every team had a large bath where after training and on match day, all players stripped naked and bathed in each other's mud and dirt. I must also confess that occasionally certain players found it funny to defecate in the bath and we were always on the lookout for brown coloured floaters. I can only imagine the furore among today's pampered players if the practice of communal bathing would be allowed or supported.

\*\*\*\*\*

Another episode involving a linesman happened just after I'd joined Arsenal as an apprentice. We'd played a youth team match in the morning – we beat our great rivals Spurs by three goals to one – and it was customary for us to attend every home game at Highbury for dressing room and support duties. This entailed being on hand to assist with any kit matters, and to clean the dressing rooms after the game. It was a great education for us and allowed us to get backstage and access all areas in both the home and away dressing rooms.

I was sitting just behind the dugout for the game against Liverpool, when youth coach Ian Crawford came up to me and said that I had to go into the dressing room corridor to help Tony the kitman. "The linesman's pulled a muscle," he casually added.

Dennis Drewitt was the chap who had got himself injured, and I must have been en-route to the dressing room when an announcement was made over the tannoy asking if there was a qualified referee among the crowd. The match was on the verge of being abandoned.

When I got to the dressing room, Tony was talking to TV pundit and ex-player, Jimmy Hill. I thought it was simply a coincidence that Jimmy was there. Little did I know that Jimmy was the qualified referee that was needed to ensure the game was played to a conclusion.

Tony was from Ireland, so we had a Celtic connection. He said, "Dave, get up to the laundry and get a large coach's kit, light blue tracksuit, black sweatshirt, shorts and black socks. Oh, and a grab a pair of boots from the boot room too."

I scurried up the stairs to the laundry room, gathered the kit plus a towel, then ran back down via the boot room, where I lifted my new size 8 boots.

Tony nodded his head in approval and Jimmy shook my hand and went into the referee's room. He emerged five minutes later wearing all the gear that I had collected, including my boots. *At least my boots have made their Highbury debut*, I thought, as I made my way back pitch side. I found out later Jimmy was a size 10 and changed boots at half time, but I appreciate the fact that he broke mine in for me!

Jimmy had a quiet game despite the array of stars on view, and the uneventful encounter finished goal-less. At the end of the season, Liverpool were crowned champions, while we ended up three points behind them in second place.

I watched the highlights later on *The Big Match* to see if I appeared in any footage, but sadly I didn't. Jimmy couldn't resist advising that he had a flawless performance and his tip to linesmen was to listen for the sound of the ball being kicked to better judge if someone's offside. What would the refereeing fraternity have done if Jimmy hadn't given that advice? Jimmy Hill was a true showman who recognised an opportunity when it came along.

## CHAPTER 2
# INJURIES AND THE POWER OF RECOVERY

I FACED AND surmounted a number of challenges in my career, but some of the most demanding were medical ones.

Injuries are a common occurrence in a contact sport like football, and as a defender, the added physicality of tackling put me at risk every time that I went on the park. I never shirked a challenge, though, despite the risks involved.

So many players have had their careers ended prematurely by injury, so I consider myself fortunate to have spent two decades as a professional and only missed around 100 games due to injury.

The misfortune I had, though, was that when the injuries came, they did so at crucial points in my career. My pathway in football may have been considerably different had I not suffered the injuries when I did.

I first experienced the physical and mental anguish that goes hand-in-hand with being an injured footballer when I was with Arsenal.

By this point I was spending most of my time at full-back. One of the pre-requisites in that role is that you were expected to either clear the ball to safety or play it forward to the creative players in the midfield and attack. Bertie Mee liked to adopt a 4-4-2 formation, and the full backs were encouraged to hit the two strikers from the back, with the midfield then pushing forward to support.

The first-team forwards were two colossal figures, John Radford and Ray Kennedy, and Bertie wanted to replicate that partnership in the reserves and youth team too. This meant that I was trying to hit guys like Frank Stapleton and another young prospect called Gary Goodchild.

When I had the ball wide or when I ventured forward, my instruction was to play the ball into the channels so that Frank or Gary could gather the ball and hold up play until the midfielders got forward.

This was the doctrine every single day. It was drilled into us such that it became second nature, and very quickly it became a key component in our style of play.

But playing this way made me more susceptible to injury. The opposing winger would invariably try and close me down and attempt to block the pass forward. I've lost count of the number of times a winger's studs met with the top of my foot, and that impact led to time out of the side. I think over a couple of seasons, I had four broken bones in my right foot which sidelined me for up to eight weeks each time.

Metatarsal injuries were commonplace, but it was only when David Beckham sustained the injury in a Champions League tie against Deportivo La Coruna in April 2002 that they were talked about widely in the public domain. There was a real furore too, as he was injured in a challenge with the Argentine player, Aldo Dusher, prompting some to suggest that it was a ploy to ensure that the talismanic Beckham would not make the England squad for that summer's World Cup in Japan. As it was, Beckham's recovery mirrored mine – eight weeks – and he was fit for the opening match against Argentina in Saitama. He scored the only goal of the game too.

My own metatarsal breaks were the first serious injuries of my career, and as I recovered, I discovered that it wasn't just your physical fitness that was affected. Being out of action had a detrimental effect on your mental wellbeing too.

Being 400 miles away from my home and family made the eight-week recovery period very lonely. I couldn't even seek solace by going into training, as I was initially ordered to take three weeks rest in my lodgings. That meant long days devoid of any real stimulus as I tried to cope with the injury and the toll that it was taking on me mentally. These days clubs are much more conversant with mental recovery, but back then it was very much "give yourself a shake and get on with it."

My misery was compounded by the fact that I had been identified by Bertie Mee as one of the emerging talents at the club. The injuries stalled my progress, and I recall being pretty low when it was announced that my room-mate, Frank Stapleton, was being promoted to the first XI. I should have been delighted for Frank, but I recall sitting alone in my room, mired in misery, listening to his debut match on the radio. But when Frank returned to the lodgings after the match against Stoke City, he was buzzing and after "giving myself a shake" I shared in his joy.

Frank and I were like chalk and cheese initially. He was a Celtic-supporting Catholic from Dublin, while I was a Rangers-supporting Protestant from Glasgow. Growing up we had both witnessed the hatred and division that religion can create. But that was never an issue for us. Despite our cultural differences we became good friends, and Frank was a great help during my periods of recovery from injury. He'd come home and talk about what had happened at training, which helped provide some much-needed light in what was an extremely dark period for me.

As dark as it may have been I did learn a lot. The experience of recovery from those early injuries gave me strength that I was able to call upon when I had to recover physically and mentally from the other injuries that I experienced later in my career.

The first of many operations came in March of 1976. I had just signed for Dundee and was signposted to make my first-team debut against Celtic at Dens Park. But I had to prove my fitness first, so I was selected to face the Celtic reserves at Parkhead a few days earlier. During a game that we lost 4-0, I took a knock on my ankle. I couldn't walk for days afterwards as the pain was excruciating. I eventually had an X-ray which concluded that a flake of bone had been detached in a tackle and it was lodged in my ligament. An operation was quickly arranged, and I rested and recuperated during a Scottish summer that was sunny AND warm!

Upon my return to training, the pain returned, and I had another X-ray. The diagnosis this time was that during my recovery, the ankle had grown a spur which meant I was going under the knife again.

The operation this time was deemed to be a success but, as a consequence, my left leg was now shorter than the right and I had a terrible limp. Worse was to come as the surgeon suggested that he had done all he could – and my career could be over!

With the guilt of making the wrong decision to leave Arsenal still to the fore, this was another body blow. And that blow wasn't softened when I read that Arsenal were indeed doing what Bertie Mee had said and introducing young players into the team!

My mental health suffered as a result. I was desperate and spent many long days in a very dark place. But suddenly, out of left field, came salvation. The legendary Jackie Husband, who made nearly 400 appearances for Partick Thistle, was a friend of the family. When he retired, Jackie had taken up physiotherapy and psychology; he was now back at Thistle as the reserve team physio, and among the staff he worked with was my half cousin, Donnie Mackinnon, whom after an illustrious playing career, had become first-team physiotherapist.

Jackie contacted me and said he thought that he could help. After limping through training in the morning at Dens Park, I drove to Renfrew to meet up with Jackie. He was a colossus of a man with hands the size of shovels and he had a kind, welcoming disposition.

"Right," he said. "Let's get you fixed."

He told me to lie on a bench and asked if I believed in hypnosis. The only hypnosis that I'd seen was on the TV, but I said yes.

I don't think I was hypnotised, or have been since, but I felt an amazing, serene calmness as Jackie counted down from 10. I could hear his words but couldn't answer.

He told me that my limp would be cured when I returned to Dundee, and that I would be able to run uninhibited. He also told me I'd retain my form and go on to play at the top level. I thought the session lasted only a couple of minutes, but I was told later that I had been with Jackie for over an hour. Jackie bade me farewell and said that we'd meet again. He also said I shouldn't tell anyone at Dundee of my experience, but I'd notice a big difference at training. I thanked Jackie and drove the 105 miles back to Dundee.

The next day at training I led the warm-up and amazingly my limp was gone. Tommy Gemmell, who was now the Dundee manager, shouted at Eric Ferguson the club physio. "What the fuck have you given him, Fergie? Yesterday he was for the knacker's yard and today he's running like a show horse!"

"Nothing," shouted Fergie. "It's a miracle."

I eventually made my first-team debut in a pre-season friendly against Inverness Thistle – I scored in a 3-2 win – and made nine appearances in the First Division during the 1976/77 season. My league debut came in a 6-1 win over Falkirk at Brockville – Gordon Strachan got one of our goals – and the following season saw me turn out 27 times in Dark Blue. I scored three times too, netting against East Fife, Montrose, and Queen of the South.

My last appearance for Dundee came at Parkhead on 16 August 1978. Ironically, I signed for Partick Thistle a few days later, the club at which the late, great, and wonderful Jackie Husband had found fame. I will always be grateful to Jackie; he saved my career.

\*\*\*\*\*

I signed for Bertie Auld's Thistle side in time to make my debut against Dundee United. We drew 1-1, and over the next couple of years, I established myself as a mainstay in the first XI. I was respected by my peers and was eventually awarded the captaincy.

That Thistle team were punching above their weight. We regularly finished in the top six of the Premier Division, and we were able to call upon top players like Alan Rough, Brian Whitaker, Jim Melrose, Colin McAdam, Doug Somner, Andy Anderson, Jackie Campbell, and Maurice Johnston.

My consistent displays saw me gain international recognition too, when Jock Stein selected me to play for the Scottish League against the Irish League. The match was played at Windsor Park in Belfast, and the Scotland XI included Billy Thomson of St Mirren, Andy Ritchie of Morton, Jackie McNamara of Hibernian, and my Thistle team mate, Jim Melrose. There were no representatives from the Old Firm as Celtic were in Spain preparing to face Real Madrid in the European Cup, while Rangers had a league game against Dundee United at Tannadice.

It was a great honour to be chosen, a wonderful feeling that I felt almost vindicated about my decision to leave Arsenal. We won the game 4-2, and my confidence was boosted when big Jock told me after the game that I wasn't far away from the full squad. There were high calibre players in my position at that time, though, with Danny McGrain, Ray Stewart, John Brownlie, Sandy Jardine, and George Burley in contention for the right-back berth. Perhaps Jock was just being nice.

Nevertheless, I returned to Thistle with a spring in my step.

If I was on the fringes of the national team, then I had to focus on trying to improve my game. With the teachings of Alan Ball and Pat Rice still to the fore, I suddenly started to find the consistency of performance that I had always wanted.

But four months after that night in Belfast, I returned for pre-season training and felt terrible. I had no energy and was really struggling for fitness. On 30 July 1980, we played Rangers at Ibrox in the Anglo Scottish Cup. When I went to the toilet at half time, my urine was crimson-coloured. Jim Melrose was in the toilet too and saw the blood. Before I knew what was happening, I was substituted. It would be SIX months before I was called upon to play for the first team again.

As the weeks passed, my energy levels and stamina disappeared. I'd also lost a stone in weight and for someone who tipped the scales at around 11-stone, I started to look gaunt.

Weekly hospital visits became the norm, although I was still attending training. But during one session, I collapsed and was rushed to hospital. After undergoing further tests, a student doctor on a ward round finally postulated, "I think he's got tuberculosis." The lead doctor nodded and said that I would need to be tested. Less than 24 hours later, it was confirmed – I had tuberculosis!

I had also been experiencing excruciating pain in my right side, so following a test where dye is delivered into your kidneys via a radioactive drink and a camera is shoved up a delicate piece of one's anatomy, a decision was taken to remove my right kidney. I was 24 years of age with a young daughter. I was devastated.

My kidney was removed by a wonderful surgeon at the Southern General Hospital. In those days surgical methods weren't as intricate as they are today, so part of two of my ribs had to be removed to open up the area.

As I came around from the operation, I was moved into a side room. It had a TV and on Saturday evening I watched *Scotsport*. As the news section came on, announcer Andy Melvin said, "Dave Mackinnon, the Partick Thistle captain's career is over tonight after the removal of a kidney."

I was on my own and the words hit me like a sledgehammer! My head was spinning. I had seemingly gone from being touted as the next right back for Scotland to the soccer scrapheap in less than six months.

As Melvin's words started to sink in and I contemplated a future without football, there was a commotion outside my room. I could hear loud voices and then the door to my room burst open. There was a plume of cigar smoke, so I knew who was entering my room before I saw them; it was the Thistle manager Bertie Auld, with his trademark Cuban cigar dangling from his lips. As well as the smoke, I could also smell the unmistakable aroma of cognac, Bertie's favourite tipple.

Bertie bellowed, "I was at the restaurant and Phil (his best friend) told me of that report on the telly. Forget it, son, you've got the spirit to come back, you're still my captain."

He smiled as a nurse came into the room. "Mr Auld, David needs some sleep so if you could give him the time to rest it would be appreciated."

"No problems, darlin'. Keep him positive," he said. "Davie, I've spoken to the Chairman (Millar Reid) and he's agreed to pay for some sun on your back. I'll sort it."

That short period of time summed Bertie up. He was a class act, and despite being a hard task master, he was a great motivator when he needed to be.

His visit had the desired effect. As my thoughts drifted to sunnier climes, I felt better about the future and my road to recovery. Such was my focus on Bertie's words, I had holiday brochures delivered to my room so that I could be inspired.

Two weeks later I was discharged and sent home. An hour after I arrived home the doorbell rang, and I felt well enough to answer it. I opened the door and a delivery driver said, "Sunbed for Mr Mackinnon, where do you want it?" Bertie's promise of a holiday had been a false one – he had wound me up – but his kidology had done the trick in getting me to stop thinking of a future without football and focus on overcoming this next challenge.

As I recuperated, I received countless letters and messages of support. I had over 100 sent from supporters and people who, like me, have had a kidney removed. The letters contained positive messages, and I recall one in particular from a 70-year-old man living in Aberdeen:

*Dear David,*

*I read about your operation and the removal of a kidney. Let me tell you that I also had a kidney removed as a young man in my twenties following an accident. Like me you will recover and gain full fitness as your remaining healthy kidney will do the work of two.*

*I wish you good health and a full recovery. I'll be watching your return to your career as a professional footballer.*

I drew great strength and positivity from the messages in each of the letters, but one touched me more than most.

I was intrigued from the outset as the envelope had a Madrid postmark stamped on it. Inside was a letter handwritten in Spanish accompanied by a typed transcript in English. Scanning to the signature at the bottom, I couldn't believe it when I found out the letter had been penned by the great Real Madrid striker Carlos Gonzalez, known simply as Santillana.

Santillana signed for Real Madrid in 1971, and was with Los Blancos for 17 years, amassing 645 competitive appearances. He won nine La Liga titles, four Copa del Reys, and the UEFA Cup twice. In addition, he won 56 caps for Spain, representing his country at the 1978 and 1982 World Cup. Santillana was also part of the Spanish side that finished as runners-up to France in the 1984 European Championships.

As I read the transcript, I felt emotional and was humbled that such a great player had taken the time to write to me. Santillana had seen the news in a newspaper and wrote in his letter to me that when he was 20 years old he had taken a knee in the stomach during a match. The result he said was excruciating pain and blood in his urine.

Several tests were carried out and it was discovered that he only had one kidney instead of two. He went on to say that it is estimated that 10 per cent of the world's population are born with only one kidney and they are generally unaware of it until it's identified through examination or illness.

After a few months out, Santillana returned to action, defying medical opinion in the process, and went on to forge a long and distinguished playing career. He retired in 1988 when he was 36.

He finished by saying that he wished me a full recovery and hopefully that we'd meet sometime in a European tie. That hasn't happened yet, but perhaps one day we can meet and I can thank him personally for the kind words that provided a real fillip as I recovered from the operation.

Whilst Bertie Auld used his guile and humour to take the first steps on the road to recovery for me, his next move was a brilliant piece of psychology.

A couple of months after the operation, I was deemed fit enough to take part in a reserve game at Firhill. The fatigue that I had experienced pre-op had left, and I was in a much better place physically and mentally. In the first half of the second XI fixture, I was full of running but my customary tackling and physical drive seemed to have deserted me. Bally would have been disappointed. In hindsight, I didn't feel confident enough to test out taking a blow to my right side. The stitches had healed and been removed, but subconsciously I was protecting the area. At half time Bertie said nothing so I thought I'd got through it.

Early in the second half our goalkeeper, a lovely young guy called Dougie McNab, tried to throw the ball out but only succeeded in gifting a corner to the opposition. I gave him a scowl and picked up my winger at the back post. As the ball came into the box, I moved to head clear and then I felt a bang into my side. It was big Dougie's knee and I collapsed into the turf.

Dougie was distraught and blurted out, "Wee Bertie told me to do it, Davie, are you OK?"

The physio came on and gave me a rub with the 'magic sponge' but there was no pain and I started to laugh. I grabbed big Dougie and gave him a hug and a peck on the cheek. I was back and Bertie's ruse had sorted out the psychological challenge.

A few weeks later I was included in the first-team squad for our Scottish Cup third round replay against Glasgow rivals, Clyde, at Shawfield. The date was 28 January 1981, and after almost six months on the sidelines, during which time I shed, and put back on, THREE stone in weight, I led my team out once again. I was back!

We won the match 4-2, but by then Bertie had left us to join Hibernian. Peter Cormack was our new manager. I was always indebted to Bertie for his support, and I was really sad to hear of his death in November 2021. He was one of a kind. I could write a book about him and his man management – good and bad!

But Bertie isn't the only key figure in my career who is no longer with us, so I want to take an opportunity now to reflect and pay tribute to them.

# CHAPTER 3
# MAY THEY REST IN PEACE – PLAYERS

*March 2022*

I WAS STILL waking up each morning to blood-stained pillows. They provided me with a stark reminder that I was very much still in recovery.

I had been told by the medical staff at the hospital, that in the scrum to save me, they had to glue the top scar in my head to stem the flow of blood. The other scar on the left side of my temple was less of a problem and the 10 stitches woven in, still tightening and healing, had done their job.

As I convalesced after my fall, my mind drifted to the past. That resurrected memories of time spent with players and managers that I'd played with and who are no longer with us. My therapist and doctor told me that this was to be expected as my brain healed and reset.

When I looked back and thought of my own mortality, there were some who weren't as fortunate as me. There were others, too, who for various reasons had taken the decision to end their lives.

Throughout my life I have often experienced dark days when I questioned my value and worth. But however dark things got, I always pulled myself back from the brink. I didn't want that to be my legacy, and that gave me the resolve to power through and overcome the negative thoughts.

This was almost like reverse psychology. I'd had those early life experiences centred around my mother, and I was steadfast when I told myself that if bad times were programmed in my brain to follow good times, then consequentially good times could follow bad. That was the guiding light which I used to navigate my way through the dark times, and I'm so blessed that my brain, although traumatised, was able to process in that manner.

My experiences did encourage me to talk about my feelings and now I actively look for signs from others and encourage them to talk. It's imperative that everyone is aware of those around them, and if we were all to have that awareness, then I'm sure more people would not contemplate taking their own life. Over the years, I've done some work with the Scottish Association of Mental Health and if you or anyone that you know is facing these challenges this organisation is a great place for solace and support.

Football now has a network of chaplains who are around clubs to give players and staff independent support. The man leading the chaplains in Scotland is Mark Fleming. When I was at Kilmarnock as General Manager, I introduced one of the first chaplains into a Premier League side. This was through Mark, and Neil Urquhart, a minister from Irvine, was introduced to the management, staff, and players.

Jim Jefferies, the Kilmarnock manager at the time, was very accommodating, and not long after Neil came in, Jim invited him to join the players at training. After his first session I went down to the training ground, and everyone was talking about how well Charlie had done.

"Have you signed a new player behind my back?" I asked Jim. "Who's Charlie?"

Jim burst out laughing and said, "That's what the players call the minister, Dave. Charlie, as in Charlie Chaplain!"

\*\*\*\*\*

## Erich Schaedler
### 6 August 1949 – 24 December 1985

We called Erich 'Shades' and he bounced into Dundee in 1977. He was an amazing but complex character who had incredible courage, both on and off the park. He lit up any room that he entered, and I was fortunate to get to know him as well as he would allow.

When he signed for Dundee, we were preparing for a cup tie. Although staying away the night prior to a game is commonplace nowadays, it was rare back then. But the club had decided that we would have an overnight stay in Dunblane Hydro on this occasion.

Shades, a Scottish international, was my roommate, and this arrangement was to become a permanent fixture. We shared rooms all over the world, including hotel rooms in Australia and New Zealand when we embarked on a tour at the end of season 1977/78.

But that first night in Dunblane was enlightening, and Shades and I forged a great friendship from that moment on.

As we retreated to our beds for the night, and before I fell into a deep sleep dreaming about the game ahead, we shared some small talk, which included Erich telling me that he was a black belt in karate. *As long as Erich was my sidekick, I would be protected*, I told myself.

But in the early hours of the morning my dreams seemed to take a strange and sinister turn. Chanting echoed in my ears, and as I woke in pitch darkness in an unfamiliar hotel room, my stomach was churning.

I fumbled around and found the bedside table lamp switch, and when I turned it on, there was Shades, upside down on the far wall, his head on a pillow and his legs stretched up the wall. He was chanting like a Tibetan monk!

Dazed and a little confused and fearful, I asked Shades if he was OK. "Yes, David, I'm meditating," was his reply. "Don't try and wake me, I'm in a deep trance."

Almost nonchalantly I then said, "No bother, Shades, see you in the morning," and promptly turned out the light and fell back asleep.

When I awoke in the morning, Shades was sitting at the bedroom table reading a newspaper. On the table was a pot of coffee, two cups, and several croissants accompanied by those squares of butter and jam you get in hotel rooms. There were two bowls of fruit segments and two glasses of orange juice too.

Shades was smiling.

"I've been down to the dining room and thought I'd surprise you, mate," he said laughing. "Sorry about last night, I'm having some problems sleeping. I've got a lot on my mind, you'll no' be saying anything to anyone will you?"

I agreed to keep schtum, but I asked Shades if he wanted to talk about it.

"Naw," was his swift reply. "Women problems."

Shades having that black belt in karate gave rise to an amusing incident with one of the younger lads. During a training session, this young upstart shouted, "Oi Shades, show me the death grip."

Shades moved towards the group of players and grabbed the young guy by the neck. He immediately collapsed to the ground and lay motionless. Another young player bent down beside him and put his hand against his neck. "Shades," he shouted. "You've killed him. He's not got a pulse, phone an ambulance."

Shades thought he'd killed the young guy and shouted, "Get an ambulance." I suspected this was a ruse and went over to the young player and kicked him in the backside. He promptly squealed and sat up.

Everyone started laughing but Shades shouted, "Ya wee bastard," and chased the youngster around the training pitch until he caught him and duly administered the same kick up his backside that I had.

I spoke with Shades after training and the conversation gave me a further insight into the man.

"That was a terrible wind-up Shades, are you OK?" I asked.

"Davie," he started. "They did the same trick at Hibs, and I really thought I'd killed the guy."

"If you knew it was a wind up, why did you act as if it was real?" I asked.

"Davie, it was going to happen sometime or other and I thought, let's get it out now and I don't have to worry about when it would happen in the future, so I played the long game. It's always about the long game, Davie, remember that and you'll do OK."

He smiled and went in for a shower.

On the pitch Shades was a revelation and quickly became a favourite of fans and players alike. He reminded me of Alan Ball, zooming out of the traps at the start yet still being the last man standing at the end.

Watching on from the other flank, I was in awe of Erich's levels of energy and commitment. His enthusiasm sparked something in me. I was still carrying that Arsenal-sized chip on my shoulder, but I still tried to emulate Erich on the park.

He was an inspiration to everyone. He and I would take turns bombing forward into opposition territory, and we complemented each other, although I think the others thought that we were having some sort of bromance as we were getting stick about being so close.

That season was memorable, but ultimately without success. We had a shot at promotion going into the final day of the season, but although we defeated champions Morton 3-2 at Cappielow, Hearts scored a last-minute equaliser at Arbroath to squeeze us out by one point.

I remember being utterly dejected after the game. It was a case of so near, yet so far. But I also recall the gratitude shown by the Dundee fans. As Shades and I walked over to the car park, a bus full of fans stood up and applauded. That helped to ease the pain somewhat.

After a week's rest, we were off on our travels. Our destination was Australia, New Zealand, and New Caledonia. Again, Erich and I roomed together; the bromance was back on.

We played nine games on the tour and bonded as a team. I have no doubt that tour was the catalyst for winning promotion the following season. Sadly, though, I wasn't part of it.

I should have seen my departure from Dundee coming. On a flight from Auckland to Noumea, the capital of French colony New Caledonia, I was seated beside our assistant manager, Willie Wallace. One of the fabled Lisbon Lions, Willie had been brought in by our manager and fellow Lion, Tommy Gemmell. I sensed fairly early on that Willie didn't rate me as a player, and he confirmed that during the three-hour flight. He didn't hold back and said that I wasn't good enough and should be looking to find a new club. In fairness, they'd said the same to Gordon Strachan when they appointed him, so I was in good company!

Brutal honesty was part and parcel of football in that era, but in hindsight, I'm glad that Willie was so damning in his appraisal. No player wants to stay where they aren't wanted, so I knew then that it was time seek pastures new and develop elsewhere.

As fate would have it, we played a double header against New Caledonia, and we were defeated 2-1 in the first game with the soon to be famous Jean Tigana running the show.

The management team were clearly less than enamoured with our display, as the next day we got both barrels and told that we weren't good enough. To illustrate their point, Tommy and Willie decided that the New Caledonia players needed a lesson, and they both decided to play in the next match.

We won 2-1, but my abiding memory is of Tommy kicking Tigana up and down the park before he was eventually red-carded for a particularly crude attempt to curtail the magic of the French wizard. All hell broke loose as photographers tried to capture the moment as Tommy walked off. A camera was broken in the melee, and we had to sneak out of the stadium at the end.

Once the dust had settled and we had found sanctuary in the hotel, I shared my conversation with 'Wispy' – Willie's nickname – with Shades.

He laughed and said he'd been told the same thing and that it was an attempt to motivate us. We laughed out loud and I felt better. Shades was good at doing that.

On Christmas Eve 1985, Erich was found dead in a forest in the Scottish borders. He'd taken his own life. He was just 36 years of age. I was at Rangers at the time and I cried when I heard the news.

He was such a lovely man, but sadly one who was unable to deal with his demons.

## Ian Redford
### 5 April 1960 – 10 January 2014

I first met Ian Redford when he signed for Dundee in August 1976. He was a young, emerging talent who was quiet and unassuming, and after his first day training with us it was clear to see that he was supremely talented.

He was an athletic, elegant, thoughtful midfield player and he added his fair share of goals too. In season 1977/78, he chalked up 10 goals in 41 appearances, and by the time Reddy left to join Rangers in February 1980, his final total of goals scored in competitive matches stood at 39 in 105 appearances in a dark blue jersey.

Although he was four years younger – I was 22, Reddy was 18 – we became friends and socialised together. I was a regular visitor to his family home in Errol too. The Redford family owned half the land in the area and were farmers. His mum and dad were always very welcoming.

The family had suffered a heart-breaking loss five years earlier when Ian's younger brother, Douglas, had passed away after battling leukaemia. The family had done everything to ensure that Douglas had as good a life as possible and had installed a swimming pool in the grounds of their house.

When I saw the pool on that first visit to Errol, I asked Ian if he swam in it, but he said no one in the family had been in it after Douglas had died.

Douglas's death had left a huge void in the family, and I could tell that Reddy carried the weight of losing his brother on his shoulders.

Reddy and I enjoyed some memorable moments off the park. One that springs to mind was at Christmas in 1977. Reddy asked me if I fancied a goose for Christmas dinner, and although my family had enjoyed the tasty turkey from Arsenal a couple of years earlier, the idea of gobbling up some goose made for a nice change.

In the week leading up to Christmas Day, Reddy told me that he'd bring the goose into training. One day he ushered me to the away dressing room and his cousin Gavin was standing over a large cardboard box. "Yir goose is in there," he said. I opened the box and there were about 10 fully feathered dead geese, their heads intact and flopped to the side.

"You'll have to pluck it, but I'll gut it," said Gavin.

I put my hand into the box and pulled out a goose at random. Its lifeless glassy eyes seemed to be focussed on mine. "How the fuck do you pluck them?" I asked. "I'm fae a tenement in Glasgow."

Reddy laughed and grabbed the bird and pulled a hand full of feathers from the breast and then threw the goose towards me. "That's how you do it, schemie."

Both he and Gavin laughed, and I spent the next hour or so removing the feathers. Other players who'd expressed interest in taking home a goose started arriving and followed suit. It didn't take long for the dressing room to be festooned with feathers.

Once I had plucked all the feathers, I handed the bald corpse to Gavin and he disappeared, before returning five minutes later with my Christmas dinner in a paper bag. There was blood dripping from the bag all over the dressing room floor. Thinking that the other lads would have a similar issue, I went to the groundsman's shed as I knew there was plastic sheeting there. I found the roll and thought it best to bring it back to the dressing room to put on the floor.

When I arrived back the guys were throwing clumps of

feathers at each other; it was carnage. The dressing room door suddenly burst open, and it was George, the groundsman.

"What the fuck?" he shouted. "Get this cleaned up, we've got a game here on Christmas Eve."

He left and returned a couple of minutes later with a bucket, brush, mop, and a metal bin. "Get that shite in the bin and get some disinfectant or I'll call the gaffer."

The guys moved fast and within an hour the place looked almost spick and span again. However, we must have missed some feathers as after the game on Christmas Eve against Morton, our visitors complained that pigeons must have infiltrated the dressing room as the players had found a dead bird. Clearly the guys who found it weren't into ornithology as I would have thought it was quite difficult to confuse a goose for a pigeon!

Back on the park, Ian's game kept improving and he soon established himself as our talisman. It was no surprise, therefore, when he was transferred to Rangers for £210,000 – at the time a record transfer fee between Scottish clubs.

When I was at Thistle, I played against Reddy on numerous occasions, but he rarely engaged on the park and when we shook hands before and after the game, it was as if he was a stranger.

Two years later I signed for Rangers, but even then, the friendship and camaraderie that we had at Dundee was never fully rekindled. I think Reddy wanted to forget the past.

By then he had become even quieter, and he was content to go about his own business. This wasn't the guy I'd known at Dundee, but who knows what was going around in his head.

He lived in a flat on the southside of Glasgow with a very talented young player called Billy McKay.

Billy, whose promising career was sadly curtailed by an injury, was a livewire both on and off the park and he seemed to bring Reddy out of his shell. Their exploits were legendary and they were always getting up to mischief off the park.

I remember one particular day when the pair of them didn't turn up for training and our manager, John Greig, said they'd called in sick. An upset stomach upset caused by a dodgy takeaway was given as the reason for their absence. We all looked at each other wondering whether we should laugh. At that point,

Davie Cooper's magnificent dry wit broke the silence, "Gaffer, when did Chinese takeaways start delivering lager?"

Greigy simply shook his head and muttered something about them getting fined a week's wages.

When we were both retired from playing, I bumped into Reddy from time to time at games when he was doing some scouting. But we didn't really keep in touch, and I hadn't heard from him in years when suddenly out of the blue, he contacted me via Linkedin in December 2013.

He said he was writing a book and he'd mentioned me in it. He said it wasn't complimentary and he wanted to apologise. He told me that he had written that I wasn't as good as Sandy Jardine. I burst out laughing. I had a good career as a full-back, but Sandy was on a different level to me, so I told Reddy there was no need to apologise as he was telling the truth.

We shared a laugh or two and I asked him where he was living. He told me he'd moved to Irvine because of a golfing job. As I lived not far away in Gourock, I said I'd come down and see him. He thanked me and said he'd send me his number over Linkedin, and that we could meet up in the New Year as he was flitting between Irvine and Perthshire.

I was at a Burn's Supper at the start of January 2014 when I received a text from my friend Billy asking me to call him. As I dialled his number, I wasn't prepared for what he was about to tell me.

"Have you heard about Ian Redford?" he asked. I hadn't. I was left numb when Billy told me that Reddy had been found dead in the woods in Irvine.

I left the Burn's Supper immediately and cried as I drove back home. The next day I downloaded Ian's book and read it in one sitting. In it, Reddy gave an honest appraisal of his life and the challenges that he had faced. He bared his soul and I felt sad that such a wonderful man had left us. He was just 53 years old.

### Brian Whittaker
#### 23 September 1956 – 7 September 1997

Brian Whittaker was a special individual. He was handsome, polite and was also a very talented footballer with whom I forged a tremendous relationship at Partick Thistle.

For reasons I don't know, he was nicknamed 'Piggy', and the lads in the dressing room loved him. He lifted us all with his humour and energy, and he was always on the lookout for his next jape at some poor soul's expense.

I'd been transferred to Thistle from Dundee in August 1978 for what seemed like a paltry sum of £18,500 with a £3,500 signing on fee. However, that outlay was the second highest fee that Thistle had paid for a player in their history. The player that pipped me for top spot in terms of expenditure was Alex O'Hara, Thistle having 'broken the bank' a year earlier to sign him from Rangers for £25,000.

When I joined Thistle, they were part-time, although the manager, Bertie Auld, never alluded to that during our negotiations. But that didn't really matter to me as I sat between two Lisbon Lions, Bertie and the Dundee manager, Tommy Gemmell, for the signing photograph. I was signing for a club in the Scottish Premier Division, and I felt that my career was now moving on an upward trajectory. The millstone round my neck – my reckless departure from Arsenal – seemed to lighten somewhat too.

As I entered the Thistle dressing room, I recognised some familiar faces and I immediately felt at home. That dressing room was one of the happiest that I experienced in my career. We all had a mutual respect for each other, with fun and mischief making being a daily occurrence.

It took me less than a week to switch on to the latter. The main protagonists when it came to piss taking were the likes of Piggy, Roughie [Alan Rough], Mello [Jim Melrose], wee Mac [Ian MacDonald], Ally Love and Gibby [Ian Gibson]. They combined to make sure that the dressing room was a sanctuary, a proper happy place.

What surprised me, though, was that wee Bertie was perceived as the Prince of Darkness by this group.

After I trained with the lads for the first time, the team sheet for the home game against Dundee United on the Saturday was pinned to the notice board. As I peered at the sheet, I noted that we had to gather at 10.30 a.m.

"It's a 3 p.m. kick off, why have we to meet so early?" I asked Roughie.

He laughed and simply said, "Wait and see."

I reported to Firhill just after 10 a.m. and was promptly told by big Donnie Mackinnon to get my training gear on. As the rest of the players started to arrive in the home dressing room, I noticed that there were a lot more present than those listed on the team sheet. For example, there were several reserve team players sat with their training gear on.

Bertie appeared and read out two teams. He included himself, Pat Quinn, the assistant manager, first team coach Davie Provan, and Donnie, the physio. And without further ado, Pat distributed bibs and we were told to get on to the park.

Brian Whittaker was beside me as I walked down the tunnel, and I asked him, "A practice match before the game, is it just a tactical walk through?"

Brian simply repeated the words Roughie had uttered the previous day – "Wait and see."

Bertie had just turned 40, but he looked as fit as when he was in his pomp. He lined up the two teams and chose to play in the midfield of the side made up of Pat, Davie, Donnie, and the reserves. I was included in the first team at right back so I realised at that moment that I would be starting against United.

Bertie blew the whistle and play started at a fierce pace. I was up against a winger called Ronnie Sheed and he ran towards me at pace. But he overhit the ball and I was able to gather easily. At that moment, I thought the move was over and stood with my hands on my hips with the ball under my foot. Big mistake!

Almost immediately, my ears were ringing as I heard the shrill sound of a whistle. Bertie ran towards me and bellowed, "What the fuck are you doing, Mackinnon? At this club we train as we play. I bought you because you make tackles so start fucking making them!"

Another blast of his whistle signalled the restart of play, but not long after that Brian Whittaker wiped out Pat Quinn with a sliding tackle. It was at that point, some four hours before we were due to face United, that I switched on – this game was serious.

I liked to rampage forward when the opportunity presented itself, but when I did so in this game, wee Bertie, aimed a kick at me. As a full-back, I expected to take the odd kick or two, but I was left bemused on this occasion as Bertie was my manager! Fortunately, I saw the challenge coming and rode it before teeing up Jim Melrose who curled the ball into the net. As I jogged back into position, Bertie flashed a smile and said, "Good job you're fast, Mackinnon, but I'll get you the next time."

Over the next few weeks, I realised that when we played at Firhill this 'game' was a regular feature. I learned quickly that I was expected to tackle and slide-in in the manner which Bertie expected from his right back, and I did that, so much so that I soon became a regular in the number two jersey.

I liked Bertie's mantra of training as we played. My respect for him as my manager grew, although that was challenged when I experienced his interpretation of what was referred to at the time as 'the coffin'.

'The coffin' was a running exercise where two players are placed on each side of the half-way line, each corner flag, and various other points. There were twelve positions in total. The first run was a sprint to the next point followed by a half pace full lap jog back to the starting point. You were then expected to sprint to two points followed by a half-paced lap to the starting point.

As we reached the last run – a full paced lap – Bertie's whistle suddenly peeped. He hollered, "Right, Roughie you're slacking, everyone back to the start!"

At that moment, I then realised why the players were so tight knit as a group. Although it could have been perceived that he was trying to create division within the ranks, with the benefit of hindsight, it was an inspired piece of man-management by Bertie. I vividly recall the phrase, "Ya wee bastard," being uttered by all the players and echoing round the empty ground. I looked over to Bertie for his reaction and he started to laugh. He had achieved his objective; in the spirit of *The Three Musketeers*, it was 'all for one and one for all'.

Piggy and I were kindred spirits as players. We were both very fit and always filled with attacking intent. Piggy was on the left, I was on the right, and we quickly developed an almost telepathic relationship. When he attacked, I would hang back and vice versa.

We also developed a strategy at corner kicks. We picked one of the posts and stationed ourselves there steadfastly. Over the course of about four seasons, we must have prevented something like 20 goals each season using this tactic. Watching games now, I am left perplexed that teams don't employ this tactic, as you often see goals scored when the ball sneaks into the net at an unguarded post.

Brian was always full of fun and I remember we were both selected to play for the Scottish League in a double header against Eire and Northern Ireland. We shared a room on the trip, and when we were in Dublin, Brian decided the night before the game that he would have a few pints of the black stuff, Guinness.

I told him that he wasn't taking the game seriously, but Piggy just laughed. The following day he was a standout performer, running down the left flank from start to finish. He was a natural athlete and even copious amounts of alcohol couldn't hold him back.

Brian was a party animal, but there was a superstitious side to him too. I recall one game in February when it was freezing, yet he arrived at Firhill in a pair of luminous yellow shorts, a pink vest, and a pair of white espadrilles as if he was going to a beach party after the game. He looked like something out of a Wham video and strolled about the dressing room pre-match much to the consternation of wee Bertie.

He said, "I'm fining you a week's wages, Piggy, as yer no' wearing a suit." At that Brian produced one of those black Ralph Slater suit bags and promptly put on a white suit over the vest and shorts. As the team was announced the white suit was dispensed with and Brian walked seductively about the dressing room in his trademark, and lucky, leopard skin underpants! The boys were in stitches and it certainly eased the tension as we were playing Celtic that day.

When Piggy went to the toilet, his pants were thrown onto a peg. Roughie, lithe-like in his movement, pulled down his shorts, removed his white slips, and pulled on Piggy's leopard skin pants before redressing.

As we emerged from the tunnel, the heavens opened, and the two goalmouths quickly turned into a muddy quagmire. But as a team we played magnificently and Roughie saved a penalty. With only a couple of minutes remaining, Celtic forced a corner. Someone was down injured, so the physio was called for. As was customary, I was on the right-hand post and Brian the left. Roughie rubbed away a chunk of mud and shouted, "Oi, Piggy. Do you recognise these?" as he pulled down his shorts to reveal the sodden and muddied leopard skin pants.

Brian ran to the centre of the goals and started wrestling with

Roughie to try and get the pants off him. Here we were, just minutes to go in a crucial game against Celtic and two of our top players were wrestling in the mud. I was the captain and as the referee moved in, I dived in and pulled them apart. "That's it sorted," I said to the ref. "I think it was a dispute over the penalty."

"No bother, Davie," said the referee and he blew his whistle for the game to restart. The corner came in, Roughie gathered the ball safely and we saw out the remaining time to earn a 1-1 draw.

In the dressing room after the game, Roughie removed the pants and Piggy ran into the bathroom to clean them. They were his 'pulling pants' and he wanted them to be clean when he donned them under those yellow shorts that night at the Savoy. What a legend!

I was transferred to Rangers and Brian was transferred to Celtic. We bumped into each other occasionally and I'd ask if he had the lucky pants on. That always brought a smile and he would give me a cuddle and say "Version number two, Davie, I gave my auld pair to Roughie and they've given him some luck. The ugly bastard needs it."

Brian retired after an illustrious career which saw him play at Thistle, Celtic, Hearts and Falkirk, before venturing into commercial management.

He was killed in a car crash on 7 September 1997 at the age of 40. He was one in a million and there's not a day goes past when I don't think of him.

### Colin McAdam
#### 28 August 1951 – 1 August 2013

Colin McAdam was a monster on the pitch but an angel off it. He was a lovely guy, one you'd always want in your corner. As a player, he was courageous, fearless and a true and loyal friend.

I first met Colin when I signed for Thistle. He was a PE teacher and the discipline from his day job seemed to bring with it some decorum among the mayhem and carnage in that Thistle dressing room. I was amazed at his strength, and he was very skilful for such a big man. Equally adept at centre forward or centre back, he wreaked havoc among defenders when a cross came into the box for him to attack, but he could also repel anything an attacking side could throw at you.

Colin established a potent partnership with Jim Melrose, and after scoring 34 goals for the Jags, it was no surprise to any of us when Rangers paid £165,000 to take him to Ibrox in the summer of 1980.

That immediately looked like money well spent. Colin scored his first goal for Rangers against Thistle on what was only his second appearance for the club, and between 27 August and 24 September, he grabbed goals in seven successive matches. A double in a 3-0 win over Celtic at Ibrox in November helped endear him even further to the Rangers followers; by the end of the season, he had found the net 21 times in all competitions.

Two years after Colin left Thistle, I followed him across the River Clyde to Ibrox. By then he had shown his talent by playing in defence, but, as I also found to my cost, having the ability to play in several positions gets you the unwanted tag of being a 'utility man'.

In my opinion, Colin was at his best when he played up front. He was the archetypal 'battering ram' centre forward, and in that first season at Ibrox, I don't recall too many players in Scotland that could match Colin.

In addition to being a great friend and team-mate, Colin could look after himself too and the lads and I were thankful on more than one occasion that he was in our corner. And the man who is rightly regarded as Rangers' greatest-ever goal scorer, Ally McCoist, had cause to be grateful to big Colin after the Ibrox faithful turned on him following a 1-0 defeat against Dundee in the Scottish Cup in 1985.

Coisty's predatory instincts had deserted him that afternoon and he spurned chance after chance. As we sat disconsolate in the dressing room after the game, we could hear an irate crowd outside on Edmiston Drive. They were venting their anger using the full repertoire of blasphemous words and one song, in particular, must have chilled Coisty to the core. The lancing lyrics were: "Ally, Ally, get to fuck, Ally get to fuck."

We changed out of our kit and got ready to head home, but realised pretty quickly that the crowd wasn't going to disperse any time soon. We were faced with the prospect of running the gauntlet to get to our cars when the stadium security manager came into the dressing room and suggested that we leave it for a couple of hours. But Colin and Derek Johnstone stood up and flanked Coisty. "Don't let them intimidate you, Coisty, we're going to leave together as a squad and walk with our heads held high to the car park," announced DJ.

"And don't rise to them," added Colin. "Keep the head high and don't talk to them."

We all left the dressing room feeling like we were lambs to the slaughter. We exited through the main door at Ibrox and were soon in the midst of a crowd baying for blood. I ploughed through, but recall looking across and seeing Colin grabbing a guy and throwing him out of Coisty's path. *So much for not rising to the bait*, I thought! However, at that point the hostility seemed to subside. I think the fans must have taken one look at Colin, nostrils flaring – a sign that he was angry – and suddenly the fans stepped aside in a scene that was reminiscent of Moses parting the Red Sea. We all made it to our cars and drove to our respective homes.

Coisty was dropped to the reserves the following week. He could have been swallowed up by that whole experience, but he was made of stern stuff. He got back among the goals in the second XI and returned to the first team before the season ended. I think he scored something like 10 goals in the last nine games too. He never looked back after that and it is unlikely that anyone will match or better the 355 goals that he scored in competitive matches for Rangers.

Colin wasn't actually involved in the match against Dundee. He had played what would be his last game for the first XI some nine months earlier.

Rangers had embarked on a World Tour at the end of season 1983/84, spending five weeks travelling around Australia, New Zealand, the USA, and Canada. We played in over 20 matches, but early on, the tour earned a new title, 'the leg break tour'. Bobby Williamson, who had joined us from Clydebank the previous December, broke his leg in an incident that happened off the field of play, while Colin sustained his during the third game of the tour against Australia at the Sydney cricket ground.

From memory, Colin was introduced to the action from the bench midway into the second half, as big Jock Wallace tried to curb the threat posed by the talented striker Davie Mitchell, who signed for Rangers shortly afterwards.

What would have been the wicket when cricket was played

at the arena traversed the centre circle and it was like concrete. The ball was played into that area and as it bounced wickedly, Colin and Davie collided and the two of them collapsed onto the hard surface. Davie tried to pull Colin up after the tackle, but Colin grabbed him and shouted, "I've broken my leg."

Colin was stretchered off and his tour, and indeed his time as a first-team player at Ibrox, was over.

Colin had played sporadically in season 1983/84 – mainly at centre back – and had come off the bench when we defeated Celtic 3-2 in the League Cup Final. He had also netted a vital goal against Dunfermline Athletic in the Scottish Cup. But I didn't get the opportunity to play alongside Colin in any of the 11 games that he played, as my season was disrupted by illness and suspension.

Between late November 1983 and April 1984, I only made one appearance for the first team. Jock Wallace had taken over as manager after John Greig had resigned and around mid-November we played Aberdeen. I was one of the only players that ate raspberries and there was an outbreak of Hepatitis A at the hotel in Aberdeen where we had our pre-match meal.

Shortly afterwards we were playing Hibs and Jock took me for a walk around the track. He asked what was wrong with me as he felt I had lost all my energy. I then went to the toilet and my urine was black which meant I had Hepatitis. That was a difficult time, but Jock used to phone me every Saturday night and told me how the game went. I couldn't go out of the house and my diet meant that I lost a lot of weight.

I missed the League Cup Final too, but that wasn't due to Hepatitis. I had recovered from that, and the manager said that if I could prove my fitness in the reserves I would be back in the squad. I played against Dunfermline at East End Park in the Reserve League West and I was captain. Jock was there watching. I tackled someone, won the ball, but the referee booked me and, believe it or not, that took me past the points threshold, so I was suspended for the Cup Final.

Colin and I did play alongside each other in season 1984/85, but those appearances came in the reserves. One of those matches was instantly forgettable too; a 5-0 thrashing at the hands of Celtic Reserves at Parkhead.

Colin joined Adelaide City after he left Rangers, but he would come back to haunt Rangers when he returned to Scotland, scoring for Hearts in a 3-2 win at Tynecastle in January 1986. I didn't play in that game as I was recovering from a knee injury, but the defeat in Edinburgh in the third round of the Scottish Cup effectively ended our season.

I bumped into Colin a few times after he retired and he hadn't changed. He still had that positivity he'd had during his playing days.

He survived a heart attack in 2013, but sadly, suffered a brain seizure. He passed away on 1 August 2013 aged 61.

### Davie Cooper
### 25 February 1956 – 23 March 1995

Davie Cooper was a genius. He didn't get on with everyone, but for some reason, he saw something in me that he liked and I was proud to be a friend.

We first crossed paths as opposition players. With Coop playing on the left wing for Rangers and me at right back for Thistle, we were direct opponents and it didn't take me long to recognise that he was a tremendous player. But when he faced me for the first time, he wasn't aware of the lessons that I had learned from Pat Rice in the nascent days of my career at Arsenal.

Coop had similar attributes to George Best. He had perfect balance and was both brave and confident. His left foot was almost wand-like too. And Coop also had the same technique as George of being able to beat an opposing defender using the movement of his body. I quickly realised, therefore, that Pat's mantra of 'keep your eye on the ball' would stand me in good stead up against Coop.

When he first approached me, Coop swivelled his hips and dipped his shoulder, but with my eyes transfixed on the ball, I took it away from him. Confidence started to course through my body and Coop was rattled.

After the game he made a point of walking off the park with me. And in a touch of class that summed the man up, he complimented me, offering his hand and saying, "Where did you learn that? I'll need to watch you, son." I played against Coop numerous times when I was at Thistle and he never lost that graciousness. But I have to admit that the Pat Rice doctrine didn't always work.

We played Rangers at Firhill on the opening day of season 1981/82 and he nutmegged me. The only option was to bodycheck him, so down Coop went. Penalty to Rangers was the decision of the referee and up stepped Tommy McLean to score what proved to be the only goal of the game. As we trotted back to restart the game after wee Tam scored, Coop ran past me and said with a smile, "I see you've grown too comfortable, never underestimate the Coop."

In the wake of the match, I had to feel sorry for my team-mate, Donald Park. In their match reports, both the *Evening Times* and the *Glasgow Herald* identified him as the culprit when it came to halting Coop in his tracks. The advent of YouTube exonerated Donald, though. There is footage of the game on there that clearly shows that I was the one responsible for conceding the penalty kick.

Shortly afterwards, Coop and I became team mates when I signed for Rangers in June 1982. It was the greatest day of my life.

When I signed, the manager, John Greig, advised me that some players were coming in a couple of days a week to keep fit before pre-season started. I decided that I would do the same and went in one day to do some running and meet a few of the players.

On that first day, Coop and Bobby Russell were there and it was great to be welcomed to the club by two guys who weren't just outstanding players, but brilliant human beings too. Coop, in particular, provided support and encouragement and said that he was delighted that I had signed as it now meant he didn't have to play against me.

But despite Coop and Bobby's kind words, there were some huge personalities in that Rangers dressing room, so I was apprehensive when I walked into Ibrox on the first official day of pre-season.

I needn't have worried; Coop broke any ice that there may have been in his own inimitable style. When I walked into the home dressing room, he said, in a loud, staged whisper, "Thank fuck you're on our side now, I don't need to get my shins stitched!" He burst out laughing, gave me a welcoming hug then announced, "Guys, meet Davie Mackinnon, he'll run through a brick wall for us."

Any lingering apprehension or nerves were blown away when Coop said that. I felt that they gave me a status in the dressing room and Coop knew that too. He was a wonderful and thoughtful human being and I will always be grateful for the words that he said that day.

After I settled in at Rangers, one thing that surprised me was the lack of focus on sports science. Sports science is now an intrinsic part of any football club, with hydration, diet and training capacity among myriad things that are measured and analysed on a daily basis.

But in the 1980s, only some clubs emphasised that. For example, after my kidney was removed, the physio at Thistle ensured that my hydration levels were always high, providing water for me at training and on match days. But when I went to Rangers, that didn't happen and I had to make my own arrangements for our first home game during pre-season against Spurs.

I had mistakenly assumed that water would be available, particularly as the temperature that afternoon was in the mid-20s. Prior to going out for our warm-up, I asked if I could get a bottle of water and was told that there was a tap in the toilet!

Minus a receptacle to dispense water into, I followed the instructions given, but found that the taps in question were part of a sink that was in one of the toilet cubicles. The cubicle was occupied when I went in – one of my teammates was emptying his bowels prior to the match – so I ended up shuffling in and putting my mouth under the tap. I was promptly christened 'lavvy sniffer' so elected to sort myself out for fluids for the rest of the season.

While the Spurs game was my home debut, I'd made my full debut a few weeks earlier on 27 July 1982 in a pre-season tournament in France called Le Tournoi du Nord that had been arranged by Lille. Also taking part were Lokeren and St Etienne, and our opening game was against the latter.

In their ranks was the very talented Dutch player, Johnny Rep. Johnny had famously scored against Scotland in the 1978 World Cup in Argentina and was one of the most confident and assured players that I'd encountered.

He was my direct opponent and I remember that he spoke for the whole game. My ears were burning by the end of a match we edged 6-5 on penalties after a 0-0 draw. John McClelland, Jim Bett and Colin McAdam missed from 12 yards for Rangers, but our goalkeeper, Peter McCloy, was the hero, saving four spot kicks. My fellow debutant, Craig Paterson, netted the decisive penalty, and Craig and I both drew praise from Hugh Taylor; in his match report for the *Glasgow Herald*, stated that Rangers had turned in a 'tremendously satisfying performance, especially in defence, where Paterson and the other Ibrox new boy, McKinnon [sic] from Partick Thistle, were outstanding.'

The tournament came at the end of three gruelling weeks of hard graft in pre-season, which included my first experience of the infamous Murder Hill at Gullane in East Lothian. Jock Wallace had taken several successful squads there during his tenure and John Greig was doing likewise. The hill is a near vertical sand dune and the players were tasked with undertaking numerous runs up and down the shifting sand.

I have never experienced strain and pain in my legs like I did at Gullane, it was without question the hardest training that I ever endured. I know now that the purpose of the trip was both physiological and psychological as completing the course meant that you were at peak fitness and ready to face the challenges of the season ahead.

But a consequence of Gullane for me was the development of painful blisters on both feet. They hadn't healed before we faced St Etienne, so the chairman, Rae Simpson, a retired and respected surgeon, decided to visit me in my room to rectify the issue.

He brought his medical bag with him and laid a surgical sheet on my bed that I was to lie on. Within seconds, he sprayed anaesthetic on the soles of my feet, and a shiver ran down my spine as I switched on to what was about to happen; Mr Simpson felt it best to cut away the blisters.

The pain was excruciating as Mr Simpson sliced the skin and it wasn't long before a pool of blood started to surge on to the surgical sheet. As he finished, Mr Simpson once again sprayed the anaesthetic onto the soles of my feet. It felt like I had been struck by lightning or received an electric shock. Pain coursed through my body and I nearly hit the roof when the anaesthetic hit the raw and exposed wounds on my feet.

I had to bite my lip to stop me from shrieking due to the pain, but as Mr Simpson tidied up his tools, he peered over his half-moon spectacles and said, "That's the blisters sorted. There will be a bit of pain for a couple of hours, but I'll get the physio to make up some padding and you'll be right as rain for tonight's game."

In order to help get me immersed in the ethos of Rangers Football Club, John Greig had paired me with an experienced pro as a room-mate. As I writhed and wriggled on my bed trying to get comfortable, he uttered the words, "The chairman was a good surgeon in his time, but he shouldn't get involved now, so I'd watch your feet don't get infected. He tried that on me and I told him I wasn't doing it."

At that point, I thought that sleep would be the best medicine, but as I drifted off, there was a knock at our room door.

"You get it," instructed my room-mate. I hirpled to the door, and when I opened it, a hotel waiter was on the other side. He said, "Ice as requested, sir," and handed me a bag of ice cubes.

My initial reaction was to be thankful. I thought my room-mate had been sympathetic to my plight and ordered ice to help my feet. I was wrong.

I brought the ice bag into the room and my room-mate, a player who had made several hundred appearances for Rangers, stood up and took the bag from me. He said, "I'm going to give you a career lesson here, Davie, something I've used throughout my life and it has prolonged my career."

He added, "I was given this lesson as a young player by a Scottish international who was a Rangers legend so I'm now passing it on to you. I'm sure you'll get great benefit for what I'm about to teach you."

At that moment he went into the bathroom, put the plug into the low-slung wash hand basin before pouring in the ice and topping up with cold water. As the ice swilled around the sink, I couldn't wait to get my aching feet into the soothing, ice-cold water.

But as I prepared myself, my room-mate suddenly dropped his shorts and announced, "Before every game, Davie, you have to do this an hour or so before kick-off." He then grabbed his testicles and dropped them into the cold water.

I thought it was a wind up, but he appeared serious. He continued, "You see, Davie, the cold water and ice pulls your testicles up into your body and gives you incredible strength. It will lengthen your career and give you great power."

At that he pulled his testicles back into his slips, pulled his shorts back up and said, "I'll leave you to it," and closed the bathroom door. I didn't oblige, and to this day, I still believe it was part of some sort of initiation prank which the players would be in on.

Fast forward a few hours and it was game time. I was still in a great deal of pain post Mr Simpson's operation, but I had waited my whole life to pull on that Rangers jersey. Raw feet weren't going to deter me, so I summoned up the necessary strength to bust the pain barrier and play. I remember that we wore white socks against St Etienne, not our traditional black with red tops, and by the end of the match, my wounds had bled so much that my socks had turned crimson. There was a pool of blood in my boots too.

But as eventful and enlightening as that trip was, I will always look back on it fondly as that was where my boyhood dream of playing for Rangers was realised.

Two days later, I was back in blue as we faced Lokeren in the final of the tournament. We led 1-0 with 10 minutes to go and I remember striking the frame of the goal with a shot, but the Belgians scored twice to win the trophy. Hugh Taylor was once again effusive in his praise, though, stating that 'there was much to admire in Rangers' play and new centre half Paterson and right back McKinnon [sic] showed that they will be excellent captures.'

After I hung up my boots, I took up various executive roles in football; and it was only then that I got to realise how important proper nutrition and its subsequent impact on energy and performance was. It's a pivotal part of preparation nowadays, but when I was playing, my pre-match meal varied from a sirloin steak in my early days at Arsenal to scrambled eggs on toast latterly. Perhaps had we paid a bit more attention to what we were eating then the doleful period that Rangers endured in my time there may have been avoided. If only we had in place even a fraction of the expertise that can be called upon today things could have been different.

When I was at Rangers, I felt the team's best performances were in evening games, particularly the European nights under the lights. I remember having a huge amount of energy during the night-time games and that must have been down to the amount of fuel that I had on board.

If we were at a hotel or indeed at home, we would have three solid meals inside us, breakfast, lunch, and pre-match. We would also have an afternoon nap to conserve energy. The combination of the calorific value of those meals and that sleepy siesta must have had a significant effect on performance. But the penny didn't drop then with anyone at the club or any of the players. Knowing what I know now about nutrition, I kick myself for not realising it at the time. Who knows what the impact would have been?

As the games started to come thick and fast, I witnessed first-hand the chemistry between Coop and Bobby Russell. Two hugely intelligent players, they instantly knew where each other was going to be, particularly in the final third of the pitch. From my vantage point at right-back, I was often mesmerised by the genius that they produced on a consistent basis.

As my first season as a Rangers player gathered momentum, I was able to tune into that telepathy occasionally. This is best illustrated in a winning game at Pittodrie in September 1982 when I claimed an assist for a goal scored by Robert Prytz.

We had started the season unbeaten and three days before we went north to the Granite City, Coop had scored four times when we defeated Kilmarnock 6-1 at Rugby Park in the first leg of the League Cup quarter final. We therefore went to Aberdeen imbued with confidence, despite the fact that Rangers hadn't won there since the inception of the Premier Division in 1975.

As always, there was a huge swathe of Rangers supporters located in the Beach End at Pittodrie. They were in fine voice as always and they spurred us on to achieve that elusive first win. I was involved in both the goals we scored too.

DJ scored our first when he headed home a corner kick that I had won, but it is my involvement in our second goal that I am most proud of.

Coop bamboozled a couple of Aberdeen defenders and played a cute reverse pass to Bobby Russell. Bobby cushioned a pass into my path and I went to the by-line before floating a cross to the far post. Prytzy rose highest to send a header beyond Jim Leighton.

I was having a good game prior to that moment and much of that was to do with how I was dealing with a player that had been my nemesis, a very talented winger called Peter Weir. I always seemed to struggle against him when I was at Thistle. He was not one of the stereotypical 'move the body' wingers that Pat Rice had taught me to deal with; Peter moved at pace and drove past full backs.

Peter came on as sub that day shortly after DJ had scored for us. Alex Ferguson was clearly sending out a message that his side were going to attack us. But this was going to be my day. I had realised in our previous encounters that whilst Peter was brave, he often retreated if he knew that his opposite number was on his game. With that in mind I tackled him early on and repeated the tackles on several occasions. As a result, Peter started to look nervous and rather than look to run at me when the ball was played to him, he instead looked for a quick pass inside. I knew at that point that I was going to have the upper hand.

Aberdeen halved the two-goal deficit when Gordon Strachan scored a penalty after Jim Stewart was adjudged to have fouled Mark McGhee, but we were worthy winners in the end.

As the Rangers fans celebrated, we headed for the tunnel which at Pittodrie is in the corner next to the Beach End. As we trooped off, I suddenly became aware that Alex Ferguson was moving towards me at pace. His face was contorted with rage and he shouted, "Ya dirty bastard," at me. I thought I was set for a confrontation with Fergie, but John Greig diffused the situation by stepping in and ushered me into the dressing room.

The following week, I found out that the chemistry on the park between Davie Cooper and Bobby wasn't solely down to telepathy.

After training on the Monday, Coop said to me, "Skippy, do you want to join me and Bobby for a kick-about?"

As the players drifted away from the Albion training pitch, Coop and Bobby grabbed a ball and moved into the final third area of the pitch. Coop took the ball inside, working back to the half-way line and Bobby moved into various positions to receive a pass then return the ball. It was like poetry in motion as these two magnificent ball players moved with almost balletic grace to hone the accuracy of the passes that they so often interchanged with each other.

"See," said Coop to me. "This is what we do to create space to open up a cross into the box. You got lucky on Saturday but keep watching and you'll learn something."

They say that 'practice makes perfect' and that's something that had been drummed into me from my Arsenal days. You were told that you had to work together to develop an understanding of how each other played and the positions your team mates would take up during games.

We would often reap rewards from that and a perfect example

was Coisty's record-breaking goal against Celtic in the early part of season 1983/84. It was the first of 27 that Ally would score against our Old Firm rivals, but the genesis of the move that created the goal came on the training ground.

In the week leading up to the game, Robert Prytz and I stayed back after training to practice free kicks. Prytzy was a very intelligent player and said that if we won a free-kick in the middle of the pitch, he'd take it quickly and play me in down the right.

Coisty had only just signed for us, but I approached him and asked if I had the ball where would he want me to cross it to. "Play it between the six-yard box and the penalty spot," was his answer. "Put it there and I'll score."

Within seconds of the kick off, Roy Aitken clattered into Sandy Clark just inside the Celtic half. Referee David Syme awarded us a free-kick and Prytzy grabbed the ball and nodded towards me. I scampered down the right wing and met his perfectly weighted pass just before the dead ball line. I rapped the ball into the penalty area as Coisty had instructed, he met it with his right foot and slammed it into the net. A mere 27 seconds had elapsed and it was another example of how communication in football is one of the keys to success.

During my time at Rangers, I was also Coop's warm up man.

Coop lived in Hamilton, but he didn't drive. If he couldn't get a lift then that meant a train and subway journey to Ibrox, yet he was always one of the first in for training in the morning.

I lived in Renfrew and usually arrived at the same time. There was a tennis court set up under the stand where we used to play head tennis, and not long after I joined the club, Coop challenged me to a game.

The court was adjacent to drainage pipes on the wall and when serving Coop would scoop the ball against them before delivery into my side of the court. It meant that it was difficult to track the trajectory of the ball and he would laugh as I ran about like a headless chicken trying to get the ball back to him. Nine times out of ten he would win 21-0! By then the better players had arrived looking to take the King's crown while I exited stage left with my groins and hamstrings aching.

I bumped into Coop many times after we both left Rangers and I always got the same rhetoric from him; "How's my warm up man? Still doing the slide tackles?" He would laugh and we would embrace.

Like so many others, I was stunned when I heard Coop had passed away on 23 March 1995. He had collapsed while coaching kids after suffering a brain haemorrhage. He was just 39 years of age.

## Tommy Burns
### 16 December 1956 – 15 May 2008

Thomas Burns was an exceptional human being. We crossed swords on many occasions in the heat of an Old Firm battle, but I always considered him an honest and fiery opponent.

In 1989, I signed for Kilmarnock following a successful four-week spell on loan from Airdrie. I joined a Kilmarnock side that had fallen on hard times. The league structure in Scotland at that time comprised Premier Division, First Division and Second Division. The Ayrshire side was second bottom of the lowest tier when I came in. Essentially, Kilmarnock was the second worst team in Scotland.

Jim Fleeting was the manager, and he had an excellent backroom team comprising Jim McSherry, Frank Coulston and my ex-team mate Jim Stewart. They were all very good coaches with superb man-management skills, but they'd been left with a team of young players who had talent but lacked experience.

I remember my first game on loan clearly. It was at Stenhousemuir and I was asked to play centre midfield. Either side of me and up front, were young energetic players, full of desire and commitment, but they didn't know the basics of the game. They were unsure when to go and when to stay, and after 10 minutes, they were running erratically all over the pitch, leaving gaps for the opposition to exploit.

As an experienced pro, I quickly had to reign them in. After a bit of coaching and cajoling, we won comfortably, 3-0.

This proved to be a watershed moment. Kilmarnock had taken four points from their opening five league games, but we won the next three games of my four-game loan period with good victories against Berwick Rangers (2-0), Stirling Albion (1-0), and Montrose (1-0).

This moved Kilmarnock up the league, so it was no surprise

that they found the £15,000 that Airdrie wanted to make my move permanent.

I was delighted. It was clear that the new Airdrie manager, Jimmy Bone, didn't want me, so I was relishing the prospect of joining a club that did. And in December 1989, I was joined in the ranks at Rugby Park by Tommy Burns, who came from Celtic for £50,000.

Tommy's arrival gave the club and the supporters a huge lift. I moved back into defence and Tommy took on my mantel of coach in the middle of the field.

Both of us used to talk constantly about the team and what influence our experience could have on the players. We both had the drive and determination that playing for the Old Firm had instilled in us and we were now both in our 30s; this gave us the experience to guide the young players and encourage them to reach a higher level.

Jim Fleeting and his coaches were fantastic with us too, and my time at Kilmarnock is one of the most enjoyable periods of my football career.

Tommy made his debut for Kilmarnock on 16 December 1989 against East Fife in Methil and it proved to be one of the most eventful of his illustrious career.

For trips through to Fife, some of the lads would meet at Rugby Park and get the team bus, while others like me would drive through to Coatbridge and meet the bus there. But on this particular afternoon, snowstorms and falling temperatures were causing carnage.

The team bus duly left Rugby Park on schedule, but as it reached Fenwick, it broke down. After a short delay, the bus was back on the road, but broke down again as the driver tried to traverse the treacherous Eaglesham Moor. A collective effort managed to get the bus going again, but a further stop was required in Eaglesham when one of the window wipers broke.

The bus driver carried out some repairs, although he almost got himself killed when he staggered out into the road after striking himself on the head with the broken wiper.

In the meantime, I was in Coatbridge waiting on the bus with a few other players. We had planned to meet for a pre-match meal, but as time went on, there was no sign of the bus. I received a phone call from Jim Fleeting to tell me about all the shenanigans and he assured me that they were now en-route.

I was working for the Tennent's Brewery as Kilmarnock were only part-time, and as chance would have it, the operations director of the company, Ian Clelland, owned the hotel where we were having our pre-match meal. There were around nine of us who'd travelled in cars to the rendezvous point, so we quickly had our meal and prepared for the team's arrival.

But by 1 p.m. – two hours before kick-off – there was no sight of the bus. It was at least an hour's journey to the Kingdom of Fife, but in the snow it would be longer. I spoke to Jim again and he told me to travel to the ground and that they would catch us up. It transpired that the bus had broken down again and the group were waiting for a replacement.

The Coatbridge collection looked to be making good time, but as we left Cowdenbeath, the roads suddenly got narrower and more treacherous. As we travelled, we listened to the radio. Game after game was postponed and the East Fife v Kilmarnock game turned out to be one of just six that went ahead in Scotland.

Despite the alpine terrain, we eventually arrived at the ground at 2.30 p.m. The players rushed into the dressing room and I went to see referee, Sandy Roy. He was a very decent man from Aberdeen, and I knew him well as he had refereed many games that I'd played in.

"Hi Sandy, we've got a bit of a problem," I said.

I explained the position and he said if we can name the nine of us who've arrived, he'd allow last minute changes right up to kick off. I don't know if this was in the SFA rules, but Sandy had applied common sense and we quickly tried to get our game heads on.

I called Jim and he said they'd be there at 2.45 p.m. The replacement bus hadn't arrived, so they were now heading to Methil in taxis. The nine of us at the ground didn't have any kit as that was on the bus, so we had to wait. The lads and the kit hampers duly arrived at 2.45 p.m. and we quickly got changed and ran out on to the pitch. We didn't have time for a warm-up, so Sandy blew his whistle and the game started.

But from the start, I could see that the trauma of the experience was affecting the players and very quickly we went behind. And as we moved into the second half things hadn't improved. As the sleet and snow bit into our faces, a defeat loomed as we were 2-1 down.

I was soaked through and started to shiver as the cold got to grips with me. Tommy came up to me and said, "Davie, you look terrible, are you OK to continue?"

I was the coldest I'd ever been in my life and I felt the energy drain from me, a combination of freezing temperatures and the anxiety of the journey hitting home. I remember slumping down on to the turf with my teeth chittering and chattering uncontrollably. By this time Sandy Roy and our physio, Hugh Allan, were by my side trying to raise me to my feet.

Hughie said there was just 15 minutes to go if I could hold out. At that moment, Tommy appeared and said to Sandy, "Ref, as you'll know Davie had a kidney removed when he was younger and the players are worried he might have hypo. Hypo. Hypo..."

"Hypothermia," Sandy finished for Tommy. "That's serious. I was thinking of abandoning the game, but this has confirmed it."

Sandy approached both benches, informed them of his decision and the match was abandoned. It's fair to say that the East Fife players, management team and supporters were less than enamoured with Sandy's decision, one that was going to rob them of two crucial points. And as Hughie walked me off, I bore the brunt of a fan's ire. Remarkably, he was dressed in a short sleeved East Fife replica shirt and he proceeded to bawl at me, "Mackinnon! Yer supposed to be a hard man? Ye wouldnae last two minutes doon the pit, pal". Hopefully the fact that East Fife won the rearranged fixture in January by four goals to two cheered him up!

When we were together at Kilmarnock, Tommy and I were always talking about football. I was captain, but Tommy and I worked in tandem on the pitch, ensuring that there was a link between the defence, midfield, and forward line, such that we worked as a unit. The arrangement worked well and the team gelled, but I have to admit there were one or two occasions when Tommy and I were at loggerheads.

Tommy was never one for tracking back which meant that on a few occasions, we would have an overload at the back. Frustration got the better of me one afternoon when we were playing Cowdenbeath, and I roared, "Fuck sake, Tommy! Work back the way."

Now Tommy was deeply religious and didn't use profanities. His response to me was simply, "I don't respond to that, Davie, so don't use that language again."

Disputes like that happen all the time in football, but it's important that a line is drawn under them after the game has ended. It's not healthy for them to fester. And Tommy and I settled our differences after that match at Cowdenbeath by having a laugh. I apologised for swearing and said it wouldn't happen again to which Tommy replied, "Davie, I'll make a good Catholic out of you yet." We laughed and we were back on track.

I had the honour of playing for seven different teams in my career and we were fortunate to have a vibrant and positive dressing room atmosphere at all of them. Having that is one of the rudimentary things that you need if you want to be successful. Each of the dressing rooms I was part of had a resident joker, and at Rugby Park, that role was taken on by Robert Reilly.

Robert was a very good player. He should have played at a higher level but didn't want to give up his day job. He had a bubbly personality and exuded positivity, even when things weren't going well for the team. Robert was also the team's social convener, and one Saturday evening, he arranged a party at his house after a game. I believe the popular phrase for such occasions is 'team bonding', and I think that night was instrumental in helping us come together and win promotion at the end of that season.

Tommy and I attended the party and that allowed us to indulge in something else that he and I had in common, we both loved to sing. Robert embraced that passion by doing karaoke, playing backing tracks for 'Ruby Don't Take Your Love to Town', which was my party piece, and 'Mac the Knife', which Tommy was famous for. It was like an episode of *The Voice* as we both put our heart and soul into our renditions. Tommy just edged it on the night, the lads voting him as the worthy winner.

Tommy Burns, a compassionate man who was devoted to his family, was loved and respected by the players. After I left Kilmarnock, I met him many times and he always greeted me the same way. "Hello, diamond," he said. "Are you still banging the penalties down the middle?"

This was a reference to a penalty kick that I took while we were at Kilmarnock – one of the defining moments of my career

– but the first time he said that to me, I was more interested in why he called me 'diamond'. I assumed it was because I had played for Airdrie, but he simply said to me, "No, Davie, it's because you're a good guy."

That made me feel like a million dollars and Tommy Burns made countless others feel the same way.

Tommy Burns died of melanoma skin cancer on 15 May 2008, aged 51. Another lovely man with an exceptional spirit who was taken from us far too soon, he is sadly missed.

### Alistair Dawson
### 25 February 1958 – 26 July 2021

I first met Ally Dawson when we were youngsters playing in football for the Paisley and District Life-Boys' team. Our team also included Gordon Boyd who, like Ally and me, would eventually play for Rangers.

Although we had to embark on a long bus journey to meet up – I stayed in Renfrew while Ally was from Johnstone – that was never an issue and we both chased our dream of becoming professional footballers together.

Ally was only 16 when he signed for Rangers. By then I had already signed for Arsenal and as we couldn't call upon the same communication technology that we can today, we didn't see each other again until I signed for Thistle and we crossed swords on the pitch.

Ally was highly thought of at Rangers – Jock Wallace took him on a world tour with the first team squad in 1975 – and in the early 80s, he was made captain by John Greig. Rangers had a squad full of leaders at that time like Sandy Jardine, Colin Jackson, Derek Johnstone, and Alex MacDonald, so this was an incredible accolade and testament to what Ally brought to the team.

Although he favoured his right-side, Ally was comfortable at both right back and left back. He was a very strong and steady player and I was pleased to see my old pal doing so well.

After captaining Rangers when they won the Scottish Cup in 1981, Ally sustained a fractured skull on a post-season tour of Canada. But he was resolute, a fighter, and he overcame his own challenges and came back stronger, not only to play again for Rangers but also to win caps for Scotland.

When I signed for Rangers, the friendship between Ally and me was rekindled and we stuck up for each other on and off the park.

Ally had been in and around the first team at Rangers since 1975 so he knew what was expected of a Rangers player. He had played alongside totemic figures like Derek Johnstone, John Greig and Sandy Jardine, and that coupled with his time as captain of the club meant he was perfectly placed to pass on words of wisdom about the traditions of the clubs and the levels of expectation. And when Robert Prytz and I signed for Rangers in 1982, Ally was our go to guy when it came to learning about all things Rangers.

As a fan himself, Ally knew how important the club was to the supporters. One of the first things he instilled in new guys like me was that we made sure we acknowledged the fans and thanked them for their support, particularly when we played away from home. Rangers fans travel far and wide to follow in the footsteps of their team, and Ally was sure and steadfast when it came to making sure the fans knew that irrespective of whether we won, lost, or drew a game, the players appreciated the vocal support we had received.

I can remember one particularly poignant experience too which epitomised Ally. After training one day, John Greig came into the dressing room and called Ally out into the corridor. After five minutes Ally returned and told Prytzy and I that a young teenage fan was ill in hospital, and his family had asked for players to visit. The youngster had a brain tumour and was very poorly, but as he was Rangers daft, his family knew a visit would lift his spirits.

We jumped into Ally's car and following a quick visit to the Rangers Shop, which was situated around the corner from the stadium, we drove the short distance to the Royal Infirmary in the Townhead district of Glasgow. On arrival, we were directed to a private room on the 2nd floor where we were introduced to the father of the teenager. He explained that while his son was still lucid, he had deteriorated badly in the last 24 hours. Doctors feared that he may not see out the afternoon. That news hit the three of us hard. We were three fit guys in their 20's, yet we were here to see a chap younger than us that could be dead by the time the day ended. It was a sobering moment.

After the father left to prepare his son for our visit, Ally told us that this wasn't his first time in a situation like this. During his time at the club, he'd regularly met seriously ill fans in hospital.

And he told Prytzy and I that our attendance would give the family support at a time when they needed it most.

Ten minutes later, a nurse entered the room and told us what to expect when we entered the patient's room. She advised that we talk to him as we would normally speak to any young fan and at that point, the nurse stood up and asked us to follow her.

As we entered a room along the corridor, the boy's father introduced us to his wife and his son who was lying on the bed.

"James. Ally Dawson, Robert Prytz and Davie Mackinnon are here to see you."

The young man tried to raise himself up but slipped back into the bed. I looked at Ally and he moved over to the bed and took the youngster's hand and placed it into his. Typical of the dry wit that he had, Ally said to James, "Sorry I couldn't get any decent players to come and meet you James, Prytz and Mackinnon will need to do."

Tears appeared in James's eyes and Ally grabbed a handkerchief from the bedside table and wiped the youngster's cheek. We each spoke in turn to James, and when we gave him the signed football and poster we'd got from the Rangers Shop, his face lit up.

We stayed for around an hour before the nurse told us they needed to work on James. James's mother and father warmly thanked us for taking time to visit and we hugged them as we left. When we reported to Ibrox for training the next morning, John Greig asked to speak to the three of us. James hadn't made it through the night, but despite being gripped by grief, his parents had called and asked the club to thank us. I remember being overcome with emotion, but on what must have been a very trying day for the family, I was glad that I had had the opportunity to bring some respite for them and cast some light into the last few hours of James's life.

In my first six months at Rangers, I played at a consistently high level. Under the guidance of John Greig, ably assisted by Tommy McLean, we were coached to play out from the back. Our goalkeeper, Jim Stewart, would roll the ball out to either Ally or me and we instantly played in our team-mates. When I received the ball, I had several players showing for a pass. Coop would be out wide and inside I had the option of Bobby Russell, Jim Bett or Robert Prytz, while across the backline I could find Craig Paterson

My mother and father lived in impecunious times, but they steadfastly held true to their principles of love and respect and set standards that I have lived by ever since. Here they are at the start of their journey.

Kicking a ball aged 3 at my grandparent's croft on the magical Isle of Skye.

Alongside Ally Dawson, a future Rangers team-mate, before an under 12 BB select game circa 1968.

**F.A. YOUTH CUP SEMI-FINAL**

Ian Crawford talks to his squad.

In Action: Richie Powling, John Matthews, Frank Stapleton and David MacKinnon.

Some pre-match PR as we trained before the FA Youth Cup semi-final against Spurs in 1974.

Pictured second from the right in the front row, I was part of the Arsenal youth team that played in the Iran international tournament in 1975. I was joined by the likes of Frank Stapelton, David O'Leary, Graham Rix, Richie Powling and John Devine.

Action from the match against Iran in February 1975, a fixture that attracted 30,000 partisan Iranians.

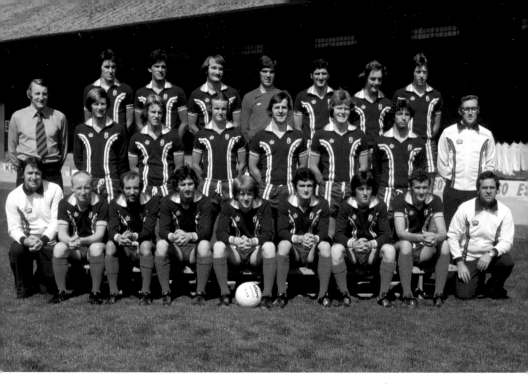

Managed by Tommy Gemmell (middle row, far left), I was part of a Dundee squad
in 1977 that included Gordon Strachan and Jimmy Johnstone.

Flanked by two Celtic legends, Bertie Auld (left) and Tommy Gemmell (right),
I sign for Partick Thistle in August 1978.

Watching on as Alan Rough saves from the late Johnny Doyle when Partick Thistle faced Celtic in front of a packed Firhill.

I got a number of stamps on my passport during my career, but this was one of the more obscure ones when we visited Nova Scotia in July 1979.

I was capped by the Scottish League. Managed by Jock Stein, we beat the Irish League 4-2 in Belfast.

My Scotland cap from the game
against the Irish League.

Tussling with the talented St Mirren
forward, Frank McGarvey.

Celebrating in the Partick Thistle dressing room after beating Celtic 1-0
to win the Glasgow Cup on 30 April 1981.

Putting Hibernian's George Best (7) on his backside. He was my boyhood hero.

Alan Rough is beaten, but I save the day with a left foot goal-line clearance from Rangers' Tom Forsyth.

I made the front page of the Daily Record with my two-year-old daughter, Kirsty, following my return to action after having my right kidney removed.

**With Ibrox in the throes of reconstruction, I keep my eye on the ball (as taught by Pat Rice) against the magnificent Davie Cooper of Rangers.**

**Slide tackle incoming as I chase down Aberdeen's John Hewitt at Ibrox.**

My cousin Murdo Macleod decked me but thought I was someone else! I convinced the ref not to book him.

Another tackle coming in on Tommy Burns in the usual Old Firm madness

Executing a spectacular overhead kick off the line clearance against Celtic in the 1982/83 League Cup Final at Hampden. We lost 2-1.

or John McClelland. Worst case scenario, I could send it long and hit Derek Johnstone who was supported by John Macdonald.

Each and every one of us were comfortable on the ball and it was a pleasure to play with such top-quality players. After I chose my pass, I'd run forward and get into the final third with the intention to cross into the box. I'd make the occasional tackle – usually a sliding one – and my game rose to another level. The fans were superb too, every tackle made being cheered to the rafters.

We were flying high. As 1982 was drawing to a close, we were on the verge of making the League Cup Final and we had lost only one of the opening nine league games. But on 3 November, our season turned sour.

In the UEFA Cup, we'd beaten Borussia Dortmund over two legs, drawing 0-0 away, then winning 2-0 at Ibrox, thanks to goals from Coop and DJ. Coop's goal came on the stroke of the referee's whistle and the effervescent Ibrox crowd gave us a rousing reception as we went back up the tunnel.

I saw Greigy run ahead into the dressing room, and as we entered, he stood in the middle of the room and unusually stuttered and stammered. He couldn't get any words out and Tommy McLean had to step in as John went for a seat. John was a great manager and coach, but it was clear the pressure was getting to him.

We were on a high, though, and we went out and blew them away in the second half. The game was probably my best in a Rangers jersey, and after the match my confidence was boosted further when I encountered my direct opponent that night, the Dortmund winger Heinz Eggeling, as we left the pitch at full time.

I felt I had played him hard but fair and throughout the game he had graciously applauded me whenever I slid in and took the ball from him. He was substituted 20 minutes into the second half, but as we took the acclaim of the Rangers supporters, Eggeling came up to me, shook my hand and said, "I'm glad you don't play in West Germany. Nobody tackles like this; you should come to Dortmund." That was a real compliment and I relished getting another opportunity to pit my wits against a West German side when we drew FC Cologne in the next round.

Our performance over the two legs against Dortmund had us living up to the lyrics in the famous Rangers song, 'Keep the Blue Flag Flying High.' We really did 'fear no foe', and we thought that we had a real chance, not just of defeating Cologne, but going all the way and winning the tournament too.

To progress, though, we would have to find a way past a goalkeeper who had achieved notoriety five months earlier. Toni Schumacher had come hurtling out of his goal and almost decapitated Patrick Battiston with a horrendous head high kick in the semi-final of the 1982 World Cup. How he wasn't ordered off I will never know!

The first leg was at Ibrox, and as we warmed up in the red blaes area under the Main Stand that we used for stretching, Schumacher was kicking a ball against the wall and catching it. As I ran past him, he turned and kicked the ball into my face. The red mist descended at that moment, and even though he was a big guy, I grabbed Schumacher and pulled him to the ground.

We rolled about trying to land punches while exchanging insults in German. I had learned some of the language while I was on tour with Arsenal, so I called Schumacher 'schwanzkopf' which means moron, and he uttered a barrage of swear words at me too. Eventually, big Peter McCloy arrived and pulled us apart.

That didn't stop Schumacher's verbal volleying, though. He continued to shout in German and I didn't need a phrase book to tell me that he wasn't being complimentary. But as he got angrier, I started to laugh then fired the parting shot of 'verdammter schwanzkopf' (fucking moron).

Ibrox Stadium is a special place, but on a European night under the lights, it goes to another level. The atmosphere was electric as we kicked off, and inside the opening minutes, Prytzy released a pass that sent me scurrying deep into their half. As I tried to get on the end of the pass, the ball ran into the box.

Out came Schumacher and it was a race to see who would get there first. With our altercation in the warm-up area still fresh in my mind, I wasn't going to let the big bastard intimidate me. As I reached his six-yard area, the ball ran beyond Schumacher and he launched his foot towards me. My leg was also outstretched, and we collided, his studs crunching into my chest. My studs connected with him in the same area too.

Cue round two of the verbals. We were still going at it when the laid back referee from Sweden arrived. He diffused the situation admirably, simply saying, "Now boys, play nice or I'll have to send you off, OK?"

We won 2-1, but I almost grabbed a rare goal late in the game when I got sight of the target when the ball landed at my feet 25 yards from goal. The connection was good, Schumacher leapt across his goal and turned the ball round the post.

When we arrived in Cologne for the next leg the atmosphere was toxic. Ally and I were sharing a room, and as we entered, we both stopped as there was a large lump under the covers in one of the single beds. "What's that?" asked Ally as he put his hand on the lump and moved it. I pulled back the covers and there lying prostrate on the bed was a dead rabbit.

This was clearly an attempt at intimidation by our opponents and all stemmed from a headline from a German newspaper. The day after the first leg the newspaper implied that I would have kicked a rabbit if it ran across the pitch – evidently my style of play had irked them – but suffice to say I wasn't ruffled in the slightest. Ally and I simply grabbed our bags and went back down to reception and were allocated another room.

As we warmed up, we kept an eye on the other end where the diminutive Pierre Littbarski was firing crosses into the box that were being volleyed into the net by his fellow forwards. "You'll need to kick him early on," I said to Ally.

Twenty minutes in, that volleying practice paid off. Four unstoppable shots whizzed past big Jimmy Stewart. I also gave away a penalty, although I thought the foul had occurred outside the box.

We eventually lost the game 5-0. It was a horror result and it sapped almost all of the confidence that we had built up since the season had started. The following Saturday, Jimmy Stewart rolled the ball out to me as usual. But while I'd had a plethora of options to pass to prior to Cologne, it was now as if no one wanted the ball. We never recovered our poise and a season that had promised so much delivered nothing. We finished third in the league, 21 points behind champions, Dundee United, and lost in the final of both the League Cup and Scottish Cup.

Although we struggled as a collective, I was still maintaining a decent level of consistency. I had made the number two jersey my own, but I picked up an ankle injury early in 1983 that ruled me out for six weeks.

The following weekend we faced Falkirk in the Scottish Cup and Ally moved over to occupy my right back berth. I went to the game and Ally was sensational. I knew at that moment that upon my return to fitness I would have to find another position as his performance was greater than anything I could produce.

As he came on to the bus after the game I gave him a round of applause and shook his hand, "Magnificent mate". I remember saying. If it had been anyone else, I may not have been so magnanimous, but Ally was my mate and I was genuinely happy for him.

When I was fully fit, I returned to the team in centre midfield and had some success, but I felt that I was better and more comfortable playing at right back.

When John Greig left and Jock Wallace came in, I was also deployed at left back and centre back. I was soon earning that unwanted tag of 'utility player' and I recall Jock saying exactly that in an interview which he did with one of the national newspapers.

In season 1984/85, I got some game time on the right of our defence, and one game of note was the visit of Inter Milan to Ibrox for a UEFA Cup tie. We had been battered 3-0 in Italy, but in the return leg, big Jock played me at right wing back with Ally fulfilling the same role on the left.

We were magnificent in the opening half and at the interval we were 3-1 up. But I was annoyed at the antics of the Inter winger. He would switch from right to left and he also pulled the hairs on the back of your legs as the ball approached. He would then collapse theatrically onto the turf looking for a free-kick. It was both frustrating and painful, as if you've ever had hairs pulled out of your thigh, you'll know how sore it is.

Ally and I sat together in the dressing room at half-time. I said, "What about that wee bastard, Ally? He keeps pulling the hair out of my legs."

"He's done the same to me," replied Ally, "I'm going to do the wee bastard."

As we moved into the second half, Ally broke out of defence with the wee winger in pursuit. But as he closed in, Ally's elbow caught him in the mouth. Cue more theatrics.

As the referee approached, I think Ally felt that he was about to be ordered off. A card was indeed brandished, but it was for the little play actor who received a yellow for diving. I remember looking at Ally and we each had a wee smile of satisfaction on our faces.

We used to call Ally 'Dozy' as he liked to sleep a lot. He was a wonderful man.

Ally and I both contributed to a book written by a friend and this book's editor, Alistair Aird, called *Rangers FC in the 1980s – The Players Stories*. After the book was published, Alistair set up a WhatsApp group chat which allowed us to share memories of our time at Rangers and to stay connected with each other.

We found out that Dozy was ill and spoke openly about it. I would call him regularly to see how he was, and although there were times when his speech was affected as his illness kicked in, he was always positive.

On one of our calls, I suggested that we meet up and Ally invited Coisty and me down to his house to come and shoot the breeze. At that point I knew it was only a matter of time before Ally passed away, but I still hoped to receive the invitation. It never came. Ally's health deteriorated rapidly, and he was admitted to a hospice for palliative care.

On 26 July 2021, the sad news reached us that Ally had died. He was 63 years of age.

# CHAPTER 4
# MAY THEY REST IN PEACE - MANAGERS

*April 2022*

I HAVE UNDERGONE several tests including an MRI scan and some cardio analysis. The brain surgeon wants to see if a heart rate blip caused my brain lesion/stroke. Sure enough, they detect an anomaly in my heart rhythm. They tell me that it might actually be linked to my playing career.

I learn soon afterwards that John MacPhail, who I had played with at Dundee before he went on to play for Sheffield United and Sunderland, has had a similar fall. John fell down the stairs in his house, but he hasn't been as lucky as me; he has lapsed into a coma.

The news has a profound effect on me. I pray that John recovers and I suggest to a mutual friend that we organise a fundraising dinner for John.

And when the news reaches me, I take time again to reflect once again about my mortality, although this time, I choose to reflect on the managers that I have been lucky to work with who are sadly no longer with us.

*****

**Bertie Auld**
*23 March 1938 – 14 November 2021*
Robert 'Bertie' Auld was a unique individual. He played at the highest level and won countless honours with Celtic, including the European Cup in 1967. Once he hung up his boots, he became manager of Partick Thistle in 1974. It seemed like

destiny since Bertie had been born and raised a free kick away from Firhill on Panmure Street where his mother owned a shop.

Jackie Husband was the man that first made me aware that there might be an opportunity to move to Thistle from Dundee. Dundee were due to play Inverness Caledonian in a pre-season match and Jackie called me to say that Bertie was coming to see me play.

That night I was playing centre midfield and was up against a hero of mine, Andy Penman. Andy had played for Dundee and Rangers, I watched and admired him many times as I was growing up.

During the warm-up, I sidled up beside him and smiled. He drew me a look and said, "What are you wanting, ginge?"

It wasn't what I expected and said, "You'll find out shortly."

It wasn't quite the exchange of pleasantries I had anticipated, but it gave me a lift. I felt as if Andy had thrown down the gauntlet and that motivated me to show my hero just what I could do.

As we came out for the start of the match, I saw wee Bertie on the terrace and the words of Alan Ball came to the fore.

*"You can run and tackle so what I want you to do is run and tackle in the first minute and run and tackle in the last minute. People at the game – fans, managers, scouts – remember the start and finish of a game so if Mackinnon's the guy that catches their eye in the first and last minute then you're the man."*

I started out with a solid tackle and a shot at goal and I ran for the whole 90 minutes. I've always thought attitude and conviction played a huge part in performance and I played what I thought was my best game for Dundee that night.

The next week Tommy Gemmell called me into his office and said that he'd accepted a bid from Thistle. Tommy travelled with me to the Salutation Hotel in Perth where I was to meet Bertie to discuss and hopefully agree personal terms. Although Thistle were part-time, they were in the Premier Division, and wee Bertie made me an offer that would see me double my wages. He also offered a generous signing-on fee. It was a no-brainer; I signed on the dotted line flanked by two Lisbon Lions.

I'll admit that my career was in limbo when I signed for Thistle. The hangover from the decision to quit Arsenal was still lingering and I hadn't made the impression at Dundee that I had wanted to due to injury. But Bertie immediately made me feel wanted and I had a feeling that the move would resurrect my flagging career.

Bertie brimmed full of enthusiasm, and when he outlined his plans, he did so making use of vivid imagery. You could picture in your own head what he was planning due to the way he put his message across. As he spoke, he described the Firhill pitch and how he would set his team out. He made reference to each player, highlighting their strengths and weaknesses, while telling me where he thought I would fit in. That sort of visionary thinking certainly whetted my appetite and I was determined to play at the top of my game for Bertie.

My first pre-season at Thistle was tough. We would gather on a Monday, Tuesday and Thursday evening and also for a full day session on Saturday. We ran countless laps around the track at Firhill and pounded the pavements of the surrounding streets too. For the first three weeks, we didn't see a ball. No one was exempt, not even Alan Rough who wasn't long back from Argentina where he had represented Scotland at the World Cup.

As I've already alluded, we had a vibrant and bubbly dressing room, so although the sessions were arduous, the mischief makers were never too far away. Bertie encouraged that. He was very much an advocate of the 'carrot and stick' approach.

A regular routine on a Tuesday evening saw Bertie, stopwatch in hand, wave us off from Firhill in pairs to embark on a run that took in most of Possilpark and Lambhill. One particular night I was paired with Roughie as Bertie wanted me to stretch him. As he clicked his stopwatch and logged the start time, I set off at pace, running up Firhill Road towards Panmure Street, leaving Roughie panting in my wake.

As we turned the corner, I noticed a black taxicab sitting at the side of the road with its engine running. "Davie, stop," hollered Roughie. I stop at the taxi and Roughie comes panting behind and stops. The taxi driver rolled down the window and opened up the back door. Roughie jumped into the back seat. I was startled and said, "Hey, Roughie, what's going on?"

"Fuck that running Davie, that's no fur goalies," was his reply. "Do you want a lift?"

I paused for thought, but immediately visualised Bertie and his reaction if he caught us. "Na Roughie, you go ahead," I said, and I started running again.

I must have covered another half mile when I saw the taxi drawing up alongside me. Roughie rolled down the window and said, "I'll get you at the Ruchill Park end of Bilsland Drive, Davie. We'll then run into Firhill together." The window went up and the cab sped off towards Possilpark.

Half an hour later I arrived at the rendezvous point at which point Roughie jumped out of the taxi and started running towards Firhill. His time resting in the back of the taxi meant that the big bastard was ahead of me, and he must have been some 75 yards in front when we turned into Firhill Street. As he reached the stadium, I'd reduced that to 30 yards. Roughie reached the main entrance of the ground where Bertie was standing with his stopwatch and theatrically 'dipped for the line' as he passed Bertie.

I arrived shortly afterwards at which point Bertie shouted, "I would never have believed Roughie would outpace you, Davie. I thought you were fitter than that." He then turned to our physio, Donnie, and said "Donnie, 12-minute run for Mackinnon."

By this point, Roughie is doing some exaggerated running on the spot, and as Donnie takes me through the front doors for my 12-minute pounding, Roughie shouted, "You'll need to up your game Davie, you're no' at Dundee now." He was smiling as he knew that he had got one over on me!

Roughie is a great guy who has a wonderful sense of humour. Away from the dressing room pack, I saw a trait that would have derailed his perceived persona amongst the guys; he had great empathy with people. I first noticed this side of his character when we were both asked by the club physiotherapist, Donnie Mackinnon, to come into the club one afternoon. Donnie had been commissioned by the hugely talented film producer and writer, Bill Forsyth to assist as a football mentor in a new production he was creating. The film was to be called *Gregory's Girl* and it was a coming-of-age comedy film set in Cumbernauld.

The cast were largely made up of young unknown teenage talent, and Donnie thought that the experience of working with professional players would give them a better sense of the game.

Cue Roughie and I to get into our training gear and give the pair some basic coaching on the pitch at Firhill. The two main characters, Gregory and Dorothy, played by John Gordon Sinclair, or Gordie as he asked us to call him, and Dee Hepburn, were nice kids who didn't know at that point the influence the film would have on their careers and fame. They were awestruck as we took them on to the pitch. In the film, Gordie was to be replaced at centre forward in the school team by Dee, and he was to become the goalkeeper. Dee had been practising keepy uppy and had a decent touch.

We had a laugh and a few drills on the pitch for an hour and they both genuinely thanked us and said we'd helped them. Particularly as Roughie had been deliberately diving the wrong way at shooting in. At a break I said "Roughie, you're having a mare, try and get near some of these shots".

He just smiled and said, "Not a word to anyone, Davie, I'm just trying to give them some confidence". It was a side of Roughie I'd never seen, and I got it that he didn't want the squad to know he had a heart. I was extremely honoured to see that side of him and when we both returned to the madhouse that was the Thistle dressing room, I kept the exchange between the big man and me quiet. In all we worked with Gordie and Dee for around six weeks, and I think they both pulled it off in the film.

*Gregory's Girl* went on to be a worldwide success and brought the two actors into the spotlight. I met Gordie years later and he hadn't changed, still a thoughtful and nice guy. Produced on a working budget of under £200,000, the film generated worldwide box office revenue of £25.8Million. Now that was a result!

Back to Partick Thistle and one of our first league games was away at Aberdeen, and as the day unfolded, it quickly became one of the craziest ones that I experienced in my entire career.

Roughie turned up for the bus with a white suit on and sat near the front beside the talented winger Bobby Houston. Bobby was wearing a black leather suit, so the contrast was stark.

Bertie had arranged for us to have our pre-match meal at Stonehaven, so as the bus pulled into the car park of the Queen's Hotel, both Bobby and Roughie got up to stretch their legs.

I was seated diagonally opposite and as Roughie turned towards me, I noticed there was a black mark down his jacket and trousers. I pointed it out to him, saying that his seat must have been dirty. "Ah fuck, I just bought this yesterday from Slaters," was the big man's reply before he had a go at the driver, walked off the bus and headed for the hotel dining room.

Roughie was raging and kept standing up to look at the damage to his suit in a full-length mirror. Suddenly, one of our midfield players, Ally Love, stood up laughing. "Roughie!" he hollered. "Badger (Bobby Houston's nickname) has just told me the reason for the black mark. Go on, Badger, tell him. Roughie will no' mind."

Bobby had tried to stop Ally from spilling the beans by putting his hand over his mouth, but the cat was out the bag so, with reluctance, Bobby got up and said, "Roughie, Margaret (Bobby's wife) thought my leather suit was looking a bit shabby, so she gave it a wee polish this morning. Sorry big man, I'll get your suit dry cleaned."

Shortly afterwards, Bertie came into the dining room and said we were to go for a walk along the nearby beach. We walked to the shore and sat on a wall as the tide started to turn.

Brian Whittaker, always on the lookout for some fun, said. "Roughie, you like a bet big man, so you've got a chance of saving this gold bracelet of yours I found on the floor. I've got a tenner here that says you can't grab this before the tide comes in."

The North Sea was lapping towards the wall we were on, so Brian moved to the water's edge and placed the bracelet on the sand. Roughie got up, stretched his legs then prepared to jump onto the sand.

"It's all about timing, Roughie," I shouted.

Roughie watched as the tide came in then went back out again. As it was retreating, Roughie leapt onto the sand and immediately dropped into a hole that Brian had prepared in advance. Roughie managed to grab the bracelet and pull himself out of the hole, but his white suit trousers were now caked with wet sand!

He was oblivious to this, though, and he shouted, "Right Piggy, gees the tenner."

The players laughed, but Bobby probably more than most of us. The state of Roughie's trousers now meant that a couple of flashes of polish were the least of his concerns.

We got back on the bus and Bertie came on and clocked the state of Roughie's white suit. "Donnie, get a pair of trackies for this arsehole," he said tersely.

Donnie retrieved a pair of black and red tracksuit bottoms from the hamper and threw them at Roughie. He put them on, and half an hour later, we had reached our destination, Pittodrie.

Gathered outside the ground was a pack of journalists and one of them grabbed me to ask me how I was settling in at Thistle.

As I start to reply, Scotland's international goalkeeper emerged from the bus. Suddenly, nobody wanted to know how David Mackinnon was settling in at Thistle! Instead, the flashbulbs were popping as attention turned to Roughie, strutting towards the players' entrance, with his trademark blond curly perm, white stained jacket, and a pair of black and red tracksuit bottoms on. Roughie didn't have a care in the world, and I realised at that moment how happy I was at Thistle, both on and off the park.

We drew the match 1-1 against Aberdeen, and in the home XI was my old friend, Gordon Strachan. As we warmed up, I asked Strachs how he was settling in at Pittodrie. "The fans hate me," he replied.

I thought he was at it. I knew first-hand how much ability Gordon had and I thought he was lulling me into a false sense of security. But not long after the game started, Gordon received the ball and boos echoed around the stadium. He would eventually achieve legendary status at Aberdeen, but it was clear at that point that he had some work to do to win over the discerning home support.

The competitive skulduggery between Roughie and Piggy (Brian Whittaker) was legendary at Thistle. I do think that Piggy edged it though during a pre-season trip to Nova Scotia in 1979. We had unexpectedly been invited to a four team tournament in Halifax, which we subsequently won, and flew out from Prestwick airport midway through pre-season training. We were staying on the university campus and were roomed in one-bedroom apartments. My apartment was set between the two protagonists.

Roughie had bought a white Stetson hat at a local store on arrival, and he had taken unbelievable stick from the squad. It was though the fuel that energises the big man and he wore it on all occasions, including training.

One night we were allowed out for a couple of beers, with a strict 11.00 p.m. curfew. As manager Bertie Auld and his assistant Pat Quinn, checked the rooms to ensure everyone kept to the curfew, I noticed that Roughie hadn't made it back.

As the management pair made their way along the corridor, I stuck my head out of my room to see Piggy walking out of Roughie's room. "The big man not back?" I asked.

"No," answered Piggy, "and you've not seen me, right?"

As the words left Piggy's lips Bertie arrived on the scene. "Right Pat, mark Mackinnon and Whittaker present," Bertie said as they walked passed us and stood outside Roughie's room. "Ok, Pat, this must be Rough's room?"

"It is Bertie," said Pat as he opened the door.

As Piggy and I stuck our heads out of our door, we heard Bertie shouting. "Fuck Pat, he's not here, put it down as a fine. But Pat what's that smell, it's stinking?"

Piggy and I ventured into the hallway of Roughie's apartment to hear Pat reply. "Its coming from that white hat up on the wardrobe Bertie". Pat stretched up and pulled the hat off the wardrobe. "Oh Bertie, someone's done a shit in the hat," he shrieked.

Piggy grabbed me by the arm and pulled me back into the corridor. "Remember you didn't see me in Roughie's room did you?" He winked and we went back into our rooms. Safe to say Roughie never wore the white Stetson again. Game set and match to Piggy!

The turn of the year into 1979 brought the worst winter in years. After drawing 1-1 with Motherwell at Fir Park on the 22 December 1978, we were second in the table, just three points behind leaders Dundee United with a game in hand. I genuinely thought that we had a shot at the title.

But then the big freeze set in. We didn't play again in the league until 17 February, and during that spell of inactivity, we couldn't train properly. We had to flit from school hall to school hall to try and maintain some fitness and sharpness which was far from ideal.

When the games resumed, we went into freefall, losing 10 of our last 18 league matches. We finished in eighth place, comfortably clear of relegation, but that Arctic blast probably cost us a place in Europe at the very least.

I last saw Bertie in January 2019. I was a director at Hamilton, and we were at Parkhead for a league game against Celtic. It was a day rubbing shoulders with celebrities for me; I was introduced to the wonderful Billy Connolly by my long-term friend, Tony Roper, and had my photograph taken with Martin Compston, the very talented actor from Greenock who found fame in the BBC drama series *Line of Duty*.

Bertie was in the boardroom and was laughing. He said to Martin, "Do you know this guy used to play for Rangers, Martin?" at which point Martin made a face and said, "I wish you'd told me that before the photo, Bertie."

As a manager Bertie always kept some distance between

himself and his players. But that day as he made a beeline across the boardroom towards me, I saw that he had changed. He was ebullient as always, but back in the day, he wouldn't have given you a hug or anything like that. However, as he strode towards me, his arms were outstretched and he gave me a big cuddle. "How are you, my son?" he asked. "I'm well, gaffer, how are you?" was my reply.

He smiled and said, "I'm great son, a couple of health problems but God's looking after me." At that moment the referee's bell sounded and we went back to the directors' box to watch the second half of the match.

"Tell the family Bertie was asking for them, son. God bless," was Bertie's parting remark to me. He seemed to be at peace and in a good place spiritually.

Bertie Auld was a special man. He died on 14 November 2021, aged 83.

### Tommy Gemmell
### 16 October 1943 – 2 March 2017

I first met Tommy Gemmell when I came up on loan to Dundee from Arsenal. Dundee trained at Strathmartine Psychiatric Hospital and I was in the passenger seat of Tommy's car as he drove to training. The journey was an eye-opener for me to say the least.

Tommy was a compassionate guy who could mix humour and pathos in the same sentence. He was a bundle of energy and that was mirrored in the way he drove a car. I liked him instantly although during journeys in his car my hands were firmly welded to the seat.

As we journeyed through the streets of Dundee, he said to me, "If you're at a loose end anytime in your digs, just let me know and you can come to the hotel."

Tommy, who was on the final lap of his playing days when I joined on loan, owned a hotel in Errol, the same village that Reddy lived in. For a seasoned pro to make that gesture to a young player was very unusual in those days, but it proved quickly to me that Tommy was a caring human being.

Tommy had a reputation as a hard man, but he was also renowned for his ability from the penalty spot. Still in the nascent days of my career and a sponge when it came to soaking up knowledge from my peers, I wanted to know his secret. I seized my opportunity during that first session when we were both trying to make our mark from 12 yards.

"Any tips on taking penalties, Tam?" I asked expecting to get a lesson in the art of taking the perfect penalty.

But Tommy simply smiled and said, "It's simple, son, I just run up and hit it as hard as I can. I haven't a fucking clue where it's going, and if I don't have a clue, then the goalkeeper has no chance!" At that point, he turned round and battered one into the top corner.

This was another valuable lesson, one I used on many occasions when I was called upon to take a penalty kick, usually as the last member of the team in a penalty shootout. The advice also came in handy when I was asked to take the penalty kick that would make or break Kilmarnock's chances of promotion in 1990.

Tommy took over from Davie White as manager of Dundee on 12 June 1977, and looking back now, the transition from player to manager must have been difficult for Tommy. The dressing room was his domain after all. He was a player's man and the leader who, more often than not, spoke to the club's hierarchy on the player's behalf.

I remember one occasion when we were playing St Johnstone in a Scottish Cup replay. We were offered what I thought was a decent £100 each should we secure progression into the next round. But Tommy was adamant that it wasn't enough, and an hour from kick off when Davie White read out the team, Tommy, who had been out injured since December, assumed the role of shop-steward and delivered an ultimatum.

He stood up and told Davie White, "Boss, the players aren't happy about the bonus and unless the chairman increases it, they're not playing."

At that he sat down and I witnessed several of the senior players taking their boots off and throwing them onto the concrete floor. I was one of the two substitutes listed that day. For me, £100 was decent, so I didn't join in. I was also just in the door and I had been schooled by my father not to challenge people in authority.

Davie White, usually a quiet, dignified man, was livid and stormed out of the dressing room.

Tam stood up and gave another impassioned speech. The club were "taking the piss" he said before adding, "We've had two sell-out crowds and there's a chance of getting either

Rangers or Celtic in the next round. They can afford it so you're not going out until the bonus increases."

It was my first experience of player revolt and I sat in the Dens Park dressing room wondering what would happen next. I would get my answer when Davie White came back in to address us 20 minutes before kick-off.

He told us, "I don't accept the way you've done this. Nobody is bigger than the club. I have though had a chat with the chairman, and he's upped the bonus to £150, but this is the last time this ever happens, right Tam?"

By this point, Davie was six inches from Tommy's face, but the big man simply smiled and said, "The lads better win then."

Looking back, I believe that Tommy had planned this confrontation as he quite openly made it clear that he wanted the manager's job. Six months later he got it.

In the meantime, we beat St Johnstone 4-2. I replaced one of our goalscorers, Bobby Hutchison, with 20 minutes to go, and Dundee actually got to the semi-final before being defeated by a strong Celtic side 2-0.

The defeat to Celtic was on 6 April 1977. Around five months earlier, I got married for the first time. It was midweek and the previous Saturday, Tommy had organised a whip round for a present, which was a great gesture. He also organised a pub crawl, or a 'smoker' as they called it in Dundee, a couple of days after we drew 1-1 against Morton at Dens Park.

I have to admit that I was apprehensive. There was a drinking culture at most clubs in that era, but I wasn't a big consumer of alcohol. My limit was usually a couple of lagers, but even they were diluted with a dash of lime.

In the second pub that we visited, Tommy insisted he bought a round and asked me what I wanted. I said a lager and lime and he said "No, a spirit."

I didn't have a clue but for some reason I asked for a dry Martini and lemonade. Tommy laughed and called a waitress over. "Five vodkas and Coke, five Bacardi and Coke, and a Martini and lemonade for the lady," he said pointing to me.

We finished our drinks at which point Tommy announced, "Right lads, next pub." He got up to walk out, but he was met at the door by the manager of the pub.

"Eh, Mr Gemmell, you'll need to pay for these drinks before you leave," he said holding Tommy's arm.

Tommy brushed the manager's arm away and said, "Na son, for your cheek, I'm no' paying."

Tommy stepped into the guy's space and rubbed his own nose and said, "If you want it, take it oot ma nose."

The guys started laughing, but the manager came back with a classic. "Have you nothing smaller, Tommy?"

The blue touch paper had been lit.

Tommy was the double of the Hollywood actor Danny Kaye. Both were handsome, charismatic characters and Tommy would occasionally give us a rendition of some of Danny's songs. But they also shared another characteristic, they each had a very large nose. As I got to know him, I could sense Tommy was a bit self-conscious as he often had a kick at players, team-mates and opposition, who ribbed him about the size of his nose. In fact, he told me his infamous kick at Helmut Haller in a World Cup qualifier against West Germany was because he was wound up as Haller had called him a 'big nosed twat' throughout the game. That may have been a Gemmell urban myth, though.

I could see Tam was raging with the pub manager, but he didn't show any emotion as he threw a tenner and a fiver on to the table – pub prices were a little lower back then – and said, "That'll cover it, but anything left get yirself a wee bit of ointment to clear up that ugly puss of yours."

When Tommy was appointed manager, he was very supportive of me. In his first full season, 1977/78, I managed 27 appearances in all competitions and scored three goals. The first of those was the winner against East Fife at Dens Park in October. At that stage of my career, I needed games to flourish and I was grateful for the faith that Tommy showed in me. He was also ahead of his time to an extent as he deployed me as a right-wing-back and encouraged me to get forward as much as possible.

I was enjoying my football, and after losing 4-3 to St Johnstone on 2 January, we were unbeaten in our next 11 league games. The run was ended by a 2-1 defeat against Dumbarton at Boghead and that proved costly. We finished third, a point adrift of both Morton and Hearts.

It was tough to take as Tommy had us playing in a cavalier style that was attractive for the fans. That boosted attendances, and we averaged around 6,000 at home and scored 91 goals in the league. Our principal marksman was Billy Pirie, a natural goalscorer in the mould of Coisty. He notched an incredible 38 goals that season.

I made my last appearance for Dundee against Celtic on 16 August 1978. I joined Thistle, and as my first season at Firhill drew to a close, Tommy was leading Dundee to promotion as First Division champions. I was delighted for him and sent him a congratulations card.

Tommy Gemmell, one of the Lisbon Lions, died on 2 March 2017, aged 73, after a long illness.

### Jock Wallace
### 6 September 1935 – 24 July 1996

I can still vividly recall the first time that I met Jock Wallace face to face. He had just been appointed as the manager of Rangers following John Greig's departure and having recently been manager of Motherwell. Jock also penned a column in the *Glasgow Evening Times*, and the week before he came back to Rangers, he had commented favourably about me in that column. He had written, "Mackinnon is the type of guy I'd want in my team. He'd run through a brick wall and he epitomises what it means to be a Ger."

When a new manager comes into a club, their arrival naturally breeds uncertainty about whether you would be part of the plans going forward. But Jock's words had banished any of those notions for me and I walked into Ibrox full of confidence on the day of his appointment.

There was an air of anticipation as the chat buzzed around the dressing room that morning as we prepared for Jock's arrival. I remember donning my training gear quickly and sitting with the others waiting for this colossal figure to join us. I had taken a bit of ribbing from the lads about Jock's column – the general consensus was that I must have paid the big man to write what he did – but I will admit that his words were at the forefront of my mind. That was my first mistake. My second was only minutes away too.

Dressed in a blue tracksuit and red socks pulled up to his knees, Jock entered the dressing room and the first impression was that he had immense presence. I remember thinking that his hands were huge too. The room fell silent as the big man stood behind the treatment table in the middle of the room, his big arms engulfing the headboard.

"Right, listen in," he said.

At that moment, his piercing blue eyes met with mine and in his trademark booming voice, he hollered, "Mackinnon, out here!"

I was stunned. I stood up and was immediately conscious that some of my team-mates were making less than complimentary hand gestures. I moved towards the treatment table and big Jock moved towards me. I'm not sure what I expected to happen at that point, but I certainly wasn't ready for one of his massive hands grabbing me by the neck. Cue raucous laughter from my team-mates. I was on the spot!

Jock turned me to face my team-mates, his hand slipping to the back of my neck. "I need to give you a warning, son," he said in a voice that reverberated around the room. "I was a jungle fighter, so don't move for your own safety."

"Too tippy-tappy, too many touches," was his assessment of my game. "Two touches is all I want from you, one to control it and the other to fuck it up to the striker, got it?"

I was still thinking about the positive comments in the newspaper column, though, and I made a face which increased the levels of laughter from the players. And at that moment, I made the second mistake, and this one could have been fatal.

"I can't do that, gaffer," I said, his grip on my neck tightening as the words came out. I can't recall who it was, but one of the players made a sign of a throat being cut and shook his head.

"Ye cannae dae that? "Two touches?" said Jock aghast.

"No," I said, "I need three touches, two to control it and one to fuck it up to the striker!"

Silence.

Big Jock turned me around. My mind flitted immediately to the team-mate who had made the throat-cutting gesture. Was my relationship with my new manager about to end before it had even started?

Fortunately, it didn't. Big Jock released his vice-like grip and said, "I'll say this for you, son, you've got some balls". He slapped me softly and I walked back to my seat, my first encounter with big Jock over. I'd say it was a score draw!

Jock's first game in charge was against Aberdeen at Pittodrie.

He tried to lift the spirits by having us stay overnight prior to the game and changed the blue socks back to the traditional black with red tops. The club was subsequently fined for wearing the socks as they weren't registered colours.

As we drove into Aberdeen, the Rangers fans were, as always, out in their numbers. Big Jock moved to the front of the bus and put a cassette into the tape deck. 'The Sash My Father Wore' blasted through the speakers, and Jock walked up the aisle shouting, "Sing, sing". As he passed a silent Robert Prytz he shouted, "Sing Prytzy, sing".

Prytzy, in broken English, shouted "I no sing gaffer, I not know the words".

"Sing it in Swedish then," roared Jock. Prytzy started singing something in Swedish and big Jock was happy.

Despite Jock's efforts we lost 3-0. This was our eighth defeat in the opening 12 league games and we occupied eighth place in the 10-team Premier Division. We were 12 points behind the Dons, who topped the table, and only three better off than St Johnstone who were bottom of the league.

As if our predicament wasn't bad enough, the trip North would prove to be even more painful for me.

About a month later, I started feeling ill. On Boxing Day, we gathered at the ground before the game against Hibs at Easter Road and I was shattered. Jock walked me around the red blaes Ibrox track and put his arm around me. He said that I looked terrible and asked if I'd had a drink on Christmas Day.

"No, gaffer," I replied. "I wasn't able to have any dinner and had to go to bed."

He promptly marched me into the treatment room where Dr Cruikshank was filling his medical bag in preparation for the game. "This boy's ill, Doc," said Jock. "Can you have a look at him?"

The Doc shone his torch in my eyes and said, "Here's a sample bottle, go and fill it for me."

I took the bottle to the toilet and let nature take its course. When it had, I looked at the contents of the bottle; my urine was black. Something wasn't right, so I returned to the treatment room and handed the bottle to the Doc. He immediately shouted for the manager and the two of them met in the corridor.

After about five minutes the Doc came back in and said, "You go home and get to your bed, Davie. I'll be in touch." I was worried by this point, so I asked the Doc what was wrong with me.

"You've got Hepatitis A, son," was his response. "There was an outbreak at the hotel we stayed at for the Aberdeen game and you've got it."

This extract from the Environmental Health Report goes into more detail:

*November 1983: An outbreak of 24 cases of hepatitis A in Aberdeen was traced to a large hotel in the city by epidemiological investigation. Food-specific questioning of those affected, their fellow diners and hotel staff, coupled with serological studies, implicated raspberry mousse prepared from frozen raspberries as the source of the infection. The raspberries were probably contaminated at the time of picking.*

I arrived back home in a state of shock and spent the next three months in isolation. It was three months of hell and my mental health hit the floor during that spell. Words like 'Aids' and 'Hepatitis' had a real stigma associated with them at that time and I remember the papers reporting that I had a 'long-term' injury. I don't think the players even knew what I was suffering from. Perhaps the club didn't want any negative publicity.

But big Jock was brilliant. He would call me without fail after each game to talk me through it and I really appreciated that. It was proper man-management and boosted my flagging spirits.

My contract was up at the end of season 1983/84, and Jock spoke about not renewing it as I hadn't played enough games. I reminded him of my isolated spell due to Hepatitis, but it seemed as if I was on my way out of Rangers.

I got a call from Sandy Jardine who was joint manager at Hearts with Alex MacDonald. Sandy had spoken to Peter McCloy who had seemingly told him that I was being released on a free transfer. He said that Hearts were interested in signing me and there was interest from England too. Billy McNeill had just been appointed as manager at Manchester City, and a journalist I knew, Jim Blair, called me as Billy had asked him to sound me out about going to City once I'd been freed.

Of the two, the move to City appealed to me most, but I was pretty pissed off as nothing had been confirmed by Rangers. I needed clarity, so I sought out big Jock. I wanted to be put out of my misery, I wanted the manager to confirm that I was surplus to requirements and would be released. But when we spoke, big Jock said I wasn't being freed and that he wanted me back fully fit before the end of the season.

Rangers were going on a world tour at the end of the season. At that point I wasn't sure that I would be included in the travelling party, but a week before we left for the first leg of the tour in Melbourne, I was handed a new two-year contract. Relief washed over me as I put pen to paper and another part of my career that tested my mental fortitude was over.

I played in most of the games that we played on our epic tour. I was still struggling for full fitness, but when we returned home, I rested and returned for pre-season raring to go. After doing our usual gruelling sessions at home, Jock took us on a tour of Switzerland and West Germany, and in the game that we played against Kaiserslautern, I found the form that had escaped me since Jock joined. Jock was delighted and grabbed me as I came off the park and shouted, "Skippy's back!"

I'd been given the nickname 'Skippy' by Ally Dawson and Davie Cooper. That wasn't anything to do with any bush kangaroos, though. I was given the moniker as I skipped into the air every time I had a shot at goal. That was a legacy of the ankle surgery I had back in my Dundee days, surgery that left a quarter-inch reduction in one of my ankles.

Another legacy of that surgery was that when I crossed the ball, I inevitably lost my balance due to my slightly shorter left leg. These days a podiatrist would be engaged by clubs to provide an insole to compensate, but in my day, you just had to try and make adjustments to your stride pattern.

I carried my good form into the new season, and by the end of the campaign, I had appeared in 41 of the 47 games played by the club. The handful of games that I missed were through suspension or injury. But a couple of the games that I was absent for caused a great deal of hurt and distress.

In the second round of the UEFA Cup, we drew Inter Milan. We had scraped past Bohemians in the opening round, losing a tempestuous first leg 3-2 in Dublin, before a couple of late goals saw us through in the second leg at Ibrox.

It would be remiss of me not to mention the build up to the game in Dublin. We were staying in a castle on the outskirts of the city and had round the clock protection from Special Branch; there has been a plethora of death and bomb threats in the days and weeks that led up to the game.

It got a bit scary at times particularly as Jock decided to take us on a walk into the countryside the night before the game. It was for character building and Jock, a fearless jungle fighter who'd fought with distinction in Malaya, took great delight in putting the fear into some of the more nervous players by suddenly stopping and saying, "Did you hear that? Somebody's in the bushes."

As we drove to the game for an evening kick off, the Irish Garda provided two motorcycle outriders. The two led the bus into Dublin, one stopping at crossroads to ensure that no sniper was present, while the other drove on. Jock was still winding us up and the nervous energy was at fever pitch.

As we came to a crossroads, one rider went left, and one went right and momentarily we were flying solo. Someone shouted, "Down! Sniper," and we all hit the deck waiting for the crack of a rifle. After a couple of minutes, we started to sit up and Coop stood laughing. "Ya bunch of dicks," he shouted. We all laughed albeit nervously.

As the crowd arrived, the atmosphere was electric, but there was a sinister and threatening edge to it. As we warmed up, I looked up to the roof of a stand, and a man in a balaclava was running along the roof, an Irish tricolour in his hand fluttering in the wind. Suddenly the roof gave way and he crashed down onto the Bohemian fans below. At the other end, Rangers fans were climbing the fence which separated the fans from the pitch.

The place was like a cauldron, so Jock appeared to get the young lads who were clambering the fences down. His arrival settled our supporters, but it wouldn't be the end of the sectarian-fuelled shenanigans.

The game kicked off and as I ran back chasing their winger, I noticed our goalkeeper, Nicky Walker, standing almost on the 18-yard line, "Get back Nicky," I shouted.

"That'll be right, Skippy," shouted Nicky in reply, "Look at the goalmouth". After I escorted the ball out of play for a goal kick, I looked at the six-yard box and there were about 20 darts sticking out of the turf. They were cleared away by the ground staff, but it did make you think what other objects could be lurking on the lush green grass below our studs.

Minutes later I made the mistake of running to the fence behind the goal to retrieve the ball. As I bent to pick it up, a fan ran from behind the fence and threw a lump of concrete towards me. Thankfully the fence absorbed most of the impact as the concrete crumbles, but shards of rock did break off and enter my eye.

The game should have been abandoned for everyone's safety. We learned later that the referee told Jock at half time that the Garda and the UEFA observer had agreed that abandoning wouldn't have stymied the issues; the carnage would simply have spilled from the confines of the stadium out on to the streets.

After progressing into the next round, we were scheduled to fly to Milan on the Tuesday afternoon before we played Inter at the San Siro on the Wednesday night. A few hours earlier, Jock had arranged a game for the starting line-up against the subs and reserves. It was unusual for the team to be announced prior to a game, but Jock ordered us not to reveal it to the journalists travelling with us.

I was delighted when I was told that I'd be playing centre midfield with a mandate to man mark an old acquaintance from my Arsenal days, Liam Brady. I knew his game well, so felt that gave me an edge.

As the game started at the Albion, Billy Davies was told to be Liam Brady. Now Billy was an exceptionally talented young player, but his style was not in any way like Liam's. Liam was a very static player who rarely left a 12 square yard area in midfield. Billy on the other hand was a livewire, a player with a great energy who ran all over the park.

As the game started Billy suddenly ran back into his own penalty box to get the ball from the goalkeeper. I didn't track him and Jock blew the whistle. "Skippy, you're supposed to be marking him," he shouted.

"But gaffer, I played with Brady for four years and he never once ran into his own area to get the ball from his keeper".

That reply to Jock cost me my place in the team against Inter. An hour before the game, Jock revealed that Cammy Fraser was now tasked with marking Brady. I was livid, and as I sat and seethed on the side lines, Liam dictated play, rarely venturing outside that 12 square yard area. We lost the game 3-0.

The next game was the League Cup Final against Dundee United, and the heavy defeat in Milan had thrown me back into contention. In a pre-match practice game at Girvan Amateurs, the nearest park to our base at Turnberry, I slotted back into central midfield. *Surely, I would keep my place in the XI this time?*

I didn't.

On the day of the game after Jock announced the team. I waited to hear 'Mackinnon', but I was left out again. I was devastated and I broke down on the way back to my hotel room. My room-mate, Stuart Munro, tried to console me, but this latest snub put me in the darkest place that I'd ever experienced as a professional footballer.

Stuart's a great guy and he went to speak to Jock to tell him I was distressed. Jock told him that was football and he sent the assistant manager, Alex Totten, to speak to me. Alex is a good man, but he couldn't tell me why Jock had changed his mind which only served to darken my mood further.

I was embarrassed as I climbed onto the bus before we made our way to Hampden. The players tried their best to cheer me up and Coop came to sit beside me to try and help. "At least you'll be sub and when you get on you can show the gaffer he's made a mistake leaving you out. You could be the hero today, Skippy," he said as he gave me a hug.

Hero? I felt closer to zero and I was about to plummet further into the depths of despair. Robert Prytz, who'd not been in the party that had prepared for the match at Turnberry, was in the dressing room. Robert was a friend and he said, "I'm a bit embarrassed to be here, Skippy. I got a call from the gaffer to say I had to get to Hampden as I was one of the subs."

My stomach lurched as I knew what was coming next. Jock read out the starting XI then disclosed the two subs, Robert Prytz and Davie Mitchell. My world collapsed.

I summoned up some sort of strength to keep it together and went around the dressing room and wished all the players well. I ignored big Jock and Alex as I vowed at that moment that I would never play for them again. I walked up into the stand and watched Iain Ferguson score the only goal of the game to win Rangers another League Cup.

At the conclusion of the match, I considered walking away and getting a taxi home, but I knew that wasn't the correct thing to do. I went down to the dressing room and congratulated my teammates. I was genuinely pleased for them, but my exclusion from the squad was still too raw for me to congratulate Jock and Alex.

Coop told me to get on the bus and come back to Ibrox for the victory celebration. I said I couldn't as I felt worthless and that I hadn't contributed to the win. Again, Coop took control and dragged me on to the bus.

I left the event very quickly and went home to think about my future. It is always very difficult to plan when matters are taken out of your control. I decided to go into the club the next morning and have an open and frank discussion with Jock. I needed to know where I stood. Today that chat would be undertaken by the player's representative but in my day you were on your own.

Ibrox was quiet when I arrived at 9 a.m. The players and staff had been given the day off after the cup success, so the only person there was Stan Holloway, the doorman. Stan was an ex-Services man who proudly wore the uniform of the commissionaire's service. He was an Englishman who'd served with distinction in World War II and was a guy that all the players respected.

As I entered, he said, "Great win yesterday, Skippy, were you injured?"

"Only my heart, Stan," was my short reply.

I quickly found some kit and a ball and went into the tunnel warm-up area. I did some sprints and then some ball work hitting the ball, ever so increasingly harder, against the wall. Around 11 a.m. the tunnel door opened and Jock stood with the cup in his massive right hand. He hadn't expected anyone to be in and I quickly said, "Can I see you, gaffer?"

He spun around back into the corridor and said, "Na son, I've been up all-night celebrating, come and see me in the morning at 9.30 a.m. before training," and he was off.

Another sleepless night ensued with me rehearsing over and over what I was going to say. I wasn't one for standing up to the management team, something my dad had rammed into me from an early age, but on this occasion, I was determined that Jock would hear me out and if that resulted in a transfer then so be it!

I was nervous as I climbed the famous marble stairs to the

manager's office at the agreed time. Outside the office was a traffic light system, not green but red and amber. I knocked the door and after a couple of minutes, the red light turned to amber.

I walked inside and Jock was sitting at his desk in his blue tracksuit with assistant manager, Alex Totten, and coaches, Stan Anderson and Joe Mason, forming a half circle as they stood behind him. I should have been intimidated as the display was meant to instil fear, but I launched into my rehearsed speech. "Gaffer, I respect you, but you haven't shown the same respect for me as you cut me from the team without even having the decency to tell me why." That was the opener which I hoped would set the scene, but Jock being the wily old fox that he was, wouldn't allow me to take control of the meeting.

He stood up to his full height and the trio of coaches behind him took a step forward. He grabbed a piece of paper in front of him and held it up to within an inch of my face. I stepped back to see the detail and I realised that it was a team sheet. "See," said Jock, "you were in the team, but I cut you." He pointed to my name with a red line through it and Cammy Fraser's was added.

"Why?" I asked, that horrible feeling of hurt rising to the surface once more.

"I had a dream the night before the match and you weren't in the team," was his response.

"What!" I shouted. "Do you think you're Robert the Bruce? Do you think I'm daft?"

Jock looked shocked and I was shocked myself as I'd never spoken to any manager like that.

"I want a free transfer. I hear Billy McNeill wants me at Manchester City," was what I thought was my final riposte.

Jock came round from the other side of his desk and pulled me towards him. "Skippy, you give me 100 per cent and that's all I can ask for, but I'm the manager and I need to pick the team. We won, didn't we?" he said with a smile. "You'll not miss another game this season unless you're injured or suspended. I left this club once and it was the biggest mistake I made, let's forget this and move on."

I started to calm down and I knew he was right. I had fought hard to become a Rangers player and it would have been stupid to throw it all away. "Ok, gaffer let's get back on track," I said.

I got up to leave, and as I opened the door he shouted, "Check your wages next week, I've told them to pay you the [win] bonus."

It wasn't about the bonus for me, but I got the message. I left the office and I played 21 games out of the next 27.

I last saw Jock in the summer of 1986. I was in Torremolinos on holiday and as I walked with a mate in the old town, a booming voice echoed around the ancient square, "Skippy!". I turned around and there was big Jock looking resplendent in a short-sleeved shirt and shorts. He had just become Seville manager and he was in great spirits. "You'll be buying me a beer, Skippy," he smiled ushering us towards a bar in the square.

"Of course, gaffer, this is my mate Billy."

We sat down and as we sipped our beers, Jock grabbed my hand and said, "You know, Skippy, I felt bad leaving you out of the League Cup Final, but we won and that's life, son."

As much as I was floored by his decision at the time, I had got over it by that point and said that to him. He smiled, those piercing blue eyes magnified through his glasses. We finished the beers and he gave me his customary bear hug.

Jock Wallace was a great man. Tough, but a diamond. He died from Parkinson's disease on 24 July 1996, aged 60.

### Walter Smith
### 24 February 1948 – 26 October 2021

I first bumped into Walter Smith in 1977 when I was at Dundee. He was coming out of a bank in Reform Street as I was going in. I recognised him as he'd recently returned to Dundee United for a second spell following a two-year stint at Dumbarton. "Have you left any money in the bank, Walter?" I laughed.

"Plenty," he replied, "Wee Jim doesn't pay much."

"How was Dumbarton?" I asked. "My cousin, Murdo MacLeod, plays there."

"Aye, Murdo's doing great, he'll get a big move soon," said Walter. We shook hands and he was gone.

Almost 10 years later, our paths crossed again at Rangers. In a bold move, David Holmes had appointed Graeme Souness as the club's first-ever player-manager. But Graeme needed someone by his side who knew the Scottish football landscape, so he picked Walter. And with Graeme still under contract at Sampdoria, Walter assumed control of the team for what remained of season 1985/86.

I can still remember his first training session. It was on the pitch at Ibrox and he was working on corners. He instructed the very talented Ian Durrant to ping a couple of corners into the penalty area and set up the defenders to try and repel them.

Durranty was normally a confident young guy, but I think Walter's presence unsettled him. Stationed at the flag between the Main Stand and the Broomloan Road stand, he had three attempts, but each and every one flew behind the goal. Walter put his head in his hands and I witnessed the great humour which was to lace his wonderful career at Ibrox.

"Fuck sake, Durranty," he shouted, "I was told you were a player, son, but I see you'll need a bit more practice".

The players laughed and, in that moment, Walter became one of us.

He took the team for a couple of the league games at the end of the season. I'm certain that he was assessing us and feeding back to Graeme, but he made every one of us believe that we had a chance of being part of the new regime.

Sadly, it didn't turn out that way for me, but when I left Walter wished me well. That was the mark of the man; respectful, sincere and genuine.

I bumped into Walter many times over the subsequent years, and although he had gone on to establish himself as one of Rangers' greatest-ever managers, he never changed.

A humble, family man, Walter Smith sadly died of cancer on 26 October 2021. He was 73.

# CHAPTER 5
# ATTITUDE AND MAN MANAGEMENT

*May 2022*

I HAD AN appointment at the hospital for an MRI scan which would be followed up with a review by the brain surgeon. My previous CT scan had shown a lesion on the right side of my brain which may have been an historical stroke, or due to the lack of blood going to my brain after my fall.

I was also receiving physiotherapy and counselling which meant that my recovery was focussed. My GP had not been very supportive, so all was arranged and paid for privately.

The glue and the cut on the top of my head continued to be problematic and visits to the GP were a waste of time, as my records didn't state if there were stitches, staples or just glue. In the end they told me to go to Accident and Emergency.

I went to Inverclyde Hospital and waited four hours, but it was worth it. The doctor who saw me was excellent. She cleaned all the glue and dried blood and saw that the wound was infected and that was why it wasn't healing. She asked if I wanted her to open it up to clean and stitch it. As a player I used to get stitches on a weekly basis as I didn't wear shin pads, so I had no hesitation in giving her the go ahead.

The doctor worked on me for around an hour and I went home with a clean wound and some antibiotics. For the first time in 10 weeks, I felt as if a corner had been turned and my health and spirits started to move in a positive direction.

I must admit that a lot was down to attitude. After the frustrations of my GP experience, the positive attitude of the

A&E doctor was uplifting, and I genuinely felt that I'd overcome the worst.

*****

Attitude plays a huge part in football too. I've seen dressing room dynamics destroyed by players with bad attitudes; while I've also been part of dressing rooms where the players were perhaps less talented, but we enjoyed success because of the positive vibes that were created. But it's not just the attitude of the players that plays a part, the manager and coaching staff have to do likewise.

When I was at Arsenal, they had a Scottish youth coach called Ian Crawford. Ian had scored two goals for Hearts in the 1956 Scottish Cup Final against Celtic and I had reckoned that as he was a Scotsman in the coaching team that I may get some preferential treatment. Nothing could have been further from the truth!

One day after training Ian decided to get all the guys together in a circle. We hadn't a clue what was going on, but it suddenly became clear as I was told to get in the middle. "Right," said Ian to the players. "What do you think of this Scottish bastard?"

Cue pelters from my team-mates. I got it from every angle, with words like "lazy", "Scottish dick", and "crap player" being bandied about. One of the lads even said that I wasn't to be trusted.

Every word was like a knife getting driven into my back, but I was determined not to let anyone know how I felt. After about 10 minutes the players got bored and started battering balls about, but when training ended and everyone had left, I sought out Ian and asked what I'd done to deserve such a public humiliation.

"Just toughening you up," he said. "You've got talent but you're too soft. Get it sorted."

He walked away at that point. Clearly Ian didn't study psychology. His approach didn't toughen me up, instead it only made me realise that I could never trust him and my relationship with him broke down.

I witnessed the same tactic 10 years later at Rangers. Jock Wallace had taken us on a trip to Baghdad following the Scottish Cup defeat at the hands of Dundee. We were told nothing about the destination, just to turn up at Glasgow airport on the Sunday. We flew to Gatwick and after a night in a hotel got the early morning flight to Baghdad.

Jock had arranged a double header game against Iraq on the Tuesday and Thursday. We stayed in the Palestine Hotel, which later became infamous as the journalists' hotel during the Gulf War and where bomb blasts were regular occurrences.

We met Saddam Hussein and Tariq Aziz, his foreign minister, at the hotel the evening before the first game. We didn't really know who they were at that point. To us they were just Iraqi officials, but I remember Saddam saying in perfect English, that the Iranians were the aggressors and that Iraqis were friendly people who only wanted peace.

After they left, Jock tried to psyche us up for the game and he started bringing players out to the front and asked the rest of the players what they thought of them. My mind immediately flashed back to the verbal volley that I got at Arsenal, and I was cringing when some of the younger lads were called up.

Among them was Hugh Burns. Hugh had broken into the first team in season 1983/84 and had really impressed everyone on our end of season world tour. But that didn't save him from getting massacred. I felt for him and stood up and walked out.

That night as we were in bed, the air raid sirens sounded, and we walked down to the basement. Iran was bombing Basra 100 miles away, but the Iraqis were taking no chances.

The next day as we arrived at the stadium, I saw something that I hadn't seen since my trip to Iran with Arsenal. Once again, the secret police were thumping poor people on the head with long bamboo poles to break up the crowd that had gathered. As we left the bus to enter the ground, a large man walked towards me with a bit of paper and a pencil wanting me to sign an autograph. He smiled and I smiled back and went to grab the pencil. Next thing a policeman whacked him on the head, and he fell to the ground, blood starting to pour out of his head. The aggressive approach from the policeman angered me and I decided to approach him. I don't where I summoned the bravery from, but I felt enraged at his malevolent behaviour towards an innocent young football fan.

But as I moved forward, I felt the tug of my sleeve. Our

interpreter pulled me back. "Please sir, let the police do their work," he said. "If we don't control these people the country will fall, this is why we need a strong leader like Saddam."

I was still bubbling with anger when we kicked off and really wasn't in the right frame of mind to play. The pitch was rock hard and the Iraqis were quick and nimble. I remember we were lucky to play out a 1-1 draw in front of 22,000 people, including Saddam.

The atmosphere after the game was terrible and the players were largely confined to our respective rooms as it wasn't the type of place where you could go for a stroll or a coffee. The Iraqis won 4-1 in the Thursday game and we flew to Jordan on the Friday and defeated Kuwait 2-1 the following day before flying home. We wondered what the club tried to achieve by putting us in a war zone, but we heard that they got £25,000 for travelling so probably someone was trying to compensate for the financial losses incurred by our early exit from the Scottish Cup.

I've already referenced the excellent man-management of Bertie Auld. He was superb and I recall another masterclass when Thistle faced Rangers in the semi-final of the Scottish Cup in April 1979.

I was captain, and we played well to hold Rangers, who were chasing what was then an unprecedented back-to-back Treble, to a 0-0 draw at Hampden. Ahead of the replay, the boys thought our bonus should be increased so I was tasked with speaking to Bertie. I went to his office after training and he was sitting behind his desk in his usual black and red tracksuit.

He said, "Aye, Davie, what can I do for you?"

"I hope you don't mind, gaffer, but the boys think the bonus needs to be uplifted," was my reply. "What's your thoughts?"

Bertie scratched his nose and opened a drawer at the back of his desk. He moved his hands into the drawer and I heard a recorded laugh echo into the room. In the drawer was a laughing bag and he'd pulled the string.

He stood up to his full five foot six inches, and said, "Davie, you go and tell your pals, that they'll be getting the same bonus and if anyone questions that, I'll drop them and fine them. OK, son, got it?"

I stood up and left the room. I was no Arthur Scargill so I knew that the game was up.

As I entered the dressing room the players stood up waiting for the news, "Well?" asked Roughie.

I proceeded to lie, saying, "I pleaded with him guys and he threatened me with all sorts, but I stuck it out. In the end he threatened to drop me and was going to cut the bonus, but I managed to get him to change his mind and it's the same bonus as the other night. That's the best I could do."

I sat down exhausted with a nose that resembled that of Pinocchio. The boys could smell bullshit. At times I hated being captain.

But just before the replay, Bertie got the players together before we walked out. "I hear you're no' happy with the bonus?" he said looking at me. "Well, I agree, and I've spoken to the chairman and got you another £200 on top."

The players were delighted and Bertie had played his motivational card. Unfortunately, it didn't work. Derek Johnstone scored the only goal of the game and Rangers went on to defeat Hibs in a Final that required two replays.

One of the strangest motivational ploys that I've ever experienced was at Arsenal when I moved into the reserves. The reserve manager was Dave Smith, an upbeat and enthusiastic coach from Dundee.

As we settled into pre-season, Dave asked us to meet at Highbury for a team-building exercise. The guys arrived anticipating a pool or head tennis tournament, but as we waited with bated breath in the dressing room, Dave appeared and outlined the plan.

"Right here it is," he said in his usual positive manner. "I will blow my whistle and I want you all to go and hide within the stadium. No cheating going a walk into Finsbury Park, just within the Highbury perimeter. If I don't find you in an hour, come back to the dressing room."

The guys looked at each other and considered this to be a morning off training. Dave blew his whistle and the guys disappeared.

I found my way into the laundry room and opened one of the big kit baskets. Inside were two players under a pile of dirty kit. I laughed and shut the basket, realising that would be the first place that Dave would look.

I decided to go outside the main building and go to the West

Stand. There were catering facilities within the stand and I managed to get access to the main kitchen. Once inside I found a cupboard and hid inside. As I sat there in the dark, I thought how crazy this was, and vowed that if I ever became a coach, hide and seek would be off the menu.

As it was, Dave only found two of the players within the allocated hour, ironically, the two that had hidden in the laundry basket.

Money and a win bonus were motivators for players in my era. This has become less of an incentive in the modern era when players at the level that I played at are almost guaranteed a monthly sum which means they won't have to work when their career ends.

When I was at Arsenal, the club had a significant cash reserve and actively encouraged players to buy property. The club would provide mortgages and allow the players to build up a portfolio.

I bumped into an ex-teammate a few years ago. He had taken full advantage of the scheme and now has numerous flats around London giving him a big revenue income. There goes that red balloon again!

The most generous bonus that I ever had was actually for a game we lost. Kilmarnock were owned by the Chadwick family, lovely people from Florida who'd made their fortune in nursing homes. Bobby Fleeting, the brother of manager Jim Fleeting, had married Annie, the daughter of Mr and Mrs Chadwick.

Bobby is a hugely charismatic man, who is instantly likeable and persuasive. He got the Chadwick's interested in buying Kilmarnock when his brother Jim was appointed manager. Both brothers were successful businessmen as well as being football guys.

In August 1990, we were drawn against Rangers in the League Cup at Ibrox. Rangers were the reigning champions and League Cup holders, and although it may have been perceived as a formality that they would beat us, a big crowd was still expected.

This was the first time that I had been back at Ibrox since I had played my last game for the club against Celtic in the Glasgow Cup Final in May 1986. Although the stadium wasn't full – a crowd of 32,671 turned up – the atmosphere was fantastic.

As often happens, the Killie players rose to the challenge and the occasion and we were magnificent. As captain I played a key role in defence blocking shots with every part of my body. On one such occasion where I blocked a shot from Coisty with a flying header and I got a standing ovation from the Rangers fans which made the hairs on the back of my head stand up. It was exhilarating.

As the cheers started to subside, I could hear one wag shout, "Ye never did that when you were with us, Mackinnon!"

Laughter rolled around the lower reaches of the Copland Road stand. I bowed and laughed too. It was a special moment.

We looked to be holding out for extra time, but in the closing minutes, Terry Hurlock sent a speculative shot into the box and my old Thistle team-mate Mo Johnston stuck out a leg and diverted the ball into the net to give Rangers a 1-0 win.

As the final whistle sounded, we walked off the park with our heads high, and to their great credit, the Rangers players and fans applauded us off.

We may have lost the game but considering that we had been in the lower reaches of the Scottish league a couple of years earlier, it actually felt as if we had won.

We stripped off our dirty kits and started to move into the showers when the dressing room door opened and in came a smiling Bobby Fleeting. "Brilliant performance boys, you deserved better," he said. "Can you all sit down?"

We sat down in various stages of undress as Bobby moved to the centre of the dressing room. "The board and I are very proud of you tonight. The club was on the flats of its arse and you guys have given us our pride back. The board has decided to acknowledge that, and we've agreed to pay you a bonus of £1,500 each. Well done troops," he shouted before heading out the door.

As I reflected on it later with my friend and colleague, Tommy Burns, we both agreed that it was a masterstroke by Bobby and would be remembered by the players as we went into the battles that still lay ahead of us.

When you are involved in the heat of a game, the last thing you think of is the bonus. A will to win comes from the person that's inside you and that's what drives players. Football is a wonderful game that builds team spirit, loyalty and friendship that lasts a lifetime. I met many wonderful people in my time in the game and that for me is more important than money or medals.

At Airdrie I had the pleasure of working under the very talented Gordon McQueen, who was an exceptional motivator.

I'd played against Gordon a couple of times and had gone out for a couple of beers with him when Rangers and Manchester United had been in the same hotel in Australia whilst on tour.

Gordon had been appointed manager of Airdrie and he'd called me out of the blue the day after his appointment. He said, "Davie, can you come up to the ground this afternoon? I haven't a clue who any of the players are and I need you to help me."

I was the captain of the team and was honoured to be asked, so I made my way to Broomfield, the old home of the club. I climbed the steps in the rickety wooden stand to the manager's office where Gordon was sitting behind a big desk, a pen in one hand and a cigarette in the other.

"Right," he said to me, "You need to pick the team, I don't have a fucking clue who anybody is." A big smile spread across his face.

I laughed and held out my hand, "Right back and captain, Davie Mackinnon."

I wrote out a team and Gordon asked me to go through the players, what they were like and how they played. I obliged and after half an hour, Gordon asked me if I fancied going for a beer. I had to decline, though.

"I'm old school, gaffer," I said. "Early bed on a Friday before the game for me."

We laughed and he said, "You've passed the first test."

I started taking him through the people around the club and he took notes. "One guy you need to pay special attention to is a guy in his 50s who does a lot for everyone. If you single him out it would make his season. He's a guy called Willie who washes the kit, lines the park, cleans the boots and I don't think he even gets paid."

"Oh, I must meet him," said Gordon.

"One thing though," I replied. "He's got one leg shorter than the other, I think he had polio as a kid, he's rightly a bit sensitive."

"I think it's always best to take the heat out of these situations, Davie and treat people normally," said Gordon. "Come in a wee bit earlier tomorrow and get the players and Willie set up about 2 p.m."

I called him gaffer for the umpteenth time at that point, and as we parted, he instructed me to call him Gordon.

I duly arrived early the next day and got the players and Willie lined up in the dressing room. "The manager wants to meet you all before the game," I said.

Bang on 2 p.m. Gordon walked in. When you find yourself in the presence of a great player, it's as if you are meeting a member of the Royal family, and when Gordon came in, the players all stiffened up and stood to attention.

I walked Gordon along the line, "John Martin," I said as I introduced our goalkeeper.

"John Martin," said Gordon. "Incredible record for this club, big man. I always think the keeper is the most important player in the team, you'll do for me, son."

John beamed as Gordon continued the platitudes as he walked down the line. The hearts burst out the of chests of player after player as Gordon made them feel like world beaters.

As we moved towards the end of the line, Willie stood immaculate in club blazer and tie. As I started to introduce him, Gordon interjected, "Davie, no need to introduce this man. I know this is Willie."

A smile spread across Willie's face as Gordon said, "I've played all around the world, Willie, and every club has top guys like you. I've seen dedication but you are a credit to yourself and this club, you come and sit in the dugout with me from now on."

Overnight Gordon had taken time to research the career of each player in the squad and that afternoon he boosted their confidence like it had never been boosted before. As for Willie? He sat proudly beside Gordon in the dugout and we went on to beat Kilmarnock. There was no team talk required either, Gordon's man-management got him the levels of motivation he required.

I was devastated when I heard that Gordon had passed away at the age of 70 following his battle with early onset dementia. It's becoming more and more common now among players from that generation. Gordon was a wonderfully funny, unique and inspirational man. He will be sadly missed by his family and all who knew him.

# CHAPTER 6
# MARBLE HALLS AND
# MEDICINE BALLS

*June 2022*

THREE MONTHS AFTER the fall, I've now returned to work. However, I am still experiencing some strange symptoms, including waking up at 2 a.m. and anxiously going through the events of the previous day before worrying about what lies ahead of me at work in the day ahead.

And while at work, I'm also having difficulties concentrating to the extent that on one occasion I was unable to read a financial spreadsheet that I'd created. I'm also having dizzy spells and experiencing the strange sensation that my nose is being squeezed at the bridge.

Keith Bishop calls and his words offer reassurance; he tells me that these things happened to him too. But I want to be sure, so I email the consultant and she confirms what Keith said. She adds that the dizzy spells and nasal sensations are down to delayed concussion and can last up to six months after the event. She also tells me that patients who have gone through the type of fall that I've experienced are normally off work for six months.

The concussion is a strange one. As a defender who would contest aerial duels countless times every season, concussion came with the territory. And in my day, there were no concussion protocols and no breaks. If you picked up a head knock, then your head would be swathed in bandages and you carried on. You would more often than not be selected for the next game too.

I played in a semi-final League Cup tie against Hearts at Ibrox in October 1982 and I sustained a horror head injury five minutes before the break. I slid in to win the ball on the halfway line, but the momentum of the Hearts forward carried him forward and his knee clattered into my head. I was wiped out and lay prostrate on the pitch as my team mates urgently beckoned our physio to come on.

The point of contact was my right eyebrow and a large cut had appeared across its line. The physio clasped a towel to my head to stem the flow of blood and led me off the field to the tunnel area. The club doctor, Doctor Cruikshank, who had been sitting in the directors' box, had hurried down to meet us.

He put up a couple of fingers and said, "How many?" My vision was blurred, and I blurted out "Four!"

To this day, I don't know how many fingers were held up, but the Doc said, "Close enough," before informing me that the gaping wound would need to be stitched at half time.

The stitches were inserted in the treatment room in the bowels of the stadium, and as the Doc was leaving, John Greig appeared and asked, "What do you think, Doc?"

The Doc replied, "I've put 10 stitches in, and he seems to have come round OK. What do you think, Davie?"

A player will always tell you he's OK, so I said, "Sure, get a bandage on it and I'll give it a go."

My current concussion episodes have brought back the feeling that I had that night, particularly the squeezing sensation at the bridge of my nose. Anyone who's had concussion will know what I'm talking about.

I had a bandage wrapped around my head and re-appeared for the second half. To be honest I can't remember much about the match, but it appears that I played well. We won 2-0, and a young talented midfielder called Derek Ferguson also made his first competitive appearance for Rangers that night too.

Three days later we played Celtic at Parkhead in the league. In the first half I closed down Charlie Nicholas, and as he tried to create some space, he elbowed me in the head. I went down and the referee, Brian McGinley, booked me for diving!

A half time examination revealed Nicholas's elbow had opened up the cut again. So much for my simulation! I pointed this out to the referee in the tunnel as he led us out for the second half, but he was having none of it.

Throughout my career I witnessed many players having

concussion, but not many went off at the first time of asking. As the game continued, you'd see them stumbling about like a drunkard while talking incoherently. The physios would come on again and administer smelling salts, but other than give that sharp burst of ammonia, it didn't do anything to sort the concussion.

The powers-that-be in contact sports are only now realising how serious concussion is and strict protocols are now in place. Many more players from my era and before are now coming forward and I wonder if some sort of compensation scheme will be set up for these players and their families who have to deal with the consequences.

I regularly see adverts on TV aimed at shipyard workers asking if they suffer from vibration white finger because of the tools that they used. I wonder if a similar campaign will be launched soon to find out if any former footballers are out there suffering due to the effects of heading medicine balls during training.

As farcical as it may seem nowadays, it was common practice early in my career for players to be expected to jump up and attempt to head medicine balls that had been hung from the ceilings. The thought process was that heading these heavy balls would strengthen the neck muscles, and if you could head a medicine ball in training then when it came to the much lighter match ball, you would be able to get some considerable distance on a clearing header.

I also remember medicine balls at Arsenal and Rangers being used in circuit training, interspersed between weights, press ups and star jump stations, where you would have to head the ball five times. I wince just thinking about it now.

One benefit of my brain injury is that I've had CT and MRI scans. These have detected a lesion on the right side of my frontal lobe, but thankfully at this juncture, there's no damage from my football days. That's a relief as I always worried that I'd be the next former footballer to declare that they had dementia. I still think clubs and associations can do more, though, and one thing they could offer is free brain scans for their former players.

As I contemplated the past during my recovery, I reviewed the impact that facilities and grounds had on the decision-making process to join a club. Nowadays, it's common practice for a player and their agent to ask to come and check out the facilities before signing. A lot of this is down to the Bosman ruling where more and more players at a lower level have been offered roughly the same wage, and the only point of difference may be what their working conditions will be for the next season. This practice is particularly prevalent in the Scottish Championship where all 10 teams are fishing in the same pond and scrapping to land a big fish for an additional £50 a week.

Arsenal and Rangers had very many similarities. Firstly, Highbury and Ibrox were designed by the same architect, Archibald Leitch. Secondly, they had the same magnificent and majestic marble entrance and stairways.

Highbury had one feature that Ibrox didn't, though: underfloor heating in the home dressing room. Trying to squeeze cold feet into boots is uncomfortable, so getting the opportunity to warm our toes on the floor at Arsenal was a luxury.

Highbury and Ibrox certainly set the standards. On the other hand, Dens Park and Firhill didn't have the same feel or mystique. In fact, the dressing room at Thistle must rank as one of the coldest that I ever changed in.

To try and bring a bit of heat to the place, the club decided to place carpet tiles over the concrete floor. The task was completed by one of the players, Ian Macdonald, who was a carpet fitter to trade. Wee Mac did a cracking job too, laying the tiles in sections of the club colours red, black, and yellow.

That gave rise to another superstition for wee Bertie. As the season progressed, we noticed that when Bertie came back into the dressing room 20 minutes before the start of the game to talk tactics, he would only stand on the yellow-coloured tiles but wouldn't stand on the black or red ones.

At training the following week, we came up with a plan. Prior to the next home game, Wee Mac would bring a couple of boxes of red and black tiles and hide them under the benches. Bertie delivered his tactical advice as usual, and when he was done, he did what he always did and went to the toilet. As soon as the toilet door closed, we mobilised and lifted all the yellow tiles around the toilet entrance door. Wee Mac quickly replaced them all with red and black tiles.

Bertie emerged from the toilet to be greeted by no yellow tiles. His face was a picture as he now had to jump from the door to the nearest set of yellow tiles that were close to the centre of the room. Once he landed, he uttered the words "Ya bastards" while we were doubled over with laughter.

I signed for Rangers in June 1982. I'd been at Thistle for four years and was happy there. But when wee Bertie left to join Hibs, Peter Cormack came in and I realised that I wasn't part of his long-term plans.

Peter told me that if Thistle received a fee of £30,000 for my services, he'd let me go. This was duly announced in the media and the next week I received a call at home from Howard Kendall, the manager of Everton. He said, "I've had you watched last season, Dave, and I think you'd fit in with my style of play. It also gives you a chance to get back to England, where my scout tells me you want to play. A few ghosts to be laid to rest after Arsenal I hear?"

I was flattered to receive the call from a man whom I had great respect for. His Everton side was about to emerge as one of the leading lights in the English game and I didn't hesitate in telling him that I was interested in moving to Goodison Park.

The prospect of the move excited me, and as soon as the phone went down, my mind was drifting. I could see myself resplendent in Everton's blue home kit running out to face Arsenal at Highbury, and I was eagerly anticipating another call from Howard the following week.

The news of Everton's interest was soon splashed all over the papers and that stimulated more interest. I firstly had a call from the manager of St Mirren, Ricky MacFarlane, asking if I'd be interested in speaking to him, and as I hung up the doorbell rang.

I'd recently bought Ranger's legend Derek Johnstone's house from him, and as I opened the door, I saw the Rangers assistant manager, Davie Provan. Standing in my doorway, Davie, who had been an excellent full back in his playing days, said, "Big Ba (Derek's nickname) told me you'd bought his house so the manager, instead of phoning, told me to come and see you."

He continued, "We hear Everton's interested but we'd really like you to sign for us."

I had been a Rangers supporter all my life and had waited my entire career for this moment. "OK," I uttered. "What happens next?"

"The manager's going to the World Cup next week, so he

wants you to come to the ground this afternoon," was Davie's reply.

I was stunned. Rangers Football Club wanted me to play for them! When Davie left, I called my dad. His reply was as I expected. "You can't turn down the Rangers," he said.

But for some reason, I was hesitant. "I'm going to see what's on offer, Dad, but I have a good feeling about Everton."

For a moment there was silence before my dad spoke. When he did he was straight to the point, "David, if you don't sign for Rangers, you and I are finished, son."

With my dad's words still ringing in my ears, I quickly changed into my best smart casual clothes and drove the short distance to Ibrox.

As I walked into the magnificent stadium, I knew that I was home as memories of the first time I walked into Highbury came flooding back.

Stan the doorman stood in the marble entrance hall. He said, "Mr Greig is waiting for you, Davie. I look forward to seeing you on a regular basis. Just make your way up the stairs and the manager's office is right in front of you."

That was a touch of class from Stan, it made potential players feel wanted.

I walked up the marble stairs, the painting of the iconic Alan Morton watching my every move. When I reached the office, I rang the bell and when the door opened, John Greig, a man I'd idolised as a player, stood in front of me. "Hello Davie, thanks for coming. Come into the trophy room, we can chat in there."

I followed John into the trophy room and he started to take me around the enormous glass cabinets where numerous medals, cups, trophies, and international caps were dotted around.

He opened one cabinet and pulled out the League Cup that Rangers had won the previous season, defeating Dundee United 2-1 in the final. As he thrust it into my hands he said, "You'd better get used to this." He smiled as he saw my glazed expression.

"Right," he said getting down to business. "Howard Kendall wants you. He's a nice guy, but Everton are a team you'll never win anything with. How much has he offered?"

There were no agents in those days, so players had to think on their feet. "Nothing in writing," I said casually although my heart was pounding. "But he was talking around £500 a week basic with a decent signing on fee."

John laughed and said, "All our players are on the same, £250 basic but £100 a point. We'll win most weeks so that's a decent wage, son."

"What about a signing on fee?" I asked, the negotiating side slipping away.

"I'll give you five grand, even though I'll need to pay £50,000 for you," was John's reply.

"But Peter Cormack says Thistle will accept £30,000 so maybe you can up the signing on fee?" I said in response.

Greigy laughed again. "OK, let me think about it," he said but I wasn't convinced that I would get anything more.

John Greig is a well-travelled guy and he's dealt with many signings, so his next line was a beauty. "OK, son, I'll be honest with you. I want you as I think you're the type of player the fans will take to but I've other options, so I need an answer today. I hear you're a Rangers fan so let me give you a tour of the stadium."

John walked me down the stairs and I felt as if Alan Morton's eyes were moving as I walked past. We negotiated our way through the corridor that led to the home dressing rooms. As an opposition player, I'd always turned left into the away dressing room, so this was a new experience.

John opened the dressing room door and the highly polished woodwork lay before me. On the far wall was a painting of Her Majesty Queen Elizabeth II. She didn't quite have the following eyes of Alan, but her presence nevertheless was intimidating. John moved into the vast bathing area where two slipper baths and a huge communal bath lay amongst a bed of marble. It was impressive.

John beckoned me back into the dressing room and out into the corridor before turning right just before the door into the foyer. This was the entrance into the warm-up area and led out on to the pitch.

As we entered the tunnel, John played his trump card. "I know you think you've played in big games but walking out of this tunnel at an Old Firm game is like nothing you'll ever experience in your life," he said.

We walked together down the long tunnel and I felt the hairs on the back of my neck rise. John had done a great job although my mind was already made up when I entered the stadium. I was ready for Rangers.

"OK," I said. "Where's the pen?"

We returned to John's office, and he called the former Rangers manager, Scot Symon, who was the General Manager at Thistle. John put the call on speaker. He said, "Hi Scot, Greigy here. I'm interested in signing one of your players and want the contract signed now."

"OK," replied Mr Symon, "Davie Mackinnon I assume?"

"Yes," answered Greigy. "How much?"

"£30,000," said Mr Symon and John gave me the thumbs up. "Done," he said before starting to laugh.

I signed for Rangers and called my dad. It was a great day and, despite not having the chance to return to England to lay a few ghosts to rest, joining Rangers was the best decision that I made in my football life.

It would be remiss of me at this juncture not to mention a great story about my late father, Willie Mackinnon.

When I signed for Rangers, he told me he was the happiest man in the world. Born on the Isle of Skye in 1926, he'd travelled the world as a merchant seaman, before settling down and rising to the position as foreman engineer at a local business in Renfrew.

He worked in the plant department at the works. The day after I signed, he walked in and his 400 colleagues gave him a round of applause and a standing ovation. He said that he felt like the king as guys were coming up and shaking his hand to congratulate him. As the applause abated, he found himself in a corner of the large building with some of his fellow workers circling him. He turned and noticed a man with his back to him brushing the floor oblivious to what was going on around him.

"Hi Jimmy," my dad said, and the guy turned around still sweeping.

"Aye, yer boy signed for the Gers, Willie?" asked Jimmy.

"Aye," answered Dad.

"I play for Rangers," says Jimmy. "I like to keep it quiet but I'm their only part-time player, I'll look after him."

Jimmy turned his back and continued to sweep.

The guys around heard Jimmy's revelation and started twirling their fingers at the side of their heads. "Jimmy's loopy, Willie," was the general consensus.

A fortnight later when the team poster came out, the same crowd gathered. Not for my dad but for Jimmy. Some apprentices had stuck several team posters on boards and were holding them up as Jimmy swept away, oblivious.

"Hoi Jimmy," shouts one of them. "You play for Rangers?"

Jimmy turned and said, "Aye, you know I dae."

"Right, here's the team poster, where are you?"

Jimmy straightens up, looks at the throng, pauses and then says, "Are you daft, who do think took the photo?"

He turned and went back to sweeping the floor.

My father was a committed family man who always tried to pull things together. When he was seven, he had a mastoid burst in his ear and was lucky to survive. This affected his hearing and he suffered abuse and bullying by schoolmates and friends as his speech development was affected.

Family was first and foremost for him, but his second love was his work. He was an engineer who had been exposed to asbestos throughout his career and this was to kill him at the young age of 60.

The firm was a huge organisation at the time, but sadly they let him down when he needed them most. As his work involved a lot of physical and manual labour, he decided that he would retire at 60.

As he moved into his last six months of his 20-year employment, he boarded an electric buggy to travel between warehouses. Just out of the building where his base was, the buggy suddenly blew up, throwing him 10 feet up in the air before landing him on his back. He was rushed to hospital.

On arrival, they carried out tests and over the next four weeks he had a full MOT. One of the X-rays discovered a shadow on one of his lungs. The doctors were unsure if it was damage caused by the accident or was something that had been there previously. A month later he was given the news that the shadow was terminal cancer and the doctors told him he had less than six months to live.

It was a devastating blow. But for my father, his focus was to ensure that my mother was adequately provided for, and with the help of a solicitor, he embarked on a claim for industrial injury; it had been proven that the accident had been caused by poor maintenance which caused the battery to blow up.

As part of the claim, my father's doctor had to provide his employers with his medical records. This is where company profits before employee's welfare kicked in. The rules at that time were that if a claimant died before settlement, then the case ended.

On seeing the medical evidence that my father had less than six months to live, the company stalled the settlement and the claim dragged on as my father's health deteriorated. At a time when he was trying to do the right thing for my mother's future, he became stressed and heartbroken that his employer was treating him so badly in his time of need.

I remember his solicitor said that he believed the company would string things out until he died leaving the case not concluded. The solicitor said that it would be best if he tried to negotiate a settlement. My father agreed and a deal was done where the company agreed liability but wanted to settle for £1,000.

Angry and hurt, my father agreed to the settlement, reconciling that "it would pay for his funeral."

He came to live with me in the bungalow that I was staying in as he couldn't climb stairs. In the two months he had left, I was fortunate to spend several hours a day with him getting to know the man that I had not fully got to know as an adult, having left home at 16.

He told me how my mother's mental illness had affected him and the impact that it had on their marriage. There were times when he felt he had to leave to save his sanity, but his love for my mother and not wanting to leave her on her own to face the demons, kept them together.

He told me of his childhood and how his mastoid had affected his confidence and development, as well as stories of his family in Skye, and how his older brother, Roderick, had died of tuberculosis at 37 years of age.

In June 1987 I was at the national centre in Largs starting my B licence with the SFA. It was a residential course and I would be there for four days. Following a first day when I was part of a team containing Aberdeen's Willie Miller and Alex Miller, a team mate at Rangers, I joined the guys in the cafeteria to have breakfast. As we started, an announcement came over the tannoy: "Would David Mackinnon please go to reception."

As I stood up, I said to the guys at the table, "My father has died." They all looked at me, but I knew I was about to get the news.

As I walked to reception, I saw a policeman walk towards me. He was about to talk but I repeated my earlier words to save him from having to tell me: "My father's died."

He nodded and shook my hand, "I'm so sorry, Davie. I've been dreading telling you as I'm a Rangers man, thanks," he said and walked outside.

I sought out Craig Brown and told him my news. "My thoughts are with you, Davie," he said kindly.

I left and drove to my home in Renfrew.

My mother was in shock as she told me the circumstances of my father's death.

She said, "He started coughing and spluttering. It was dark and I put the light on. He'd grabbed the bucket we had at the side of the bed and was holding it up to his mouth, it was starting to fill up with blood."

She then started to cry. "I took it from him and walked him into the shower-room and the blood kept coming and he managed to get his head into the sink. I put the blood from the bucket into the toilet and we phoned for an ambulance."

I sat her down and she started shaking.

"When the ambulance came, he was dead," she cried. "The ambulance man said he'd haemorrhaged."

"What am I going to do without him, David?" she asked.

My dad's body was taken to the Southern General Hospital. I got back in my car and drove to the mortuary.

I went inside and told them who I was. I was ushered into a room and a doctor came and told me that my father's lungs had disintegrated due to the cancer and he'd bled out. I couldn't shift the thought of how frightened he must have felt as the blood drained from his body. He was always a tidy man who cared about not making a mess and I imagined when the blood started to leave his mouth, the first thing he'd have thought of was making sure that he had his head in the bucket.

The doctor said as it was classified as a sudden death, the police would have to be contacted. Once they had arrived and were comfortable, then I could identify him.

The police came and were very kind. One asked for an

autograph for his son. It was a surreal moment, but it helped make it less awkward.

When I told the police about my dad's cancer, they were content that it was natural causes and left. The doctor then re-appeared and took me into a side room. Suddenly a curtain was pulled on a window and there was my dad lying prone on a stretcher. He was as white as a ghost, but I took some comfort despite the gnawing feeling in my gut. My dad, my hero, was now at peace after six months of pain.

The doctor's voice broke my focus. "Is that your father, William Mackinnon?"

"Yes, that's my dad," I replied.

He closed the curtains, got me to sign a document and a nurse escorted me back outside.

I found the next couple of months very difficult. The image of him in pain and suffering towards the end and the heartache of losing him made sleeping impossible.

I will always be grateful to have the opportunity to play for Rangers. It wasn't one of the most successful eras in the club's history, but although I didn't win many medals, there were many great experiences particularly in Europe. But above all else, I loved playing for Rangers because I knew how much pleasure and pride it gave my father.

European football was a huge highlight for all players and threw up some pretty unique experiences and strange occurrences.

In season 1983/84 we were drawn against the Maltese minnows, Valletta in the European Cup Winners' Cup. The first leg was away from home, and on 14 September we flew to Malta on a chartered plane, sharing the journey with the reigning Premier League champions, Dundee United, who'd been drawn to play Hamrun Spartans on the same day that we were due to face Valletta. Both games were to be played at the national stadium, Ta Qali.

When we arrived for the game, the mercury on the thermometer was sitting at 30°C.

United's game kicked off first and they won 3-0 in front of 12,300 spectators. The ground was then cleared, and at 4 p.m., we took the field against Valletta with 18,213 in the stadium. The temperature pitch side was 34°C.

Given the situation with my kidney, I had to hydrate much

more than I usually did, taking on several litres of water before we kicked off.

There's always the chance that you can underestimate teams that are ranked lower than you, but we didn't do it that afternoon. We sizzled in the sun and were 6-0 up at half-time.

As we entered the dressing room at the break, Tommy McLean guided us into the shower room where he demonstrated his ingenuity; the showers were on, but cold water was cascading out of them. Still kitted up, we stood under the showers and let the ice-cold water cool us down.

John Greig then appeared for his team talk. "Right, no issues with anything as you look like you can score anytime against this team. This might be a strange instruction, but I don't want you to score any more goals as we want a crowd back at Ibrox for the return."

We started laughing but Greigy was serious, and reinforced his point, saying, "I'm not kidding. All I want you to do is keep possession for 45 minutes".

Coisty, who hadn't scored any of our six goals and was probably sizing up a couple of opportunities to find the net after the restart, shouted, "The heat's gone for you, gaffer, are you taking the piss?"

As a linesman entered the dressing room to inform us that the game was about to restart, the boys were shaking their heads as we trooped on to the park.

Despite our better instincts, we rarely ventured forward and in the second half we only scored an additional two goals. My fellow defender, Dave McPherson, scored four of our eight goals.

At Ibrox in the return, the crowd only reached 11,500. Numerous changes were made to the starting XI, but we racked up double figures, John 'Solo' MacDonald netting a hat-trick in our 10-0 win. The aggregate score, 18-0, was a record at the time, but I'm certain if we hadn't had the half time instruction from Greigy in Valletta, we would have added at least another six, given how dominant we were.

There was another strange occurrence associated with European games too. It was called 'the fireman's hose' and I first encountered it after we played Dortmund away from home in 1982.

We'd had a credible 0-0 draw in the first leg in front of 54,000 at the Westfalen stadium. We stuck to the tactics, defended as a unit, and rarely ventured beyond the half-way line. It was an excellent result to bring back to Ibrox for the second leg.

The following Saturday we were due to play Kilmarnock at home in the Premier Division. As we arrived, we were told to strip naked, then form a queue and wait outside the bathing area. As you'd imagine, as 13 strapping players in their prime physically gathered in their respective birthday suits, the banter was flying.

As I was called into the bathing area, I couldn't believe my eyes. Ally Dawson was standing against the tiled wall, while Joe Mason, who coached the reserve team, stood operating a firefighter's hose. Dozy's naked body was bombarded with a ferocious, high-pressure jet of water and my team-mate was spluttering as the water battered against him. Joe then closed off the jet at which point he shouted, "Next!"

Ally walked past me and said, "You didnae get that at Thistle, Skippy" before adding, "watch your arse when you face the wall as Joe has a good aim." He laughed and left the bathing area. Meantime, I walked with some trepidation towards the wall.

I recall as the cold water hit me, I recoiled. My system went into shock, but I can vaguely recall Joe telling me to turn around. And Dozy was proven correct, Joe's aim was superb. Not only did I get a jolt to my system, I felt like I had just had an enema which nearly cleared out my pre-match meal!

I was told later that the hosing was to shock your system out of lethargy. The plan certainly worked that day, we beat Kilmarnock comprehensively 5-0 with John MacDonald scoring a double.

I doubt whether these practices had any scientific basis, but the experience certainly focussed the mind. That season after we got battered in Cologne, we came home, got hosed down and proceeded to beat Motherwell 4-0. Wee Solo clearly benefited from the experience more than others, for he scored another two goals in the Motherwell game.

In general, after away games in Europe, the management team decided that we would stay overnight in the city we had travelled to. Today, most teams charter a flight and fly home immediately following the game, but from experience, remaining in the city after a game was the best solution on two counts it encouraged team bonding and it also allowed for a full night's sleep at the normal time.

Our post-match routine followed a very strict regime. At the conclusion of the game, we would have a bath or shower, change then return to the hotel. We would have a light meal together, with a couple of beers allowed. But it was hard to switch off and relax after playing games at that level, so we would invariably go into a room and have another beer or two.

In that era, opponents would sometimes supply the beer too. In Dortmund, I recall us being gifted six cases, and when teams came to us, Rangers would reciprocate the gesture. When we played Inter Milan in 1984, I can vividly recall watching superstars such as Karl Heinz Rummenigge, and Alessandro Altobelli carrying cases of Tennent's Lager and McEwan's Lager on to their coach outside Ibrox.

But when you mix footballers and beers, after a 'couple' there are some who want to extend the session and high jinks inevitably follow. And there are a couple of incidents that spring to mind.

In the UEFA Cup in season 1985/86, Rangers were paired with Osasuna. We beat them 1-0 at Ibrox on a pitch waterlogged by incessant torrential rain, but in Pamplona, we lost 2-0 and were eliminated. The defeat came in the midst of a spell that saw us lose to Dundee and Aberdeen at home in the league and also go down 2-0 against Hibs at Easter Road in the first leg of the League Cup semi-final.

I remember that we stayed in a high-rise hotel and our rooms were on the sixth floor. In our midst were two young pups with tremendous talent, Ian Durrant and Derek Ferguson. Durranty made his European debut for Rangers in the match in Pamplona, but post-match, in the bull running Spanish city, the experienced players kept their distance as the pair were mischievous beyond comprehension.

As the senior players settled into one room to discuss the game, there was a loud bang on the door. "Let us in," shouted the troublesome twosome. Our collective response was instantaneous, "No, get to your beds," we hollered. Admission to the room would most likely witness carnage and mayhem would inevitably ensue.

After a couple of minutes, all was quiet. The pair seemed to have heeded our advice. But as we continued our post-match analysis, the patio doors slid open. The room we were situated in had a balcony, and as the doors opened, Durranty and Fergie dived in. Cue the carnage and mayhem!

"How the fuck did you get in?" asked Coop as he walked out of the patio doors to survey the scene. "We're sixty feet up, how did you get on to the balcony?"

Durranty and Fergie were like versions of the cartoon characters, Beavis and Butthead, laughing and chortling as they wreaked havoc and wrecked the room. They were still mid-flow when they both responded to Coop's question. "We climbed into each balcony from ours," Fergie chuckled. "It's six down the corridor," said Durranty a mischievous grin spread across his face.

Coop stuck his head back out of the patio door. He came back with an incredulous look on his face. "There's six feet between each balcony, you dickheads."

Durranty and Fergie were oblivious to the geometry of it all, though. They thought that it was just an adventure. As perilous and precarious as the situation was, the boys just wanted to have fun, and their frolics on this occasion ended when they shook the bottles of juice that they were carrying and sprayed the contents over the room. At that moment they were ejected.

I shudder to think what market value Durranty and Fergie would have in today's bloated market. Both were supremely talented – Durrant would have ended up playing abroad had it not been for the horrific knee injury he sustained in 1988 – but had a wee bit of devilment too. Fun was never far away when they both entered a room, although I'm not sure how big Jock would have viewed things had he witnessed two of his young protégés risking life and limb scrambling from balcony to balcony that sultry night in Pamplona!

# CHAPTER 7
# A FOOT IN THE DRESSING ROOM AND THE BOARDROOM

*July 2022*

I'VE NOW BEEN back working full-time for a month, but strange things are still happening to me. The concussion continues and a strange pattern has developed. Every morning at 2 a.m. I wake and feel as if I've had a full night's sleep. I try several methods to get back to sleep, including listening to music and reading, but my mind has long since shifted into overdrive. It's now got me reliving the events of the working day, every conversation I've had and has me conjuring up what I said and what I should have said. I worry about everything. My mortality, how I'm performing at work and people's perceptions of me. I simply can't switch off, so tossing and turning ensues until my ordeal ends when the alarm sounds at 6.30 a.m.

My wife continues to be incredibly supportive and says it's just part of the healing process. Even further reassurances from my head trauma buddy, Keith, and the brain doctor do little to lift my flagging spirit. I continue to struggle through what is becoming an increasingly unpleasant experience. I just want it to end.

When I am fortunate to be able to sleep, I strangely have dreams where I'm speaking in Gaelic. When I was young, I spoke Gaelic when we went to my grandparent's croft in Skye. Gaelic was the only language spoken. But in a football club there are also two languages: the language of the boardroom and the language of the dressing room.

In the sanctuary of the dressing room, the thinking is much more short term. Managers, and players will talk about the team, identifying, and discussing areas where it needs to improve; the manager hoping that the board will provide the necessary financial backing. Chat in the boardroom is much more strategic, with board members forecasting cash flow and looking at the possibility of being as successful as possible without going into the red.

This language difference is the primary reason why relationships break down at football clubs. How many times have you read that the relationship between the board and the manager has become untenable. At that juncture, there's only one winner and it's not the manager.

As someone who has played the game, and also operated at director level in business and football, I like to think that I have fluency in both languages. That means I have often had to adopt the role of translator between both sanctums to ensure stability at the clubs that I have been involved with.

I was General Manager at Kilmarnock and that was where I experienced the language barrier for the first time. The board at Kilmarnock was a good one, with a wide and varied make up. It comprised the former police chief at Strathclyde Police, Sir John Orr, the millionaire owner Jamie Moffat, motor vehicle entrepreneur Robert Wyper, self-made millionaire Jim Clarke, and lawyer Michael Johnston.

Sir John ran a tight board, one that rarely interfered in football matters. But, against that mantra, the internet views of the supporters started to crop up in meetings. This came to pass because of a burgeoning internet forum that was run by two good lads that were Kilmarnock through and through – Baz and Hippo. The forum gave the supporters an online platform to air their views on the team and those views started to filter into the boardroom. This was because a board member had viewed the comments directly or had been made aware of them by family members and friends.

Soon there were certain members of the board who felt under pressure to react and respond. And matters came to a head when the team, led superbly by manager Jim Jefferies and his assistant, Billy Brown, were going through what would prove to be a losing streak.

Following two defeats against teams that many felt we should have been beating, there was a discussion on the forum that

Jim and Billy should be replaced. Some members of the board suggested that should be considered, with one even suggesting that I approach Terry Butcher, who was in charge at Motherwell, to gauge his interest.

As all of this was bubbling up, I had listened but not commented. But there comes a point when you have to step in and give guidance and advice on matters that you have control over. I got the attention of the chairman, Sir John, as all comments had to go through him, a practice that many boards I've been part of that have five-hour meetings should adopt.

I started to speak, but one member soon cut across me. This wasn't protocol and Sir John quickly intervened.

"Through the chair," he said forcefully, "Mr Mackinnon has the floor."

I smiled at him and nodded. "Gentleman, changing the manager at this stage is the wrong thing to do. Mr Jefferies has had an excellent season to date and is the right man for the job. Additionally, he is supporting and being pro-active with me in addressing the reducing budget figures imposed by the bank."

I stood up at that point 'a la Rumpole of the Bailey', although I didn't quite grab my lapels.

"Furthermore, we currently have 15 players out through injury and this has been a major factor in the last two defeats. Our physiotherapist, Mr McQueen, has given me and the manager a full appraisal of the situation, and we should have at least six of those injured back in contention for the next game."

Stepping into your authority is a hugely important aspect of successful business. But it requires good leaders to recognise and allow it to perpetuate within an organisation.

As a leader or owner of an organisation, you would never question or make decisions in an area that you had little experience of. If you had an employment issue you would never dream of overlooking the experience of a Human Resources professional to decide, simply because you were the boss. Unfortunately, this necessary leadership trait sometimes doesn't find its way into football. Jamie Moffat was a good leader who acknowledged that neither he, nor his board, had much in the way of experience in football matters. He ensured that he let the people who did, like me, contribute to the decision-making process. When Jamie left the club, his successor unfortunately didn't fully adopt the same thought process.

Jamie beckoned to Sir John. "Through the Chair, Sir John," he said. Sir John nodded and Jamie stood up and added, "We employ Mr Mackinnon as GM [General Manager] because he has a business background, but more importantly because he has a football background. We are supporters but we can't let emotions rule our head. If Mr Mackinnon says we give the manager time, then I for one would back that."

Jamie beckoned to the rest of the board and there were nods of approval. One member was a little more reluctant to support the idea, though, and through gritted teeth could be heard to say, "If he loses any of the next three, we need to look elsewhere."

Sir John gave his famous put down face in the direction of the board member and the matter was ended. I loved that board and their commitment to Kilmarnock Football Club.

The last item on the agenda saw Jim enter the boardroom to deliver the manager's report. We were on the same page, as Jim also spoke about the injuries abating and players starting to come back. For me, that reinforced to the board that we had agreed the right way forward.

After any board meeting Jim and I used to go to his office for a de-brief. My language at that point reverted to dressing room parlance, although it would be laced with messages from the boardroom too.

On this occasion, I opened with, "Great the injuries are starting to heal up, Jim. It's had an effect on the last two games."

"Yeah, Davie, I think we'll get back on track now they're clearing up," replied Jim.

Mindful of the single dissenting voice in the board meeting, I next asked what Jim thought about our chances of winning the next three games.

"I'm very confident once we get the bulk of the injured back," was his reply.

He smiled and I smiled. We both knew that if Kilmarnock did win those three games, then everyone would be happy again. And that's exactly how things panned out, the team won the next three and the pressure was off.

Without having someone present that had the ability to be

a conduit between the dressing room and boardroom, boards of other clubs may have made a premature decision to sack the manager. That's not always the case, though, as I would find out when I moved to my next role with Dundee, where the ears of the board latterly refused to attune and listen to the language of the dressing room.

Jim Jefferies was a very good manager, one who was conversant with the language of both the dressing room and the boardroom. And like every successful manager, he had a very supportive assistant in the shape of Billy Brown. Billy's a character who is well respected in the game and it's no surprise that he's now the Chair of the Scottish Manager's Association. Billy is an honest man who wears his heart on his sleeve and is extremely loyal. But I can recall an incident during my time at Kilmarnock when I was able to help him avoid a touchline ban.

At the time, BBC had the rights to screen live games in the Scottish Premier League. In addition, as part of those rights, the BBC were allowed to interview a club representative live at half time.

One of their featured games was Kilmarnock against Celtic. Celtic were awarded a controversial penalty minutes before half time and tensions were high at the interval.

As part of my role, I was the liaison between the club and the BBC producer. As I went down to the tunnel just before the half time whistle, the producer said, "We want an interview with Jim Jefferies."

I attempted to fend him off by saying, "They've just been awarded a dubious penalty, you can't interview anyone, emotions will be running too high."

"It's part of the contract, Davie," said the producer. "I don't want to have to report the club for non-compliance. I spoke with Jim pre-match and he was happy to do it."

I looked at him and shook my head.

I went out of the small, narrow tunnel at Rugby Park and made my way towards the dugout just as the half time whistle blew. It came as no surprise that Jim and Billy were raging and were walking towards me at pace. "I'm not doing the half time interview, Davie, Billy will need to do it," said Jim as he stormed up the tunnel.

Billy stopped and said, "The gaffer's asked me to do the BBC interview, Davie."

"I know Billy, try and keep your head," I said more in hope than expectation.

As the words left my mouth, the BBC producer arrived and said, "Jim says he's not doing the interview. You OK for it, Billy?"

Billy looked at me. His facial expression suggested that he didn't want to do it, but he followed the producer into the boot room where the camera had been set up.

Inevitably, the first question was about the penalty. Billy was shown the incident from a few angles. "It looks a bit debatable," said the interviewer. It was like the proverbial red rag to the bull; it enticed an already irate Billy to respond angrily.

"Debatable?" shouted Billy, "They've been getting away with conning refs for over a hundred years, never a penalty."

Billy proceeded to beat a hasty retreat to the dressing room. For me, there was an air of inevitability, I knew that we'd hear from the SFA on Monday.

Having mulled over things after the game, I was angry that Billy had been put in that position. I was adamant that I would defend him when, as expected, we received notification that Billy's comments had been noted and he was to appear before an SFA disciplinary panel at Hampden.

The Chair of the Committee was a familiar face, my old Airdrie chairman, George Peat, who was now President of the SFA.

Ahead of the meeting, I said to Billy that I'd do the talking. We were summoned into the boardroom and Billy's interview with the BBC was played. I have to admit there were a couple of sharp intakes of breath from those present.

"Pretty conclusive, Billy?" asked George at which point I intoned, "I wonder if I may speak, George?"

George smiled and said, "Of course, Davie."

Looking George directly and squarely in the eyes, I said, "As a man who's had a long and successful career in football, I'm sure you'll agree that we all have a duty of care to protect people under our collective wing, George."

George nodded and said, "Of course, Davie, we need to ensure we look after people in the game."

I continued, "I know the BBC contract is important, but the

agreement to allow managers and coaches to be interviewed at half time puts enormous pressure on people like Billy. By his own admission, Billy is a very passionate football guy who wears his heart on his sleeve. He's open and honest, George. I'm sure you'll agree that whilst the BBC contract is important, it puts our coaches and managers in an invidious position and compromises our collective duty of care towards them."

George looked around the table before he replied, "Can you and Billy give us five minutes, Davie?"

Both Billy and I nodded, before leaving the room. Like Billy, George is an honest man who tries to do things properly, so I knew I'd struck a chord. Barely five minutes had elapsed when we were summoned back into the room.

We took our seats and George delivered the verdict. He said, "We've taken notice of your words and we have decided to give you another chance, Billy. We'd ask you to think closely at how your comments could be interpreted in future, and if you appear before us again, you'll not get off so easily. Have you got that?"

Billy nodded and said, "Thank you, George."

We left the room and as we made our way down the stairs from the sixth floor, Billy shook my hand. "You ever thought about a career as a lawyer?" he laughed.

It was all change at Kilmarnock as Michael Johnston became the new owner/chair as Jamie Moffat stepped back. I'd really got on well with Michael and liked his style, but suddenly it all started to change. Michael wanted to be hands on and step into areas previously under my remit.

Before joining Kilmarnock, I'd had a successful career in pub retailing. I had spent 12 years at Tennent's where I had worked with brands like O'Neill's, All Bar One and the famous Horseshoe Bar. That was followed by four years as Operations Director and shareholder with Scotland's largest independent pub group, Pub.com, which was successfully sold for £21million.

Once the sale was completed, I spent some time travelling, before deciding that I wanted to get back into football. And as luck would have it, Gerry Dunn, a director at Clyde, called me and asked if I fancied becoming Commercial Director at the club.

I'd met Gerry several times and he was a gregarious and passionate guy whose family had been long standing associates at Clyde. At that time, Billy Carmichael, a very nice man, was providing financial support, and Clyde were full time. They were competing in the Championship, and their aspiration was to win promotion to the Premier League. They were managed by the former Northern Irish international, Alan Kernaghan, who was ably assisted by the talented Billy Reid.

After meeting all the key stakeholders, I was impressed, and I took up the role in May 2002. I got work straight away and, using my connections, I managed to quickly secure sponsorship via the Italian kit manufacturer Lotto. I thoroughly enjoyed working with the board and the football management team, and we came close to realising the dream of promotion. Clyde finished the campaign on 72 points, a tally that would have been sufficient to win the title the previous season. But Falkirk chalked up 81 points to pip us to the title, and with only one promotion spot and no play offs at that time, we faced another season in the second tier.

As season 2002/03 ended, I was asked to apply for the recently created General Manager's position at my old club, Kilmarnock. As much as I was enjoying my time at Clyde, the lure of Rugby Park and the opportunity to work once again with the wonderful Kilmarnock supporters was too much, and after a successful meeting with the board, I was appointed in June 2003.

But only a matter of weeks later, just before the first home game of the season against Partick Thistle, my family were left devastated when my nephew Stuart, aged just five, died. Stuart was a lovely bright, intelligent kid, but eight months earlier, he had had a brain scan which identified an inoperable tumour at the base of his skull. And despite supportive care from a wonderful neurosurgeon called Dr Pritchard, Stuart's health soon deteriorated. My brother Alan, his wife Mary, and Stuart's big brother, David, made his final few months as good as they could for him, with love and fun being at the forefront.

Stuart loved football too, and his idol was David Beckham who was playing for Manchester United at the time. We wrote to David explaining Stuart's circumstances and sent a photograph to him hoping he would sign it. A week later it was kindly returned, David's signature being accompanied by a lovely message for Stuart and a handwritten note. When he saw the photograph, Stuart started smiling. He was overjoyed that his hero had taken the time to write to him.

Footballers have a special place in the hearts and minds of supporters. In my time, I have seen many going above and beyond to support fans, young and old, during good and bad times in their lives. David Beckham, like many, fully understood the impact he and his fellow professionals can have in the community, and I've always been proud to be part of that compassionate football brethren.

It's now 20 years since Stuart passed away, but he is never far from our thoughts. And anywhere I have worked since he died, I have always made sure that I have a picture of him on my desk. Courageous and brave throughout, he will always be an inspiration to us all.

The Park Hotel, situated in the shadow of Rugby Park, was losing money due to stock control issues and a lack of strategic management. It also carried the burden of a several million pound loan that was taken out during construction of the hotel.

Once I took up my post at Kilmarnock, I installed a good manager, supported by a robust stock system across food and liquor and things started to move towards profit. I also negotiated a near £1million sponsorship and development fund aligned for supply and sponsorship from Scottish Brewers.

I put my experience in the licensed trade to good use. After analysing the supply agreements, I realised that the hotel could increase its profits by negotiating and changing its supply terms. Brewers at that time had created a healthy competitive market to secure new business.

I knew Scottish Brewers intimately and following a review of the hotel barrelage figures and the potential to create a new permanent bar within the Main Stand at Rugby Park, a sponsorship fund was agreed. This would inject significant investment into the club to create the bar and via a sponsorship package.

The package covered a payback period which would be offset against the current and increased barrelage which included beer, spirits, soft drinks, and snacks. I carried out a survey within the Ayrshire area; the findings concluded that a new full-time bar within the stadium could gross £5,000 per week which would cover the requirements. Should the figures not transpire following a three-year review, then the sponsorship would be converted to a loan with an interest rate of four per cent. I presented this to the board and they were happy. They passed the plan and the conversion work and sponsorship started.

The bar replaced the club shop, which was re-located to a new facility in the car park, and a function room that was rarely used. And after it opened, the new bar, which also served food and screened sport on multiple screens, hit the targets. The board and Scottish Brewers were delighted.

When Michael came in as chairman, he told me that he was taking over the running of the hotel. I asked what experience he had. He said that he knew food and drink and would change the supply relationship between the club and the hotel.

I had been working to the plan Jamie and I had agreed, but now Michael was making changes without discussion. I was left with two choices at that point; bite my tongue and accept it or move on. I opted for the former.

Michael also decided to restrict the hours of the bar as he wanted to push people towards the hotel, which had a negative effect on the takings and subsequently, the barrelage return. I understand Scottish Brewers invoked the sponsorship to loan agreement at the review once I'd left.

The next area Michael wanted to have in his remit was the signing of players. His rationale was that he was a lawyer and, therefore, it made sense that he dealt with agents. And that decision was to play a significant part in the future career path of future Scotland international Kris Boyd.

As the 2005 summer transfer window was about to slam shut, Cardiff City made a substantial six-figure offer for Kris's services. Kilmarnock accepted the offer and Kris and his agent flew to the Welsh capital to negotiate personal terms. Once they were agreed, Jim Jefferies and I were all set to sign and witness the deal on behalf of the club.

I called Sandy Bryson, a very supportive man who was the Head of Registrations at the SFA, to tell him to expect the transfer agreement to emerge from his fax machine in the next hour. But at that point, Sandy highlighted a significant hurdle in getting the deal done; I was no longer one of the club's registered signatories having been removed. It transpired that Michael Johnston was now the only person at Kilmarnock Football Club who could sign a transfer agreement.

Once I ended the call with Sandy, I hurriedly called Michael's mobile. It went to voicemail. I tried several times, but he didn't answer. With the clock ticking and the deal on the verge of collapsing, I had no alternative but to leave messages asking Michael to call me urgently.

Kris and his agent were still in Wales at this point, when word got to them that there was an issue, they elected to fly back to Glasgow. Jim Jefferies made some calls and it transpired that Rangers had made Kris and his team aware that they would be making a bid for his services in the January transfer window.

Michael eventually called me back around 7 p.m. Apparently, he was attending an event in the Highlands and had no mobile phone signal. I hastily explained the predicament that we were in. Michael said that he would fix it and resurrect the deal, but I said there was no chance of that. As soon as I heard that Kris was on his way back to Scotland and that Rangers were going to make a move, I knew that the deal was dead.

Rangers were true to their word. They came back in for Kris in January 2006 and a deal was done for around £500,000. He scored a hat trick on his debut against Peterhead, and across two spells at Ibrox scored a remarkable 119 goals in 212 appearances. Looking back, though, I often ponder and reflect on what path Kris's career would have taken if Michael Johnston hadn't changed the signatories or been uncontactable on the day that the proposed move to Cardiff City collapsed.

When I was a player, there were no agents and like my peers, I had to negotiate my own contract renewal and/or transfer. It would have been very helpful to have someone by my side taking away the inevitable haggling. As the guy dealing with contracts at clubs, I recognised the requirements for an independent advisor for players and was very happy to work with agents as the majority were and are decent people.

In my time though, I found football agents to fall into three different categories:

1. Football people who knew the game and were able to work with their client and the club's objectives to reach a satisfactory conclusion for all parties.
2. Non-football people who didn't understand the game nor their player's career development and saw the role

only as an opportunity to make money.

3. Agents who were not interested in the club or their client and used it as a means to make money for themselves.

I respect the job that an agent has to do, and thankfully, the majority whom I encountered fitted into the first category. I did, however, have the misfortune to meet a couple of agents that fell into the other two categories.

Looking after a young, talented footballer is difficult as they have so many distractions on their path to achieve the best career outcome within their skill level. Very young players not only have agents vying for their business, but some also have parents who are trying to live out their own football dreams.

The expectations and pressure put on young players by their parents is occasionally overpowering. In my experience, this pressure has destroyed the potential promise of many young, aspiring players. Adding into the mix an agent who doesn't have the best interests of their client at heart makes for a toxic cocktail and explains why so many young players never graduate beyond youth level.

Whilst at a club, I remember being approached by an agent who said that he represented a friend who was looking for a move to a team in a higher league. "Why?" I asked him. "Is he ready to move?"

The agent was bullish in his reply. "I think he's better than the club he's at and he deserves to play at a higher level. He's a big, handsome guy and I've managed to get his Twitter up to 10,000 followers and got him a couple of modelling jobs. The girls are going crazy for him and getting him to a higher profile team will make him the new George Best."

"Wow," I responded.

I'd done some research on the player in question and had watched him in a game. I'd also spoken to his manager, a very good coach who had blooded several young players and taken them to a higher level. "He's got the basics, Davie," was his assessment of the next Bestie. "But he's still got a mistake in him every game. I'm working on him every day in training, and I reckon another year learning about the game will get him the move that his agent wants."

Armed with that feedback, I asked the agent to back off and allow the player some space to continue his development. If he did that his big break would come sooner rather than later.

Three months later I heard that the player had refused to sign a new contract and he signed for a team in the division above. His earnings would have gone up by around £100 per week basic. However, at the end of the following season the player was released and now, a few years later, (he is 25 years of age at the time of writing) hasn't progressed any further. It's another example of how a catalogue of situations where bad advice is given can stunt growth and ruin a talented player's career.

Thankfully, category three agents are far and few between, but in my career, I met two in particular. 'Scurrilous' is an understatement when it comes to describing some of their behaviours.

When a player currently under contract enters negotiations for a new deal, an offer is made to the player for his consideration. At that point, inevitably, the player will say that he'll discuss it with his agent.

On two separate occasions I had different agents for two different players call me and say, "If you cut the player's offer by £200 a month and arrange to transfer £100 a month to me over the period of the contract, I'll get him to sign. You save £100 a month and the player will know nothing about it."

I was flabbergasted at what was being proposed and swiftly rebuffed it, saying, "That'll never happen on my watch, the offer remains at the level discussed."

"Oh, I'm sure the chairman will not be happy if I told him that you were not going to save the club £100 a month on the deal," was the snide reply.

My hackles were now raised and I informed the individuals concerned, "If that's a threat, I'm giving you notice that I'm going to meet with the player and tell him what you're suggesting."

The phone went dead on both occasions, and we did the deal directly with the two players at the level that we were prepared to pay.

One other area that category three agents like to get involved with is transfers. They play teams off against each other and try and cut the fee for the club's player and try the same tactic with the purchasing team. This time, though, the stakes are higher as the conversation involves figures in the region of tens of thousands.

Again, on two occasions, I've had the managers of the purchasing teams call me after a fee has been agreed, telling me that the player's agent has called the chairman and said he can do a deal to "cut the fee" to make sure that the reduced offer is accepted. The agent had said his fee for this would be half of the saving.

Again, thankfully agents in the third category are few and far between, but they're doing a great disservice to their players, clubs and their profession. Hopefully these charlatans will be identified and hounded out of the game, but I suspect only UEFA intervention will sort it.

There's also been a seismic shift when it comes to signing a player nowadays. Those making the decisions have at their fingertips a vast array of data including video analysis and statistics. There are online scouting systems like Wyscout, but back in the days when I was a CEO assisting managers when they were looking to bring in players, information of that ilk was scarce, particularly for players playing overseas.

I remember Jim Jefferies and I would spend hours looking at recommended players on VHS tapes. We would watch the full game and afterwards we would decide whether or not to go to a game and see the player in the flesh.

Scouting missions can also help unearth an unexpected diamond, though. I remember on one occasion after we had watched the video footage of a player, we travelled to see him in action. From memory, he had a good game, but Jim and I were drawn to another player who we collectively felt would fit better into our style of play. We signed him and he went on to play nearly 200 games for Kilmarnock.

As mentioned, identifying players who will fit seamlessly into the team's system is the key to success. I have watched teams signing players who have a good pedigree, but it hasn't worked out for them as it appears that little consideration was taken over whether they would fit in with the club's style of play.

During my time in football administration, I worked closely with the managers when we were recruiting players. First and foremost, before we considered ability, transfer value or wages, we determined whether the player that we were interested in would fit in. I was able to play an active role in that decision-making process as I had played the game, albeit in a different era. As a result, my opinion was respected by the managers as they all recognised that I was someone who knew the game.

In recent years, the fashionable trend in football has been for Directors of Football and Recruitment Managers to be appointed. Many of them have established a track record of identifying players following a thorough online data analysis, but too often they allow the statistics to rule and dictate the signing policy. That shouldn't underpin the strategy, though. It's about understanding whether the player will fit into the system that the manager tends to utilise, as ultimately it is that which will improve the team's performance, not how good the potential recruit's numbers are.

A classic example of this approach is the successful Nottingham Forest team managed by Brian Clough in the late 1970s and 1980s. Clough was ably assisted by Peter Taylor, and after guiding Derby County from obscurity to the First Division title in 1972, they took over a Forest team languishing mid table in the Second Division. Clough and Taylor galvanised the club and turned them into First Division champions. Successive European Cup successes followed and the key ingredient in that recipe for success was recruiting players who would fit into the system.

The list of players recruited included many so-called unfashionable journeymen who had been relegated to the reserves, at either Forest or other clubs. Frank Clark, signed on a free transfer from Newcastle United, and Larry Lloyd, signed for £60,000 from Liverpool, gave the defence solidity. And Archie Gemmell, who cost £25,000, gave the midfield boundless energy which set a foundation for Clough to build upon. John McGovern and John O'Hare were also integral parts of the jigsaw. Clough and Taylor also resurrected the Forest careers of John Robertson and Martin O'Neill. On that basis, Taylor and Clough built a club that would rise like a phoenix from the ashes to the summit of English football and compete with and conquer the cream of the Continent too.

When sifting through the minefield of potential players, Taylor went to great lengths to ensure that anyone identified would not only make a smooth transition on the playing side but wouldn't upset the dynamics in the dressing room.

One player in particular fitted that bill, Kenny Burns. He had started out at Rangers but didn't make the grade at Ibrox. He moved to Birmingham City in 1971 where he was converted into a centre forward after Bob Latchford got injured.

I remember playing against Kenny in reserve games when I was at Arsenal. He was, in my opinion, a slight centre forward who lacked focus. But Peter Taylor saw potential. Despite being told by the Birmingham City chairman to steer clear as Kenny was a "hard-drinking brawler", Taylor instead did some detective work, monitoring Burns for a period of time. The upshot was that Kenny was worth a punt and he signed for Forest for £150,000 in 1977. He immediately reverted him to a centre back and he played an integral role during that triumphant period for Forest.

Garry Birtles, a centre forward, was recruited for a paltry £2,000 from amateur side Long Eaton; although significant financial outlay was required to recruit Peter Shilton, who became Britain's most expensive keeper, and the wonderfully talented Trevor Francis, the country's first £1,000,000 player, they fitted into the system both on and off the pitch.

Having that clarity in their recruitment strategy aligned with their eye for a player meant that Clough and Taylor were set for success. There was no need for any input from a Director of Football Operations or a requirement for specialist recruitment advice.

It was the same at all the teams that I was involved with. What is in their remit now was part of mine back then. It allowed me to develop and evolve the signing strategy with the manager such that we were on the same page when it came to our recruitment policy.

Managers need to trust the people working with them on recruitment. Sometimes adding an extra couple of layers to the decision-making process can breed animosity and create friction. This will invariably lead to an impasse which could see a potential new signing slip through the net and go off to ply their trade elsewhere.

Over the years I have had calls from several individuals who wanted to be Directors of Football. They've called, picked my brains then used that advice to snare the role that they were after. Not surprisingly, once I assisted them the contact with me stopped until the next time they were hunting another role in the game. There wasn't usually a long time between the calls either. If you were to analyse how long a Director of Football stays at a football club, you'll find it is only for a relatively short period of time.

*****

Back to Kilmarnock and the rapidly deteriorating relationship between Michael Johnston and me. Although two major areas of my remit had gone, my love and loyalty for the club kept me on board. But even that was put to the test when another area was removed. On this occasion,I was left with no option but to tender my resignation.

Michael arrived at the ground one evening as I was about to start an interview with the BBC to promote a new season ticket initiative. My old friend, Kheredine Idessane, was the man responsible for conducting the interview for *Sportsound*.

"What's happening?" asked Michael as he entered the stadium. "What are the cameras doing here?"

I responded by saying, "I've arranged to go on the BBC to promote the family season ticket scheme, so Kheredine has kindly agree to give us some airtime."

"Can we speak privately?" said Michael and he beckoned me into the tunnel. The tunnel at Rugby Park is narrow so as we squeezed in, Michael continued, "I'm the man in charge, David. I only want the fans to have one focal point and that's me. I'm the face of Kilmarnock now and I don't want them confused, so I'll do all the interviews going forward."

I was livid and at that moment made my mind up – I was leaving Kilmarnock. But with the values my father taught me still at the forefront, I kept my anger in check and said to Michael, "OK, but I want to see you in the office once you're finished with the BBC."

I'd joined Kilmarnock as General Manager in 2003 and such was my affinity for the club, I firmly believed that it would be a job I'd be in until I retired.

When I joined, one of the first things to arrive on my desk was to scope out how we could cut the wage bill that we had for the playing staff.

Jamie Moffat had met the bank and they were concerned that the debt had risen to around £13.5million, with a significant amount of that due to the funding requirement for the Park Hotel.

The player wage bill was sitting around the £1.8million mark, and Jamie was looking for a reduction of £600,000 over two seasons. I was fully onboard, but I knew that I'd need Jim Jefferies to work with me. It was a significant reduction, but I still wanted to make sure that Kilmarnock would remain competitive in the Scottish Premiership as the cuts were introduced.

I created a player cost spreadsheet which listed all player's basic wages, bonus predictions, National Insurance, and tax costs to the club. It was a substantial amount of work to pull all the figures together, but once I had done so, I arranged a meeting with Jim.

I explained the position and gave Jim a copy of the spreadsheet. To his credit, Jim acknowledged why we had to make the cuts, even though it would weaken his playing squad. From there it was a matter of analysing the data to establish how we could achieve the required reduction over two seasons.

I remember Jim saying to me, "You're a football guy who understands the game and business."

"Yes," I answered, "and I know the issues that we'll need to overcome."

Those issues fell into two main categories: meeting the expectations of the fans and maintaining the required levels of performance on the field. And to help smooth the way, I made a commitment to communicate with our supporters through face-to-face meetings and the media once Jim and I had agreed the plan.

Recruitment and retention go hand in hand when it comes to strategy, so I suggested that we stuck with the philosophy of trying to keep players who fit into the style of play. We had to make sure that we didn't tumble down the table and suffer relegation over the period of change.

Jim nodded in agreement. He reckoned that with the cutbacks it would be at least another three seasons before Kilmarnock could contemplate challenging for a place in the top six again. Astute as always, Jim was spot on:

Season 2002/2003 (pre-budget cut)  4th place.
Season 2003/2004                   10th place.
Season 2004/2005                   7th place.
Season 2005/2006                   5th place.

Although these decisions had a detrimental effect on his player pool and weakened the team, Jim Jefferies was extremely supportive which sums up the class and integrity of the man. He was a great motivator and had a keen eye for a player that he knew was the right fit for his system.

I considered Jim a friend – I still do – but not only was he a good

Head swathed in bandages after having 10 stitches inserted in a head wound. The Rangers fans christened me 'Rambo'.

Getting to grips with Celtic's Davie Provan, one of the many talented wingers I faced in my career.

Sweating it out pre match against Valetta of Malta in the European Cup Winners' Cup in 1983. We won the first leg 8-0 before hitting double figures in the return leg at Ibrox.

I was honoured to win 35 Player of the Year trophies from the Rangers supporters at the end of my first season at Ibrox, 1982/83.

Tackling my old Dundee team-mate Gordon Strachan in the 1983 Scottish Cup Final.

Rangers embarked on a World Tour in 1984. This is me after training with Bobby Russell in the Minneapolis Super Dome.

The first leg of the Rangers' World Tour in 1984 was in Melbourne. To my left are Colin McAdam, Sandy Clark, Bobby Williamson, Ally Dawson, David McPherson, and Craig Paterson.

Switzerland, pre-season 1984/85. Back row (L-R): Sandy Clark, Ally Dawson, Ian Redford, Peter McCloy, and Ally McCoist. Cammy Fraser is alongside yours truly at the front.

Back to full fitness and raring to go.
Rangers had just beaten Kaiserslautern
2-1 in Germany.

Guarding the post as Rangers face a
corner against Dundee United. I have a
moustachioed Derek Johnstone, on loan from
Chelsea, and John McLelland for company.

Eyes on the ball (again) as I face Kevin Keegan,
who guested for Hearts in a testimonial match
for Alex Macdonald in May 1984

Sliding in the snow at Cappielow on the day I
captained Rangers for the first time. It was an
honour and a privilege.

Iain Ferguson, Eric Ferguson, Ally McCoist and I catch up with the news before travelling to Iraq and a rendezvous with Saddam Hussein in 1985.

Keeping my eye on the orange ball in farcical conditions at Morton in the Scottish Cup in February 1985.

I joined Airdrie in 1986 and became captain and right-hand man to manager Gordon McQueen. He was an inspiring leader.

Remonstrating with referee Don McVicar. Although I never shirked a tackle in my career, I was only sent off once. . .and that was for handball!

Rising above Morton's Rowan Alexander to head clear. My time at Airdrie was thoroughly enjoyable.

Promotion is pending for Kilmarnock after I score from the penalty spot against Cowdenbeath on the final day of season 1989/90.

Party time! Kilmarnock's promotion-winning goalscorers, Paul Flexney (left) and yours truly flank a jubilant Tommy Burns.

Perfecting practice as I prepare to take a free-kick alongside the late, great Tommy Burns.

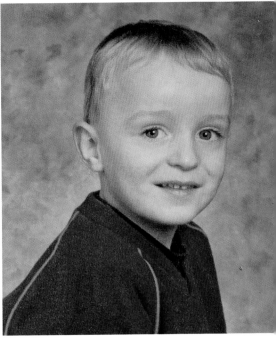

My nephew Stuart suffered a brain tumour and passed away at the age of five in 2003. He was an inspiration.

(Right) Pondering where I had put the sponsor's cheque! David Mackinnon, Kilmarnock CEO, and (left) dreaming of defeating Celtic in the League Cup when I was CEO at Dundee.

Alongside the Dundee manager, Alex Rae, I pay my respects to the Dundee United owner Eddie Thomson following his passing in October 2008.

COVID-19 presented numerous challenges for football clubs. I am with my good friend and Arbroath manager Dick Campbell.

manager, he was an excellent golfer. And the high standards that he held dear when it came to football management transferred on to the golf course, too.

I have to admit that I'm an average golfer. I've always played for enjoyment rather than seeking to reduce my handicap, so you can imagine my concerns when I was selected to partner Jim at a club golf day.

Our round didn't get off to the best of starts. As Jim addressed his ball and took his backswing on the first tee, I tried to swat one of the many wasps that were buzzing around my head. As I whacked one of them, Jim was distracted and sliced his shot. No words were necessary; he simply turned and gave me the "JJ stare" that I had witnessed many times on the touchline. I got the message and apologised.

As we moved through the course, I was pleased with my contribution and we were three under at the turn. But fate would once again intervene. It transpired that the $10^{th}$ tee was close to the first and I was reunited with the same battalion of wasps. They were still clearly irked that they hadn't managed to sting me first time around.

As Jim took his backswing, a wasp landed on my neck. What should I do? Was I more scared of the wasp or Jim? There was no contest; JJ won hands down. As Jim fired his ball unerringly down the fairway, I let the wasp sting me, all the time biting my lip to stop me squealing in pain.

Weeks later, news of our golf partnership reached the chairman, Jamie Moffat, and soon to be owner, Michael Johnston. Both were very accomplished golfers and they challenged us to a fourball at Jamie's club in West Kilbride.

To put the match-up into context, Jamie and Michael were as near as damn it scratch golfers, while Jim was playing off a handicap of two. My handicap was a healthy 18, which meant that we had to work out an aggregate handicap for Jim and me. Once that was done and the stake was agreed, we headed for the first tee.

As we walked, I whispered quietly to Jim, "I assume that even though we might be expected to throw the game, we're going for it?"

Jim smiled and said, "You're damn right we are!"

As seasoned former professional footballers, Jim and I had both developed and honed an unwavering will to win. And while others may have taken the easy option and allowed their bosses to triumph, that was never going to be the case with us.

From memory, it was very close for the first nine holes, but aided and abetted by my game, which was at a considerably higher level than normal, we started to win holes on the back nine. We were well ahead by the time that Jamie and Michael conceded on the 15<sup>th</sup> green, by which time we were four up with three holes to play.

Given my high handicap, I got the expected 'shark' comments as we shook hands and to be fair, they had a point. I can't recall ever playing a better round of golf than I did that day.

As I walked back to my office to pen my resignation letter, my mind drifted back to that moment. I laughed. I often wonder if things would have worked out differently had JJ and I lost that day.

Michael arrived at my office half an hour after our chat about the BBC interview and I immediately handed him the letter. "I'm not accepting that," he said brusquely. "You can still be General Manager, but you can concentrate on bringing in commercial revenue."

"No, Michael," I replied. "That's not what I signed up for so I'm afraid, you need to get on with it."

We shook hands and I left.

I had no bad feeling towards Michael. I liked him, but I knew that we couldn't work together. It was his way or no way, and that wasn't for me.

*****

I wasn't out of the game long either, as I reunited with another of my former clubs when I was offered the CEO position at Dundee. It was a role that I relished.

Dundee had been relegated and were in the First Division when I joined. They'd not long come out of administration and wanted to get back on track. I was approached by Bob Brannan, a guy that I'd worked with and liked. He was the CEO of Whyte and Mackay and a Dundee fanatic. He was friendly with the Dundee owner, Peter Marr, and had recommended me as he reckoned that I could help turn the club around.

I met Bob and Peter and liked what they had to say. Peter gave me full access to the club's accounts and player costs. Although they had dropped a division, Dundee hadn't reduced the player costs as they had hoped to bounce straight back up in that first season with the support of the parachute payment. As it was, they finished seventh.

The wage bill for players at Dundee sat at £1.2million, the same figure that I had been asked to achieve at Kilmarnock, so the club was out of kilter.

A number of players were on basic wages of between £1,000 and £2,000 per week. I quickly drew up a plan which would reduce the wage bill and see around 15 players earmarked for release. My plan was to approach these players and their agents and say that we'd release them from their contracts as they were Premier Division players and should be playing at a higher level. This strategy worked and around 10 agreed in principle to leave. The other five asked for a payoff which I'd anticipated.

Alongside Bob Brannan, I drew up the plan to reduce squad costs for the next three seasons to get us back on track. The aim was to reduce to £450,000 year one, £550,000 year two, then £650,000 year three.

I hadn't committed to the club at that point or signed a contract, but I agreed to attend a board meeting to present the plans.

As I entered the old boardroom at Dens Park, memories came flooding back of being in there as a player for press conferences and meetings with the manager. I felt as if I had come home.

Peter Marr sat at the head of a busy table. He was joined by his brother, Jimmy, and six other directors.

Peter stood and welcomed me and I sat down at the end of the table. He told those assembled, "Gentlemen, I've asked Dave to look at player costs and come up with a plan to get us back on track as we can't continue at this wage level."

I had come prepared, having printed off a document containing my proposals. A copy of this was distributed to each director.

"Right, gentlemen," I said as I stood up. "Peter has told me where we need to get to financially, so I'm afraid we need to cut the big earners and create a budget which is around a third of what we were operating on last season."

I held up the list of 15 players. I knew it inside out and when I announced that we had to let them go, the room fell silent. But the silence was soon broken by pleas from the directors for certain players to stay.

"He's my son's favourite player," said one.

"He scored the winning goal when we won the Forfarshire Cup," said another.

"We can't get rid of him because my company sponsors him," said a third.

I looked up the table towards Peter and he nodded. That was my cue, he had given me the go ahead, so I decided to give it my best shot.

I said, "Gentlemen, this list isn't what you want to see, I know that. But unfortunately if we don't make these changes now, the club may not survive. But if you want to go another way, that's fine but you'll need to find someone else as I can't back it."

I shut my book, gathered in the papers and started to move towards the door.

Peter stood up and said, "Dave, can you give us five minutes?"

I left the room and immediately wondered if I'd overstepped the mark. But I quickly rationalised my thoughts by telling myself that the guys needed to get the message; although they were supporters of the club, this decision had to be taken without their hearts ruling their heads.

It seemed like more than five minutes before Peter popped his head round the door. "OK, Dave, can you come back in?" he said. "The guys are ready to give your plan the green light."

Supporters of any football club want assurances when it comes to the key figures running the organisation. They want to know if they've got the best interest of the club at heart, if they have the financial backing to elevate the club to a higher level and if their involvement will ensure the long-term future and stability of the club. If they happen to support the club that's an added bonus.

The Board of Directors at Dundee at that time ticked all of the above, and this was cemented by the fact that they also had two good men at the helm, Peter, and Jimmy Marr. Peter and Jimmy were honest enough to admit that they made mistakes, but without question they were 100 per cent behind the club and their fans.

I loved my time at Dundee. The fans and the staff were great, and although the board evolved and changed during my tenure, I had an excellent relationship with the directors.

Bob Brannan, a likeable guy who combined his strategic ability with humour and empathy, succeeded Peter Marr as chairman in March 2007. Joining him in the boardroom were George Knight, Ian Bodie and yours truly.

George Knight represented the fans, but he understood that sometimes he couldn't divulge commercially sensitive information. I attended many fans' forums with George and he was a superb conduit between the board and the support. The fans understood and respected George's position and the relationship worked well.

George also had the respect and trust of the rest of the board. I have witnessed board members at other clubs viewing the supporter representatives as spies. This inevitably led to an 'us and them' mentality, which I always thought was ironic since the majority of the board was comprised of fans of the club!

Ian Bodie was a nice man who sadly passed away a couple of years ago. He was an intelligent guy who'd worked as Finance Director for some big corporations. But his greatest strength was the ability that he had to explain finance to any audience, irrespective of how much financial acumen they had.

We stuck to the financial plan that we had drawn up, and with Alex Rae in place as manager, we made progress on the pitch.

Alex had just left Rangers when I persuaded him to join Dundee. He took a few weeks to consider the offer, but whilst he was mulling things over, I wanted to have a backup plan in case Alex declined.

I was asked to represent Rangers in a testimonial match for my former team-mate, Ted McMinn, and joining me in the Rangers ranks was Derek McInnes. I sounded Derek out about taking on the role of player-manager and he seemed to be interested. In the end, Alex agreed to take on the managerial role, while Derek, a lovely guy who has proven to be a very talented manager, took on a similar role at St Johnstone.

Ted McMinn's story was uplifting. He was an eccentric winger in his heyday and he could exasperate and excite in equal measure. Ted signed for Rangers from Queen of the South in 1983, and after a short spell in Spain, he returned to the UK and made a name for himself with Derby County. Spells with Birmingham City, Burnley and Slough Town followed before Ted and his family settled back in Derby after he retired.

In 2006, Ted developed an infection while on holiday that resulted in his right foot being amputated. A few months later, he had another part of his right leg removed to allow a prosthetic limb to be fitted. When I read what had happened, I contacted him and invited him up to Kilmarnock for a game against Rangers. I collected him and his family from the airport and asked him when he was last at Ibrox. He said he hadn't been back since he left to sign for Seville in 1986.

En-route to his hotel I diverted to Ibrox and suggested to Ted and his family that we should go in. Peter, a lovely man who worked at the main reception at the foot of the marble staircase, welcomed us, and despite having no invite, Peter took us on a tour of the stadium.

During the tour we entered the magnificent trophy room. But it wasn't the sparkling silver trophies and medals that attracted my attention, it was the racing bike donated by St Etienne. It is located at the back wall and seeing it gave me an idea.

I casually suggested to Ted that he and I cycle from Ibrox to Derby for charity. He was keen and the seed was sown. But in the meantime, we ventured down to the pitch at which point Ted told a story about the epic 4-4 draw against Celtic, a match that we had both played in.

Moving towards the Broomloan Road end of the ground, Ted recalled with a smile, "I was getting pelted by coins by the Celtic fans, and after the game I ran down here and started picking up the money that had been hurled at me. I collected £32.60 and that bought me my beer for the weekend."

A week later Ted called me and said that he'd been out on a specially adapted bike and fancied taking me up on the 300-mile journey plan. Joined by around 10 friends of Ted, we left Ibrox on Saturday, 8 April 2006 and arrived to a wonderful reception at Pride Park in Derby at lunchtime on the following Friday. The money we raised went to the amputee department at the Derbyshire Royal Infirmary and the Murray Foundation, who offer support for Scottish amputees.

Three weeks later on the 1 May 2006, I played in Ted's benefit match. The likes of Peter Shilton, Nigel Clough, and Stuart Pearce were in the Derby County team, while alongside me in a blue jersey were Coisty, Chris Waddle and Ray Wilkins. The teams played out a 3-3 draw in front of a record attendance of 33,475. Around 13,000 Rangers fans attended which made for a raucous atmosphere.

\*\*\*\*\*

By 2008, our plans for Dundee had been derailed. We had finished third and then second in the league, but there was an elephant in the room. And when the bank stepped in to address it, they opened the lion's cage!

On entering administration in 2004, the bank had retained two holding accounts; one which had a £4million debt, only payable if player transfers or windfalls of over a certain level were achieved, and a second which retained the Dens Park property valued at £3million. The club meanwhile had a trading account which had no overdraft facility. Bob had spoken to the bank and they wished to write off the money for a smaller amount of around £500,000 to tidy things up. Such courses of action were unfortunately prevalent at the time as the banking system was collapsing.

Bob advised the board that former Dundee United director, John Bennett, was interested in an arrangement that would see the loan disappear. In return, he wanted ownership of Dens Park. This was the preferred option for the bank who just wanted closure.

At the start of October, we were beset with several injuries. We had gone six games without a win in the league, yet we were only six points off the top of the league. I was confident that the tide would turn once the key players returned from injury and we should hold our nerve. But on the Sunday following the latest defeat, a 2-1 reverse at home to Ross County, I received a call from Bob. He said, "Hi Dave. George, Ian, and I met up after the game yesterday. We think Alex should go as the fans are unhappy and are voicing their opinion on the forum."

I was adamant that I was going to fight Alex's corner. I replied, "I don't agree Bob. We've got a few injuries in the squad, but they should be back shortly, and we'll get back on track."

But Bob was steadfast. "It's a 3-1 decision," he said, "and as you know, that carries."

As a board that generally were on the same page, we'd agreed that if the majority settled on something then it would carry. But I still wasn't happy and demanded to know when Bob was going to inform Alex that he was being sacked. It turned out that the man to pass on the news would be me.

"I'm going to France on business, so you'll need to tell him tomorrow," said Bob. "I've arranged for you to meet Jack at Thorntons at 10.00 a.m." The phone clicked and the call ended.

I put my mobile phone down and thought about my options. *Should I hand in my resignation, or simply not carry out Bob's instruction?*

In my opinion, getting rid of Alex wasn't a football decision, so I decided to travel to Dundee to discuss the situation with the club's lawyer, Jack Robertson, at Thorntons. I didn't have to wait long to get clarity.

As I entered an office at Thorntons, John Bennett was there. He handed me a copy of an email which had the subject heading of *Conditions Regarding Offer to take over Dundee FC*. It was dated 25 August 2008 and had been sent to Ian Bodie.

This was the first time that I'd had sight of the email, so I took time to digest the salient points within it:

JMB to take a minority stake hold in the club and have an option to purchase for the sum of £1 the remaining shares available to take his shareholding up to around 60 per cent. The option to be in place for 24 months from the date of completion of the transaction.

JMB to donate to the Club the sum of £400,000 or thereby over the next 12/18 months. The said sum to be drip fed into the Club as and when required.

JMB to be installed as Chairman of DFC.

D McKinnon (sic) to resign as Chief Executive Officer. The termination of his appointment to be on the basis of an away going of three months' salary.

R Brannan to resign as Chairman and Director of DFC.

G Haggerty to be employed as Chief Executive Officer. His salary to be met by Panmure Property Co Ltd for the first year of employment.

The remaining directors to remain on the board.

"I don't know anything about this John," I said. "Why are you here?"

"I've kept Bob up to date and if I'm taking over. I want my own manager in," Bennett replied.

"I see," I said tersely. "That's just as well as I'll not be working for you."

"Did you see point five?" John asked.

I had done, but I wanted to reinforce the point that I wasn't going to be working for him.

He continued, "I've already spoken to Chiz [Gordon Chisholm] and Doddsy [Billy Dodds], they'll be in as soon as you get rid of the manager."

Gordon and Billy were in posts at Queen of the South, so I suggested that John have some sort of compensation package ready to offer the Doonhamers. If he did, he didn't admit it, ending the conversation with a direct order: "Just you do what you've been told to do regarding Alex Rae and then you can do what you want."

I left the room and immediately phoned Bob Brannan. "What's going on Bob?" I asked.

Bob told me that John Bennett had agreed to buy Dundee and Dens Park. In essence, I had no choice; I had to inform Alex that he was being dismissed then get on with it.

I should have got in the car at that point and driven home, but I decided to go up to Dens Park and see Alex. By the time I arrived training had ended and Alex was on his way back to Glasgow. I called him and asked him to come back. When he returned, I took him into the office.

"Alex," I said, "I've been asked by the board to dismiss you from your role. I am very angry, but I need to see it through."

Alex was seething – he had every right to be – and stormed off, taking Davie Farrell, his assistant manager, with him.

Me? I tendered my resignation and got in the car to drive the 110 miles home.

I got as far as the Kingsway West Retail Park, which is located just shy of 1.5 miles from Dens Park. At that point, my phone buzzed. It was Laura Hayes, the club secretary. "David, the Press are here," she said. "They've heard about Alex and want to see you."

I was back once again on the horns of a dilemma. I should have kept driving, but you can't change your DNA; my upbringing didn't allow me to run away. I turned the car around and held a media conference with the journalists and TV crew from Tayside's news outlets.

After the meeting, one journalist pulled me aside. He said, "We've re-run the tapes and you mention several times it was a board decision. Did you have any input?"

I paused before I answered, the last thing the club needed

was for the press to develop a sub-plot. I said, "Yes, it was a board decision and I'm a director on that board."

The journalist tried to get me to expand, but the hurt and emotion of the whole saga left me drained. I respectfully declined and drove home to Gourock.

As per the email, I was asked to work my notice period which I did. I left Dundee in December 2008.

On reflection, I didn't want to leave, but it was the right decision for all concerned. And it all became something akin to a house of cards unfortunately.

Bob Brannan placed an advert in *The Sunday Times* which invited investment in the club. An Aberdeen businessman called Calum Melville responded; I watched from afar as the team recovered and started to buy players on the strength of Calum's commitment. A 19-year-old Lee Griffiths was brought in from Livingston for £125,000 and Gary Harkins came from Partick Thistle for £100,000.

Calum was like the knight in shining armour, riding in on his trusty stead, but I knew that the spectre of administration still loomed large.

A property developer called Graham Gallagher, whom we'd previously spoken to regarding a development of housing around Dens Park, called me up.

He said, "Dave, I've seen what's happening at Dundee and I have a consortium that would be interested in taking over if we can get the housing development back on track."

I suggested that Graham call Bob Brannan as I was no longer affiliated with the club. I don't know if that call was placed, but in September 2010, Dundee Football Club went into administration for the second time in six years.

# CHAPTER 8
# EVERYTHING FOR A REASON

*August 2022*

IT'S BEEN SIX months since my accident. I'm still getting headaches and strangely my blood pressure has dropped to 90/60. I'm undergoing blood tests.

As part of my input to ZLX, I'd started to work with football clubs to help them submit their R&D claims while providing sponsorship as part of the agreement. Hamilton Academical was one club that I worked with and in so doing, I re-established my relationship with Colin McGowan, their CEO.

Colin is a genuine human being. He had a period in his life when drink and drugs took over, but he recovered and is now a shining example of how it's never too late to turn your life around. He now uses his own experiences to provide support to families touched by addiction.

By his own admission, though, Colin knows little about football, hence the reason for his call. He wanted me to join Hamilton as CEO, but when I left Morton, I had decided that my days in football boardrooms were over. However, once you've been bitten by the bug it never leaves you, so I suggested that Colin should consider splitting the board into two; one focussed on football, the other on commercial opportunities. I said if he did that, I would be delighted to join the football board as I'd had six great years previously at the club as media and recruitment director.

But despite the best of intentions, my recovery and recuperation from the accident meant that I wasn't involved to a great extent, particularly when it came to player recruitment. I have already indicated that getting that right is key if you want your club to be successful, so whilst I wasn't involved in the whole process, I had an indirect involvement that enabled me to identify potential signings from my extensive contacts in the game.

The Accies have some excellent young talent, so I focussed on a strategy similar to the one that I was part of as a player at Kilmarnock. That strategy saw me earmark in the main experienced players whom I thought would complement, encourage, and improve the emerging youngsters. This approach, though, didn't fit the club's strategy as they didn't want experienced players to block the young emerging talent.

Whilst I respected that approach, I believed that it would put incredible strain on the young players to perform week in and week out in the highly competitive Championship. Sadly, this was proved right as they were relegated via the play-offs.

My lack of physical presence at the club irked me as I hadn't been able to give the board and the manager the benefit of my experience often enough, so towards the end of 2022, I informed Colin that I was officially stepping back.

When the new board structure at Accies was announced to the media and the fans, John Rankin, a great young coach with a lot of potential, stepped up from assistant manager to manager. John reminded me of Alex Neil who had enjoyed incredible success at Accies before moving south to manage Norwich City, Preston North End, and Sunderland. He's now in charge of Stoke City in the English Championship.

Alex is an incredible motivator who I feel is fluent in both languages that I spoke of earlier. A prime example of this was when we travelled to Celtic Park for a league game in October 2014. Hamilton hadn't won at Parkhead since 1938, but Alex told me pre-match that he intended to set his team up to try and win the match and bust that almost eight-decade-long hoodoo in the process.

There was no reason not to adopt a positive approach. Hamilton were unbeaten in 10 games and a victory would see us move to the top of the table.

On the day, Accies were solid at the back, with goalkeeper Michael McGovern in top form. Michael was ably supported by a strong back four in Ziggy Gordon, Michael Devlin, Jesus Garcia-Tena, and Stephen Hendrie, and the team were imbued with the confidence that Alex had given them.

Four minutes after the interval, a typical free flowing passing move saw the ball fall to Ali Crawford who fired it beyond Craig Gordon from the edge of the box. Silence descended momentarily before the home fans found their voice again to try and coax their team into finding an equalising goal. It was not forthcoming, so Accies had that elusive victory and climbed to the top of the Premier League ladder.

When the final whistle sounded, I moved to the dressing room, which was what I usually did post-match as part of my media responsibilities. Alex met me in the corridor and said, "Davie, go and get the board, this is an achievement we should all share in."

I walked into the Celtic boardroom and gathered the board together and took them to the dressing room. I knocked and Alex opened the door and invited the directors in.

The board members sat down and Alex gave a speech that was of Churchillian standard. He spoke of his pride in the way that each player had played and took time to praise the performance of each of them individually. It made the hairs stand up on the back of your neck.

Even before that victory and that inspirational piece of oratory, I knew Alex would go on and further his managerial career at a higher level. He relates to players, he's tactically astute, and he listens. And each player who pulls on a shirt in an Alex Neil team knows exactly what's required of them. Players respond to that. Show and tell them how to play and nine times out of ten, they'll deliver.

The hierarchy at Hamilton is a side that know where they stand in the pecking order of Scottish football; they have board members with incredible gravitas, decent people like Bob Hay, Allan Maitland, Les Gray, Danny Docherty, and Gerry Strain, who give 100 per cent to the cause.

I was also greatly encouraged that the astute Ronnie Macdonald decided to return as CEO. Ronnie and I go back a long way and he is someone that you'd want in the trenches with you. Both Ronnie and Colin gave me incredible support in my first stint at Accies, going above and beyond as I went through a tough time in my business career, and helping me to get back on track. I'm thankful to them both for their support.

My first stint at Accies had proved to be very enjoyable and successful, and one of my first games was the last league game of season 2013/14 against Greenock Morton.

Dundee were in pole position for promotion which meant that Accies had to win by a few goals and hope that Dundee lost to give us a chance of going up.

The Rae family were the owners of Morton. The family regularly ploughed money in from their business to keep the club operating and I had a huge respect for Douglas Rae and his son Crawford.

Both were in attendance and I had a chat with them pre-match on the task ahead for Accies. Morton had already been relegated so their mood wasn't great. Douglas was a very kind man who'd handwritten and sent a couple of letters to me when I retired and joined Kilmarnock as CEO. This showed his class and I remember shaking his hand warmly as we left the boardroom to sit in the directors' box. None of us though anticipated the afternoon that was about to unfold.

Hamilton, with the likes of Tony Andreu, Antoine Curier, and Andy Ryan in the ranks, were a formidable outfit and were expected to win comfortably to put the pressure on Dundee.

The first half was one-sided affair. Accies were 5-1 ahead at half-time, but news filtered through that Dundee were 2-0 up at home against Dumbarton. Automatic promotion looked to be out of reach which meant that we would have to be content with a place in the play-offs.

Into the second half, Morton crumbled as Accies hit another five. We won 10-2, and with five minutes to go, word reached us that Dumbarton had pulled one back at Dens Park and were in the ascendancy.

Whilst our game moved to conclusion, we were all frantically trying to get updates on what was happening in Dundee. If Dumbarton could equalise and Accies could find another goal, we would edge ahead on goal difference. It wasn't to be, though. Mickael Antoine Curier missed a couple of chances to add to the four goals that he'd scored already, while Dundee needed a late Kyle Letheren save to win the title for Paul Hartley's side.

As the final whistle blew at New Douglas Park, I looked over to the Morton directors and both Douglas and Crawford were grey. I went over to shake their hands and I could see the mix of hurt and anger in their faces. Football is a rewarding game but at times it can take you to a place that you'll never experience in normal day-to-day life. This was one of those days for the Rae family.

Falkirk were defeated in the play-off semi-final, which catapulted Hamilton into the two-legged final against Hibernian. Terry Butcher, the former Rangers and England captain, a man I liked and respected, was the Hibs manager. But his side went into the game on a horrible run of form – they had gone 13 games without a win – so given the fantastic spirit in the Accies squad and the relaxed and supportive approach of the management team, I fancied our chances.

The first leg was at New Douglas Park on 21 May 2014. We had only lost once in our last 15 matches and were the highest scorers in Championship with 68 goals. In contrast, you had to go back to the middle of February for the last time that Hibs won a league game and the Easter Road side were also the lowest scorers in Premiership, having only found the net on 31 occasions. Accies were favourites, but Hibs, with their top-flight status at stake, flipped the form book, winning 2-0 thanks to a couple of goals from the enigmatic Jason Cummings.

The travelling Hibs fans were in raptures and as I made my way trackside to support the Hamilton players and management. I saw Terry Butcher punch the air in celebration as he ran towards his club's followers.

As Terry came back into the tunnel area, I congratulated him. His side had played well, but I still felt that we had a chance to overturn the two-goal deficit when we went to Edinburgh for the second leg. Terry thought otherwise, though; he told me that the tie was over.

The euphoria of victory is intoxicating and it can make you blurt out statements like Terry had made that the opposition can then use as a motivational tool. He was entitled to his opinion, but I knew if I let Alex and the players know that as far as Terry was concerned it wasn't worth turning up for the second leg, that would give us an extra edge.

When we arrived at Easter Road, Terry's confidence seemed misplaced. You could feel the tension in the air. It was tense in the boardroom too. As is customary before games the directors of each club meet and I shook hands with Hibs chairman, Rod Petrie. I'd known and respected Rod for many years. I really like his dry sense of humour, but on this occasion, he was serious.

He simply nodded and wished me all the best before moving away to the directors' box.

Prior to going into the boardroom, I'd popped into the dressing room. Despite all of the tension and the fact that the stakes were high, the Accies players were in good spirits. The gameplan was to try and score early as this would undoubtedly ramp up the pressure on the Hibs players. There would be an increased nervousness in the stands too.

Alex had shuffled the pack from the first game and brought in the experienced Jason Scotland in place of Mickael Antoine-Curier. Jason was a brilliant player who added some strength up front and it was he who delivered the sought-after early goal after 13 minutes. As the ball hit the net, you could feel the energy drain out of the Hibs players and surge through the 11 Accies players that were on the field. The Premiership pendulum had swung back in our favour.

But Hibs dug in and as the game entered the fourth minute of stoppage time, Butcher's side looked to have done just enough to stay up. There would, however, be a dramatic twist in the tale. Ali Crawford played in Jason Scotland on the left and Scotland lifted his head and spotted Tony Andreu on the edge of the box. Tony's shot found the net and levelled the aggregate score at 2-2. Extra time was cagey as neither team wanted to overcommit, so the Premiership play-off final would be settled by a penalty shootout.

As I surveyed the scene at the end of extra time, I was confident. The Hibs fans and players looked deflated. Their body language suggested that the game was already lost. And I was proven correct, the penalties taken by Kevin Thomson and Jason Cummings were saved by Kevin Cuthbert. Hamilton Accies were bound for the Premiership!

Having just joined the club, it was an incredible experience to be part of. I joined the players, management, staff and the chairman, Ronnie Macdonald, on the pitch to celebrate and it felt like we were on the cusp of a new era.

As I walked into the tunnel, I saw Terry Butcher standing with his head bowed. I'd experienced relegation as a player with Partick Thistle and it's one of the worst feelings in the world. The passage of time doesn't numb the pain. As I passed Terry, I grabbed him in a bear hug and said, "Keep positive, big man, you'll get things back on track."

Terry just nodded. It was as if he knew that the writing was on the wall and his coat was on a shoogly peg. Two weeks later, he was no longer the manager of Hibernian.

*****

As my recovery goes through its various stages, I start to think back on the turning points in my career and why they happened.

I don't know whether my mind wants closure, or the mortality question needs to be justified. Either way my mind is now bringing rhyme and reason to the significant periods of my career.

I've spoken at length about the trauma that leaving Arsenal left me with, but I've now managed to rationalise it in a way I hadn't considered previously. When I left and went to Dundee I met Tommy Gemmell, who not only taught me his penalty kick technique but showed me several times after training his approach and mindset.

He would tell me, "I get the ball and the only thing I'm thinking about is placing it properly and hitting it as hard as I can, with my head over the ball." With me standing quivering in goal, Tommy would then thump the ball into the net, never hitting the same place twice.

Fast forward 14 years to May 1990. I was captain of a Kilmarnock side that went into the last game of the season needing to win to get promoted. We'd dragged ourselves from second bottom to second top and a win against Cowdenbeath would see us elevated to the First Division.

The expectant crowd inside Rugby Park numbered 8,526. As an illustration of the upturn in our fortunes, the crowd for my home debut back in September was 1,925.

The atmosphere was superb and the old Rugby Park terraces crackled with noise when we hit the front inside two minutes. Tommy Burns swung in a free kick from the left and our centre back Paul Flexney rose and powerfully headed the ball home.

The early goal should have given us a platform to build from. We should have pushed on and made the game more comfortable, but as the game moved into the second half, you could detect that the fans were starting to get nervous. Tommy and I tried to use our experience to stop that filtering through to the players, but misplaced passes started to become a feature of our play, each one bringing howls of frustration from our fans.

With 13 minutes remaining, disaster struck. Cowdenbeath equalised. The dream was dying. But David Mackinnon had a date with destiny!

Tommy and I tried to lift the players and cajole them into making one last push for promotion. And after 82 minutes, we got an opportunity to restore our lead. Paul Flexney rose again, and when his goal bound effort was punched clear by a defender, the referee awarded a penalty.

We had missed a penalty early in the year. Davie McCabe, on loan from Airdrie, tamely hitting his effort too close to the goalkeeper. After the game Jim Fleeting and Jim McSherry gave me clear instructions; as captain, I should have taken responsibility so next time we were awarded a spot kick it was down to me to step up.

My penalty kick experience up until that point had only been in shootouts and even then, I was never among the first five selected. But in the week leading up to the Cowdenbeath game, I had a recurring dream that a penalty kick would be decisive, so I took time in training to put Tommy Gemmell's teachings to good use.

Tommy's words were at the forefront of my mind as the voices of the crowd were stilled while I made the long walk towards the penalty spot. I had 'place the ball properly and hit it as hard as you can with your head over it' running through my head on repeat as I passed Tommy Burns.

His advice? "Ye canny miss this, Davie," he said. "This is what your career was about." He then blessed himself.

"No pressure then," I laughed.

I took myself back to that Strathmartine training pitch, shut out the noise of the crowd and placed the ball carefully on the penalty spot. "Hit it as hard as you can, and if you don't know where it's going then the keeper has no chance," was now the rhetoric from Tommy Gemmell in my head.

I took a few steps back before running forward and doing as Tommy instructed. I rattled the ball towards goal, taking that customary Skippy jump, but I didn't see it hit the net as I closed my eyes! The eruption on the terraces assailed my ears and my eyes opened to a sea of blue and white. In that moment, I had some rationale, this moment was why I had left Arsenal and gone to Dundee to get that advice from Tommy Gemmell.

I had been in the game for 18 years, but the experience of getting Kilmarnock promoted was the greatest moment of my playing career. The club and its fans had been starved of success for many years and this game was the catalyst that saw a return to the Premier Division in 1993, a Scottish Cup win in 1997 and the return of European football to Rugby Park.

James Tavernier, who plays at right back like I did for a large part of my career, has now scored over 100 goals for Rangers. That is a phenomenal achievement, but the full back position has evolved since I played. I liked to get forward when I could, but the onus was very much on defending first rather than marauding down the wing to create and score goals.

As a result, I didn't score many goals in my career. But that penalty goal was actually my second in three games. On 21 April, we had faced Queen of the South at Rugby Park. Raymond Montgomerie was now resident at right back and I had reverted to the centre of the defence.

We won the game 4-1, but I'll always remember the goal that I scored. A Queen's defender cleared his lines with a long punt into our half. The ball reached me, and as I gathered it, the Queen's defence had pushed up and both sets of players were stationed within 20 yards either side of the halfway line. Seeing this, I lobbed the ball over the mass of players and ran through to collect. Suddenly, I was one-on-one with the Queen's goalkeeper, Alan Davidson.

I had now propelled myself into nosebleed territory. *What should I do? Carry the ball forward and attempt to round the goalkeeper, or take a touch and shoot?* I opted for the latter. I was something like 40 yards from goal and Alan was advancing towards the edge of the penalty area. I hit the ball with pace and it flew over Alan and into the empty goal. My name was sung and resonated around the rafters after that. I had developed a real affinity with the Kilmarnock fans and that still exists to this day.

The following season, 1990/91, wasn't to be as memorable for me, though. I'd trained hard as I always did during what was my nineteenth pre-season, but I started to have an issue with my groin. During each training session I had a burning ache and that became progressively worse when the games started.

I played in each of the opening 19 league games, but I lost a bit of mobility, and I wasn't making the same impact as I had done the previous season. It was hugely frustrating. I had turned 35 and the educated view was that the groin issue was a consequence of the wear and tear that you get pushing your body to the extreme for nearly 20 years.

Hughie Allan, the club's experienced physiotherapist, was a great support for me, and he proposed that my injury be reviewed by the top surgeon in London. That review never took place. I was nursed through the season – between 22 December and the end of the season, I only made two league appearances – and I sensed the end was nigh for me at Kilmarnock. The recruitment of several ex-Premier Division players on a full-time basis only served to reinforce that theory.

My injury became the elephant in the room as it was never discussed fully by the management. My 21st and last league appearance of the season came on 19 January 1991, a 1-1 draw against Falkirk at Brockville. In my absence, Kilmarnock finished fifth, 10 points adrift of promotion.

My contract was up at the end of the season. I met with the management team to discuss the future. I'd just turned 36 years of age and whilst it was suggested that I have rest and come back for season 1991/92, I knew that my time was up. After 20 years of playing the game that I loved, the time had come to retire.

Outside football I'd managed to climb the ladder at Tennent's and was now balancing time as their Senior Operations Manager with my football commitments. It was therefore the correct call, and I left the club on good terms.

I rested for a few weeks and was asked to coach an amateur club in Giffnock. I had no intentions of going into coaching, but this was an opportunity to stay in the game and sustain that buzz I got playing football.

But after a few weeks of training, I was amazed to find that the pain in my troublesome groin had gone. I started organising games in training so that I could participate. I quickly realised that without the pain I could potentially start playing again. I spoke with a couple of journalist friends and they kindly did a piece on a potential return to the professional game. And those articles prompted one of my old adversaries, Paul Hegarty, a stalwart in the great Dundee United side in the 1980s, to call me and ask if I was interested in playing for Forfar Athletic. Paul was player-manager at the club and after a poor start, they were bottom of the First Division.

We spoke at length about Forfar and what he wanted to achieve and I was impressed. He said that as a senior professional I knew how to maintain my fitness and the training with Giffnock would be sufficient for him. He suggested a month's trial and we agreed that would be best for both parties. The trial period went without a hitch, so I signed until the end of the season.

I made my league debut against Clydebank on 14 September. The team had lost the previous six league games, but we edged this one 2-1. That steadied the listing ship, but we were infuriatingly inconsistent which meant that we were always part of the relegation dogfight.

I played in 23 league games, a Scottish Cup tie against Dunfermline Athletic that went to a replay and a B&Q Cup match against Stranraer that we lost on penalties before my groin injury flared up again in February 1991. I had an operation to try and rectify the issue, and after a couple of months on the sidelines, I came back to help the club in the run in. But my contribution was hampered when I was ordered off for the first time in my career in a game against Hamilton Accies at Station Park.

I never shirked a tackle in my career. I picked up a number of yellow cards, but until that match on 7 April 1992, I had never been sent off. And when I eventually was, it wasn't for a mistimed challenge, it was for handball!

The game was level at 1-1 with 10 minutes to go. Hamilton, attacking the South End of the ground, won a corner on the stand side. I took up the same position that I had done when defending a corner kick throughout my career; on the right-hand post, with my right hand holding the post.

As the ball was flighted into the box, the Forfar goalkeeper, Scott Thomson, came off his line to punch clear, but Billy Stark, who had played alongside me at Kilmarnock, beat Scott to the ball and headed goalwards. I still hadn't left my station and the ball whizzed past me and cannoned off my right hand that was still wrapped around the post.

What happened next beggared belief. The referee, Eric Martindale, blew his whistle and pointed to the penalty spot. And given that Eric deemed that I had thwarted a goalscoring opportunity, he moved towards me and pulled out his red card. Understandably, I was apoplectic!

It took a few minutes for calm to be restored. I was eventually ushered off the field after several verbal volleys aimed in the direction of the match official. I seethed at the injustice and it proved to be an ignominious end to my playing career.

Hamilton scored from the spot and went on to add a third before the game ended. The loss dented our survival hopes, and with four games remaining, we were still in the thick of the battle to avoid the drop.

I eventually cooled down enough to go to the referee's room. I had no intention of apologising to Mr Martindale for what I had said after he brandished the red card, but I wanted to know why he felt the ball striking a static hand wrapped around a post constituted deliberate handball. To his credit, he said that with the benefit of hindsight it was harsh, but at the time he felt he had to give it. Harsh was an understatement and my unblemished record in terms of orderings off was gone for good.

My suspension didn't kick in for a couple of weeks, so I was involved in a 2-0 defeat at Clydebank and a 1-1 draw at home to Stirling Albion. But I watched from the sidelines as we lost 3-1 against Dundee and drew 0-0 on the final day against Partick Thistle. Our fate was sealed, Forfar Athletic finished bottom of the First Division and were demoted along with Montrose.

At 36 years of age, the time had finally arrived to hang up my boots and to end my football career. It was my intention to concentrate on my blossoming career at Tennent's, but from left field, an opportunity to remain in football came my way when I was asked to work for the BBC. My role would be to provide analysis and co-commentary on Radio Scotland; that was ideal as it allowed me to strike an effective balance between my day job at Tennent's and the media work on a Saturday and midweek on occasion too.

The media work was thoroughly enjoyable. I had some great laughs, but there are two games that stick out in my mind more than any others.

The first was at one of my old stomping grounds, Firhill. I was alongside the legendary commentator, David Begg on the gantry for Partick Thistle against Celtic; when the game finished, I was asked by producer Dougie Wernham to get an interview with the Partick manager, the larger-than-life John Lambie.

I went down to the home dressing room and John agreed to come up with me to the broadcast point, which at that time was in the old Main Stand. As I grew into the role, I felt more confident to ask questions off the cuff, but in the early days I needed the comfort blanket of half a dozen questions scribbled down on my pad.

As John and I settled down to go live to the studio, I held up my pad to deliver the first question. Next to me was my old Rangers team-mate Derek Johnstone who had been working for many years with Radio Clyde. Richard Gordon then said, "Let's go live to Firhill where Davie Mackinnon is talking to John Lambie."

As the word 'Lambie' left Richard's mouth and we went live, DJ, a renowned prankster, grabbed my pad and threw it into the enclosure. John looked at me in anticipation and now bereft of my comfort blanket I opted for the classic, "A defeat in the end John, but lots of positives."

John looked at me, smiled and said, "Davie, you're an ex-pro and you ask me that? There are no positives from a defeat, next question."

I could feel Derek suppressing laughter, but I battled on and delivered five more anodyne questions before being asked to cut by Dougie, the producer. I found out later that Derek had spoken to John before our interview and told him what he was going to do. My face radiated red in embarrassment, but I learned a lesson and never pre-prepared questions again.

A set up and a post-match interview feature in my second memorable media experience too.

I had reported on a match between Motherwell and Hearts at Fir Park. Hearts had won 1-0, and as the game drew to a close, Dougie, as always, told me who I was to interview. "Just get the Hearts goalscorer," he bellowed down the line.

I quickly ran down from the stand into the dressing room area and caught the Hearts manager, Jim Jefferies, emerging from the away dressing room. I knew Jim having played against him and I asked him if I could interview their goalscorer, a Frenchman called Stephane Paille.

Jim's a funny guy with a mischievous sense of humour and he replied with a smile, "Stephane? You want to interview Stephane?"

"Yes Jim," I said.

Jim nodded and went back into the dressing room before emerging five minutes later with the player.

"OK, Davie, all the best. Can I come up and hear the interview?" Jim asked.

I told Jim that wouldn't be a problem and I strode back to the broadcasting point alongside Stephane and Jim. Charlie Nicholas, who was working for Radio Clyde, shook Jim's hand and Jim sat down beside Charlie.

"Is it OK to get a quick word with you when Davie's finished, Jim?" asked Charlie.

"No bother, Charlie, but let's listen to Davie's interview first," said Jim who was still smiling.

With the experience at Firhill behind me, I quickly thought of the first question as Richard came to me. "Let's go over live to Fir Park, where Davie Mackinnon has the Hearts goalscorer, Stephane Paille."

"Hi Stephane, you must be delighted scoring the goal that won the game?"

Stephane stared at me and said, "Pardon, Monsieur?"

As I frantically tried to determine my next move, Jim held up a pad. Scribbled on it were the words "He disnae speak English, Davie!"

Dead air on radio is not a good thing, so it was imperative that I ended the silence as quickly as I could. I dredged up what little French I could remember from my schooldays and said, "Parlez-vous anglaise, Stephane?"

"Non!" was Monsieur Paille's abrupt reply.

My headphones crackled with the laughter that was engulfing the studio. I hoped that for salvation, surely Dougie would tell me to cut the interview. He didn't, "Keep it going, Davie," was his instruction, one he delivered in between bouts of giggles.

O-Level French leaves you somewhat limited when it comes to conversational French. But I had been told to continue, so I elected to ask Stephane a question using a mixture of pidgin English and French. I threw in some actions for good measure too. It was another error.

As I imitated kicking a ball, I said, "Oh I see Stephane, you hit la balle into the filet dons 21, vingt six, minutes, that was très bien."

"Oui, oui," answered Stephane.

Jim and Charlie were bent double with laughter by the time Richard Gordon rescued me and called time on the interview.

"First lesson in journalism, Davie", he laughed. "Always make sure the person you interview speaks English".

\*\*\*\*\*

Any footballer who reflects on their playing career will invariably recall good times and bad times. One of the latter for me was my exit from Rangers in May 1986. If you include friendlies and the like, I made 177 appearances for my boyhood heroes, and had it not been for injuries and illness, that total would have been in excess of 200. And one of those injuries occurred in the latter part of what would be my last season as a Rangers player, 1985/86.

Between 21 December 1985 and 15 March 1986, I didn't play a league game for Rangers after I tore the cartilage in my right knee when my studs caught in the turf. For some reason, the club diagnosed the injury as ligament damage and I had several aborted attempts to come back before, in early March, I had the cartilage trimmed by the new keyhole technique.

After the operation, I had a few days in the gym trying to build up my quads, but I hadn't done any cardio work. I was on the treatment table in the physiotherapist's room at Ibrox when the door swung open. It was Big Jock, and he was fuming. "That's Craigie [Craig Paterson] out for tomorrow [we were due to play Celtic at Ibrox in the league]," he shouted at no one in particular. He came over to me and grabbed my leg. "Is he fit for tomorrow?" he asked Bob Findlay the club's physio.

"No," replied Bob, "He's only two week's post op and hasn't done any training, the wound is still healing."

Jock came closer to me and grabbed my chin. "You're tough, Skippy, you're the type that can run that sort of thing off. What do you think about tomorrow against Celtic?"

Bob moved closer and said, "There's no way he's fit enough to last a game, boss, never mind one against Celtic? He wouldn't last five minutes."

Now I've always been one for the living in the moment and I've never shirked away from anything. After having my kidney removed when it was suggested that my career was over, I played every game as if it was my last and I wasn't going to turn Jock or the club down. I told him that I was in.

The weather the next day was horrendous – the rain came down in torrents – but the atmosphere at an Old Firm game can never be dampened. Just over 41,000 were packed inside Ibrox as the teams emerged on to the sodden pitch, but the noise reverberated around each of the four stands.

I was asked to play at centre back alongside Dave McPherson, and only a couple of minutes had elapsed before my knee was tested by my former Thistle teammate, Mo Johnston. Mo fell on my leg as I cleared the ball and I knew immediately that some damage had been done. But there was no way that I was coming off; grit and determination would see me through.

Against the run of play we went 3-1 down, but we stormed back and goals from Coisty and Robert Fleck restored parity. And then we hit the front with a goal that still generates debate to this day.

A corner by Coop was punched out to the edge of the box by Celtic keeper Pat Bonner. The ball looped towards me and I instinctively headed it back towards goal. Cammy Fraser, who was under the crossbar seemed to get the decisive touch to take the ball over the line. Cammy, who had scored our first goal, ran away to celebrate, but Coisty and Robert Fleck, who'd been in the vicinity, ran towards me shouting "Skippy, you've scored, it was across the line."

I was convinced that it was indeed my goal, and this was confirmed by the *Rangers News*. Cammy naturally thought otherwise and many sources credit him with the last touch. But a few years later, I got further confirmation that the goal was mine. I bumped into Pat Bonner at Glasgow Airport and he said in his beautiful Irish lilt, "You know, Dave, I have nightmares about your goal."

"My goal, Paddy?" I asked with a quizzical look on my face.

"Yes, your goal, Dave," replied Pat. "The ball was over the line."

Had the much-vaunted VAR been in operation back in March 1986 then any debate over the goal would have been ended by the analysts looking at the goal from various different angles.

But my only goal for Rangers against Celtic wasn't a winning goal. My cousin, Murdo MacLeod, rattled one in from 25 yards and the game ended 4-4.

It must be one of the few Old Firm games in history when both sets of fans went home happy. I remember walking off – well, actually I was hobbling with a wobbly knee – and I witnessed both sets of supporters on their feet applauding the players.

But this was a rare highlight in a doleful season for Rangers. We had lost to Hibs in the last four of the League Cup, been eliminated by Hearts in the third round of the Scottish Cup and were struggling to qualify for Europe via the league. Big Jock paid the price for that; within a fortnight of that epic match, he was sadly sacked.

His replacement was box office – Graeme James Souness. Graeme was one of the most decorated Scottish players in the game and he was persuaded to come to Ibrox to be the club's first ever player-manager.

I recall meeting Graeme and his assistant manager, Walter Smith, for the first time. Graeme thanked me for playing through the pain barrier, but he said that he needed me to continue to play out the remaining five league games. We still had an opportunity to qualify for the UEFA Cup and salvage something from the wreckage of the season.

In those games, Graeme asked me to play in central midfield and coach those two young bucks that had wreaked havoc in Pamplona, Durranty and Derek Ferguson. He said that he knew about my knee but said he would get me the best treatment possible during the close season. He knew the best knee surgeon in Europe and once the final game ended, he'd arrange for me to travel to Italy for a clean-up operation.

I have to admit that I was in pain training and playing, but it looked like I was going to play a part in the Souness revolution. Once again, I was all in.

Although we lost against Clydebank and St Mirren, we drew 1-1 at Pittodrie and then produced one of our best performances of the season to beat Motherwell at Ibrox on the final day. Dundee, who infamously defeated Hearts to deny the Jambos the league title, were edged out on goal difference.

Six days later, we were scheduled to face the newly crowned

champions, Celtic, in the Glasgow Cup final at Ibrox. Rumours were rife that Souness would make his Rangers debut and the match was a sell-out.

Given that I had played in central midfield of late and Graeme was a master in that position, I didn't expect to play. But on the morning of the game, Graeme informed us that clearance hadn't come through from Sampdoria for him to play so I was in the starting XI. My ecstasy would, however, be short-lived.

I met Walter in the corridor and he asked me to go and see the manager. I assumed it was to receive last-minute instructions for the game, so I made my way to the referee's room which Graeme often used as his dressing room.

As I arrived at the door, Doc Cruickshank was leaving. I didn't think anything untoward, so I knocked the door and went inside. Graeme had just come out of the shower and was sitting on a bench with a towel tied around his waist.

As I entered the room, Walter arrived and came in behind me. "I've got some bad news for you, Skippy," said Graeme.

"What's that, boss?" I asked. Graeme's reply still makes me shudder to this day.

"The Doc thinks your knee's gone."

Initially, I didn't see that as an issue. We had already spoken about my knee problem and how it was going to get fixed in Italy, but it soon became apparent that it wouldn't be happening.

Graeme continued, "I'm afraid it's beyond that, Skippy. The Doc thinks you'll need to go part-time as your knee won't now stand up to training."

It was a hammer blow. Suddenly, I had gone from thinking I had a part to play in a new era at Rangers to being in limbo. I was devastated.

Graeme then asked if I was still up for playing against Celtic. I may have plummeted to the depths of despair, but I was never going to turn down an opportunity to play for Rangers. I said that I would and left.

Driving home I tried to fathom out how this had happened. Questions bounced around my head: *should I have played in the 4-4 game despite not being fit? Should I have told Souness I needed to rest and refused to play in the final games in the league?*

I quickly rationalised that even given my time over again, I would still have played. But those decisions were coming back to bite me now.

If ever there was a game when the mantra of 'play each game as if it's your last' applied, it was this one. I was handed the number four jersey for that Friday evening fixture against Celtic, and although I was still distraught from the discussion with Graeme, I managed to focus on the game and played my heart out.

As always, the fans were magnificent that night and every tackle that I made was greeted by a roar of approval. And from two of those tackles I made in midfield the ball broke to Coisty and he slotted the chances away. He scored another to complete his hat-trick and we won 3-2 after extra time.

When the final whistle sounded, I was overcome with emotion as I reconciled with the fact that I would never play for Rangers again. It was heart-breaking!

As I milked the applause one last time, my team mates, who knew nothing of the earlier meeting with the manager, were saying to me, "Skippy, it's only the Glasgow Cup we've won, not the league. Get a grip!"

I was last to leave the field. I didn't want my Rangers career to end, I wanted more moments like this. But that ship had sailed. My voyage with my boyhood heroes was at an end.

As I joined the lads in the dressing room, Graeme Souness pulled me into the centre of the room and drew a line under my Rangers career in indelible ink when he announced, "That's Skippy's final game." And that, as they say, was that!

I went to the boot room and collected my boots, putting them in a bag before coming back into the dressing room to grab my number four shirt. I wanted one last memento from my time at Ibrox, and I headed for the door with my shirt tucked under my arm. But Bob Finlay, the physiotherapist, stopped me in my tracks when he shouted, "Where are you going with that?"

He grabbed a sleeve of the jersey and attempted to take it off me. To sum up the parsimony at that time, taking that shirt broke up a complete set of blue jerseys numbered two to 11. That was what was worrying Bob, but there was no way that I was going to surrender that shirt. I told Bob that no matter how hard he tried, he wasn't going to stop me.

My last tackle at Ibrox was not on the pitch but in the corridor as I booted Bob in a place the sun doesn't shine and left the building. I was paid till the end of the month and that was it.

Leaving Rangers was brutal. I was now unemployed and seemingly destined for the soccer scrapheap. I needed to find a new pathway, but there was no support mechanism in those days to help you to readjust. It was up to me to deal with the mental trauma that leaving Rangers gave me and attempt to get back on the proverbial horse.

Many footballers sadly can't cope with the transition and fall on hard times. Even today, I worry that the fall from grace, the rejection, has a significant effect on an individual's mental health and well-being.

Being recognised as a famous footballer was never a key driver for me. I never craved attention. For others, though, the recognition and adulation became like a drug, it was addictive. There was one young player who was starting to rise to prominence, but he craved recognition so much that he used to sit outside night-clubs, music blaring with the roof down on his convertible, dressed in his team tracksuit. He also had a mate who was instructed to follow him into public spaces, then suddenly spring out asking for an autograph or picture to gain attention.

That level of need for acknowledgment wasn't healthy and I know the lad had a really bad time when his career came to an end. The anonymity that followed really got to him.

My departure from Rangers and full-time football came to the fore again as I recovered from my fall. I hadn't even turned 30, yet my full-time career was over. I managed to get a job at Tennent's and that proved to be the launchpad for my business career. If I'd remained full time until I retired at 36, there was no way that I'd have picked up the same opportunities I have in the business world. And that was how my brain rationalised the end of time at Rangers. Once again, it all happened for a reason.

Many of the attributes I had learned in my football career were transferable into business. That made the transition more straightforward and I quickly established myself within the company.

The discipline, organisation, understanding your role and those around you, and most importantly teamwork and the part that each team member plays within the process of winning and competing, worked well. The prospect of leaving the world of playing full-time football can be daunting, but if you work hard and focus your mind opportunities will always come.

Captaining teams during my playing career helped me too. Leadership takes on many guises, but the managers who bestowed the honour of being captain on me all did so as they felt my commitment and will to win made me the perfect role model.

Some captains try and play everyone's game for them, and when doing so, I've seen some alienate their team mates, while also suffering a dip in form themselves. That breeds negativity and a downturn in results will inevitably follow, which is why I often heard captains or managers use the mantra of, "Concentrate on your own job and win the battle against your opponent". It was that simple.

Nine times out of ten, if players achieve that, then victory is won. I've been in many teams where that's worked, even when playing against teams who, on paper, were superior. But it only takes one player in the XI not to win their battle or to fully concentrate to invite defeat to the door.

That mantra is key for me. In my career I took more satisfaction when I came off the park, knowing that each of our players had played their part in victory than I ever did reflecting on my own, individual contribution. That is one of the greatest feelings in football.

I was captain of Rangers on a handful of occasions and it remains one of the highest accolades of my career. You only have to look at the pantheon of great Rangers captains to appreciate the responsibility that comes with that role. That's why being handed the armband meant so much to me.

My first appointment as captain came in a Scottish Cup tie against Morton at Cappielow in February 1985. Cappielow was always a hard place to play due to the narrow pitch dimensions and the close proximity of a partisan crowd. Morton always defended stoically too. But this particular game threw up some other challenges.

As we arrived in Greenock on a bitterly cold January afternoon, the snow and ice were piled hard at the sides of the road leading into the ground. Before the game, the players ventured out on to the playing surface to see what footwear or studs would be most appropriate. The playing surface was white, a combination of ice and snow covering each area. This and the ruts of frozen turf jutting out made for a surface that was something akin to an ice rink. With player safety a concern, the game shouldn't have been played.

The referee that afternoon was the experienced Kenny Hope. Kenny, a very good referee who had a great rapport with the players as he spoke to you as an equal, was on the far side of the pitch with his fellow officials and was digging his heel into the surface. As I walked over to him, and said, "No chance of being on, Kenny." It was a statement, not a question.

Kenny turned to me and smiled. "What! You scared, Davie?"

"No of course not," was my reply. "But it's rutted and icy, no way is it playable."

But Kenny was adamant, telling me, "The TV cameras are here, and they've sold 12,000 tickets so the game's going ahead." He turned away at that point and walked towards the dressing room.

As our players sniffled and shivered in our dressing room, the state of the pitch was at the forefront of almost all of the conversations. There was a real concern that someone could get injured. But following my conversation with the referee, I knew that we had to get on with it and realised that we had to change our mindset.

While I was nervous at being made captain, I still had to take responsibility. Big Jock liked his players to take control of situations, so as captain for the day, I stood up and said, "OK, listen in. The pitch is crap but the game's on, so we need to get our heads around that. It's going to be a battle from start to finish and the pitch will be a leveller, but if we match them and fight, we'll come out on top."

A hush descended – something of a rarity in our dressing room – so I kept talking.

"It's about us and our attitude. We're a team that fight for each other so are we up for the battle ahead?"

A collective shout of "Aye," meant my work was done.

As we changed into our kit, Coop came up to me and said, "Didn't think you had it in you, Skippy, but that's what we needed." I had played with Davie for a few years by then, but I still beamed with pride every time he praised me. But Coop, razor sharp on and off the pitch, always ended with an acerbic one-liner. On this occasion, he asked, "Have you been drinking?" We both laughed at that moment, another example of Coop at his very best.

The conditions were terrible underfoot. We opted for Adidas samba trainers rather than football boots, and it looked to have been an inspired choice, as we were 2-0 up inside the opening 15 minutes. But as the frost descended to make the conditions worse, Morton pegged us back and the game finished 3-3. We beat them 3-1 at Ibrox in the replay four days later.

*****

Throughout my 30-year business career, I used an analogy to gain commitment and understanding from staff that I worked alongside and managed.

The key to success in any business is effective communication. The business is like a wheel, with strategy at the centre driving the wheel forward. Each spoke of the wheel represents employees and each area of the business. The strategic vision is communicated from the central hub to each spoke, and the result from those instructions then feeds back down the spoke to the centre. A good Board of Directors will listen to the feedback and alter their strategic plan accordingly. This allows the wheel to run smoothly.

I have been involved in many businesses and football clubs throughout those three decades and have had many experiences of effective and ineffective communication. The worst experiences tend to come from organisations that have leaders with inflated egos who believe their opinion and word is sacrosanct. Sadly, they realise too late that they don't know it all and lose good staff who are often replaced by inferior staff who ultimately fail to deliver.

My desire to succeed and that will-to-win that served me so well in my football career is also a key component in my business life. That, alongside support from people who know their role, has resulted in many successful outcomes. Each of these lessons made the transition from a full-time football career to one that would see me work with Tennent's while playing football part-time pretty seamless.

Six weeks after I left Rangers, I signed for Airdrie. I did have offers from Motherwell and St Mirren that would have seen me remain full-time and I also had a couple of opportunities to ply my trade in Cyprus and with St Pauli in Germany. But the taster I'd had working with Tennent's had made my mind up, I would combine business with football. It was too good an opportunity to turn down.

The late Derek Whiteford signed me for Airdrie, arriving at my house with the club secretary, George Peat, to do the deal. Remarkably, although I was now going part-time, the signing on fee I got from Airdrie was the biggest of my career.

Derek was a nice man who worked hard to combine his role as Head of Physical Education at Coatbridge High School with the manager's job at Broomfield. Unfortunately, he never got the best out of me as I struggled with my knee and the transition back to part-time football. Indeed, it wasn't until Gordon McQueen arrived and I underwent a full open knee operation that my performances rose to a more acceptable level.

I really felt for Derek. He was an Airdrie stalwart, having played 438 games and scored 116 goals for the club between 1967 and 1977. He had captained the Diamonds in the 1975 Scottish Cup Final and was appointed as Airdrie manager in May 1986. But he left less than a year later. He had fallen out of love with the game, struggling to balance his football and education commitments. I will always be grateful that he gave me a chance and put a lot of faith in me. It was just unfortunate that my injury woes meant that I couldn't really pay him back in the way that I wanted.

Derek sadly died in 2002. He was only 54.

I enjoyed my time at Airdrie. I made 30 league appearances in season 1986/87, scoring a solitary goal in a 3-2 win at home to Kilmarnock. The following season, I only missed four of the 44 league games we played. But once again I would be a victim of circumstance, although looking back, it all happened for a reason.

Gordon McQueen resigned with one game of season 1988/89 remaining. I had managed to chalk up another 28 league appearances but missed a chunk of the campaign through injury.

Gordon was succeeded by Jimmy Bone, but I never had the privilege of meeting the new manager in that capacity. As I arrived for my first night of pre-season training, I was met by a man I vaguely recognised but didn't know his name. I had captained the side under Gordon McQueen and had been voted Player of the Year, but I was soon to discover that I had no future at Airdrie.

As I entered the ground and headed to the home dressing room the man bellowed, "Where do think you're going, son?"

I was perplexed and swiftly replied, "I'm a player here. In fact, I'm the captain."

"WAS the captain," he said. "Go back to your car and wait half an hour until the players leave for training. The manager wants you to do laps of the park."

I'd been around the block long enough; I knew the writing was on the wall. I was being frozen out until I decided enough was enough and leave. I was incandescent with rage. I'd played against Jimmy numerous times and thought as a senior pro, I'd earned some respect.

I demanded to see Jimmy to which the man replied, "He disnae want to see you, son, now get to your car now like I told you."

I had never been treated this way by anyone at any of the other clubs I had played with. I rationalised that he was simply the mouthpiece acting under instruction.

I went back to my car and watched as guys I had fought alongside since I had joined Airdrie left for training. A couple of them saw me and had the courtesy to come over and ask what was going on.

I returned to the stadium half an hour later, put my training kit on in the players' lounge, and started lapping the pitch. Stationed in the stand was the man who had spoken to me earlier, stopwatch in hand timing me.

I must have done 20 laps before he blew a whistle and appeared trackside. "Right, some sprints now," he barked. I ran a few times up the track past the old rickety Main Stand before I thought, I've had enough of this. I walked past him as he stood open mouthed. I went inside, put on my clothes, and left.

The next day my mobile rang, it was George Peat. George confirmed what I already knew, the manager wanted me to leave. If I could find another club. I was free to go."

"What have I done to upset him, George?" I asked. "I know we never saw eye to eye when we played against each other, but this is a joke."

"I don't interfere in team matters, Davie," replied George. "I think it's best if you get a new club. Off the record, I'd like to thank you for your time here and I genuinely wish you all the best going forward."

Despite playing in the same Dukla Pumpherston charity team with Jimmy many years later, we never discussed what happened when my time ended at Airdrie. I found that rather strange.

As it was, Jim Fleeting and Kilmarnock loomed large on the horizon and the rest is history. My old mate Robert Reilly was apparently instrumental in getting me to Rugby Park, a gesture that I've thanked him for on many occasions, and one he never allows me to forget.

Once again, I had my reason. As chastening an experience as lapping the track that day was, it led me to Kilmarnock and that date with destiny against Cowdenbeath. Airdrie netted £15,000 for my services too, so I guess that all parties benefitted in the end.

*****

I am immensely proud to have been a professional footballer for 20 years. I've had my ups and downs, but I wouldn't swap it for anything. I met some incredible people, and from Arsenal to Forfar, it was a journey that I take a great deal of pride in.

Without the support of Alan Ball and Pat Rice, I may not have been able to achieve what I did in the game. Those lessons allowed me to play against some of the game's greatest players and hold my own. There was Johan Cruyff, Karl-Heinz Rummenigge, Johnny Rep, George Best, Gary Lineker, Glenn Hoddle, Ray Wilkins, and many more.

As a young fan, I idolised the Rangers winger, Willie Johnston. His drive, enthusiasm and guile were to be admired. When I signed for Rangers, Willie was in the twilight of his career, but he retained the pace and love for the game that he had as a youngster. I also had the pleasure of lining up for Rangers against Willie when he played at Hearts.

He was nicknamed Bud and he came up to me during the warm-up on the pitch at Tynecastle. I'd played against him when I was at Thistle when he returned to Rangers for a couple of years after a spell in Canada. He had subsequently moved to Hearts, so he now wanted to excel against his former club.

Bud opened with, "Hi Davie, you're doing well at the Rangers."

"Yeah, Willie, I'm loving it," was my reply.

Willie added, "And how are you getting on with the miserable bastard from Edinburgh?"

I didn't know what he meant, but he soon alluded to whom he was referring.

"The gaffer, John Greig M.B.E. – Miserable Bastard from Edinburgh," he laughed.

"He's the best manager I've worked under," I answered.

He swiftly moved on, saying, "I hear you're fast, Davie?"

"Not bad, Willie," I answered.

"I've got a greyhound that's fast but give it a ball and he's lost," he said laughing again. "We can have a race during the game. You up for it?"

"No problem, Willie, looking forward to it," I said as we shook hands and moved back to our respective warm-ups.

Just 10 minutes into the game Willie brought the ball up to me, stopped, and set himself to sprint past me. The crowd on the Gorgie Road terracing stood silent wondering what was going on. I stooped down to mirror Bud's stance. "Three, two, one," he shouted and fired the ball down the line. I turned and followed the ball before sliding in, winning the ball, and hitting it out for a throw in.

Bud grabbed the ball and set himself to take the throw in. "Aye yer fast, but you're a better tackler than a sprinter, studs' arse." He smiled and knocked the ball off my head before throwing the ball back into play.

They don't make them like Willie Johnston anymore!

# CHAPTER 9
# COVID-19 AND
# SELF PRESERVATION

I HAD TAKEN on the role of CEO at Morton in May 2019. On Friday 13 March 2020, I received a call from Neil Doncaster, the CEO of the SPFL.

"Covid's starting to get out of control, Dave," he said. "We're suspending the league programme tomorrow so your game's off."

Despite sending out an official email with this development, I understand that Neil had called every club personally to give them the news. This was a commendable and welcome move, much appreciated by all, although neither he nor any of the recipients of those calls knew about the mess that was about to unfold in the weeks and months that followed.

I checked my watch. It was 11 a.m. The club was preparing to welcome its biggest crowd of the season to Cappielow as we were scheduled to host the league leaders, Dundee United. The players were out training on the pitch when Neil called me.

As the world had been gripped by the pandemic, we had a contingency plan already drawn up should the game be cancelled, so it was now time to action that. I made my way on to the pitch and got the attention of our manager David Hopkin. I told him the news and he gathered in the players to tell them what was happening.

At that time no one knew how long football would be out of action for; certainly no one had any idea that this pandemic would play out such that it became the biggest threat to public health since the great plagues of the 19th century.

The players were devastated and they quickly showered and went home. Anton McElhone, our assistant manager, and the sports scientist quickly drew up a remote training regime for the players.

The staff were sent home, and for the next few months, I was the only one at the stadium. I initially had to go in four times a week to check everything as part of our insurance policy compliance. The stadium was eerily quiet as I went about my business; it was surreal. And one day I was joined in the building by a fox!

My routine that day was the same as it always was. Firstly, I entered the main stand and made my way through the corridors. But as I left the hospitality lounge, the door wouldn't open. I changed direction and went into a service corridor at which point I encountered a fox lying on the floor.

I like to think I'm an animal lover, so my natural instinct was to see what I could do to help. I could see it was breathing and figured that it was dehydrated so went and got a bowl of water. I slowly opened the door and laid the bowl on the floor. The fox jumped up and I did likewise; I nearly had a heart attack" I managed to push the door closed and the fox took a drink before lying down again. It was a young fox which I'd assumed had come in from the adjacent railway through a service hatch, which was regularly left open. I looked up the SSPCA number and called them.

It took several hours for a warden to attend, and eventually after a further call, a young lady arrived. I explained the situation and watched as she put on gloves and collected a cage. I directed her to the corridor where the fox was located.

I was asked to wait outside, and for the next 20 minutes, I paced around like an expectant father waiting for the birth of a child. I grew impatient, but just as I was going to go back in to see if she was OK, she emerged from the corridor, gloves off and with the cage covered by a small blanket.

"I'm afraid the fox has died," she said quietly.

"Should I have brought it out earlier?" I asked.

The young lady held up her right hand. It had only four fingers, her index finger was missing.

"It was better you didn't," she smiled. "I had a call a few weeks ago to a fox in a garden and I didn't put my gloves on. Apparently, foxes like fingers so it was best you left it to me."

As she left, I took a moment to reflect on what looking after a club as CEO during Covid had become. It was indeed bizarre and lonely as I was the only person within the confines of the stadium for months.

When I left Morton in 2021, I took the decision not to discuss any of the events that I had experienced during my time there. But I couldn't shift what had happened when the governing bodies had taken the decision to bring season 2019/20 to a premature conclusion.

The SPFL proposal that was presented was to end the leagues with average points determined to decide the placings. The proposal was logical on paper, but once the consequences of that plan hit home, a period of acrimony developed that festered until the votes were cast on that fateful day, Friday 10 April 2020.

The SPFL had arranged separate Zoom meetings for Premiership, Championship, League One and League Two clubs to discuss their views regarding their own leagues. I believed that this was done with the best of intentions, but it led to each league having their own views which, in the end, was counterproductive. The lack of joined-up collaboration at that stage was an early indication that all would not be well when a resolution was eventually presented.

A representative and deputy was identified to attend joint SPFL meetings. Our representative was already in situ, Ross McArthur, a nice man whose only agenda was to do what was best for everyone concerned.

During this time the likes of Hearts and my old club, Partick Thistle, were vulnerable. Had the leagues been ended, both would have been relegated. There were a lot of club representatives airing their views via the media, mainly of discontent. The BBC, in particular, gave them a platform to spout their self-interest.

In my opinion the period between suspension of the games and the vote to conclude the season caused irreparable damage to the game in Scotland. Whilst I fully understood the political protocols that were enforced on two guys I consider to be competent, Ian Maxwell of the SFA and Neil Doncaster of the SPFL, I believe that they might have taken tighter control and been more inclusive as they looked to achieve the best solution for all member clubs. Instead, it appeared that they wouldn't intervene when outrageous claims began to emerge via the media, which only served to drive a fervour of self-interest.

Neil and Ian made the decision to separate the meetings; Premiership, Championship, League One and League Two. Whilst there were representatives attending who were on the SPFL board and reported back, I'm sure that a more inclusive meeting set up across all leagues with a common agenda would have produced a more informed and cohesive communication process. Instead, views on relevant issues were being diluted and ignored and that did the game a great disservice. At a time when solidarity and continuity was required we achieved the polar opposite.

*****

In our Championship cocoon, the same self-interest ideology was gathering pace and causing division. Some within our group wanted a 'null and void' scenario. That would mean no champions, no promotion and no relegation. This was first mooted at the Championship meeting on 8 April 2020.

All the teams attended with the exception of Queen of the South who were concerned about confidentiality, as items discussed at meetings had previously found their way into the media.

At the meeting, one club was asked by the Chair why a resolution was being proposed in competition to the SPFL resolution being submitted the next day. The resolution proposed was that of a 'null and void' conclusion to the campaign.

Several teams agreed with me; if this was passed then each club should receive 10 per cent of the total financial allocation for the Championship. But at that point, the debate became heated. There was division within the league. The meeting ended abruptly; it had started to get personal.

Following the meeting, the Chair produced minutes which reflected the disparity between the member clubs. That was the cue for the Championship WhatsApp group to be bombarded with a fusillade of messages. The upshot from that was a request to attend another Zoom call.

The Chair of the group called round each club to ask if they would take part. It became apparent very quickly that the majority of clubs were sickened by the tone of the dialogue that had been exchanged in the meetings thus far. Relationships between clubs were at breaking point, but for the good of the game, it was agreed to host another meeting on 9 April.

But it didn't take long for that meeting to revert to the way others had been conducted. There was awkwardness throughout, but during the session, it was indeed confirmed that some clubs were working on an alternative proposal, that the season be ended producing no winners or losers. On hearing this I re-iterated my view that if that proposal succeeded, then each club would have to receive an equal share of the Championship prize pot as in essence, the season had never taken place. Several clubs stated that they agreed with this.

We reconvened the next day, but things got out of hand when it was claimed that some members of the SPFL board had branded the proposal to terminate the season with no promotion or relegation as 'incompetent'.

Amidst all of this conflict and infighting, we had to vote. I was instructed by the Greenock Morton board to vote for the SPFL proposal of ending the league season with an average points formula determining placings. This meant that Hearts, Partick Thistle, and Stranraer would be relegated.

*****

The SPFL, who wanted responses by 5 p.m., had also committed to dialogue with clubs about possible league reconstruction if the resolution carried. If passed, the resolution would end the Championship, League One and Two seasons early, with the Premiership placed on hold until the point came when the SPFL board determined that the current campaign couldn't be completed.

As the deadline passed, the league's proposal to end the season had the necessary backing of 10 of the 12 Premiership clubs and 16 of the 20 in Leagues One and Two. Rangers and Hearts were the Premiership sides to vote against, having both publicly condemned the resolution.

Rangers said that they were going to resubmit their own proposal to free up final placing money to cash-strapped clubs without calling the Premiership season now. This was after being told by the league that their initial resolution was legally ineffective.

As it stood, nine of the 10 Championship sides had voted

7-2 in favour. Inverness Caledonian Thistle and Partick Thistle were the two clubs in the Championship to reject the proposal.

Dundee lodged a vote against the proposal to finish the lower league seasons early, but the SPFL said they hadn't received it. That raised the stakes sky high as now John Nelms, the Dundee Managing Director, and Dundee had the casting vote to determine the fate of the teams being relegated.

The days that followed were farcical as debate raged over whether the Dundee vote was or wasn't received by the 5 p.m. deadline. On hearing this, I spoke to a few people at clubs and thought that the vote should be void and another vote should take place. This wasn't possible under the rules, but the SPFL's Chair, Murdoch MacLennan, an honest and supportive man, who was continually being undermined by internal politics, advised John Nelms that he had 28 days to respond in line with league rules. Dundee would therefore have the decisive say on the outcome.

According to the SPFL, Dundee emailed them after the deadline stating that their vote should not be considered. The Dens Park side, who were sitting third in the Championship table, criticised the proposal saying it "condemns clubs to be financially worse off than they are already" citing lost revenue of up to £4million.

They added: "In all cases, current placement monies could be distributed to the member clubs in very short order while maintaining all SPFL obligations."

*****

To people looking from outside, this voting fiasco reinforced the opinion that many had held for a number of years – Scottish football appeared to be a joke. The whole sorry saga certainly did no favours to the professionalism of the league. A subsequent inquiry into why we all found ourselves mired in this situation had determined that the Dundee 'vote' had found its way into a quarantined file in the SPFL server.

But the integrity of the game plumbed new depths when private messages between some clubs who'd set up a separate WhatsApp group were made public.

John Nelms was quite rightly incensed at this leak, and I'm

sure this now public debate playing out in the media eventually made him change his mind on the Dundee vote.

Five days later John and Dundee did change their vote to support the SPFL proposal. John stated that the change of mind was made to support clubs financially at a time when the whole existence of some clubs was in jeopardy. With the proposal now supported, the SPFL released £9million to clubs as prize money.

John, like many including me, believed that there was a case to look at league reconstruction which would look to keep the relegated clubs in their respective leagues. This had been highlighted as being on the agenda by the SPFL, so there was a window of opportunity.

*****

On 17 April, the first meeting of the reconstruction committee was held. I was part of the group along with 13 others from across all leagues in Scotland, including the Highland and Lowland leagues. The meeting was constructive and it was clear that re-construction was a feasible solution to the current predicament.

There were time pressures in coming to a consensus, so the meetings took place weekly. As an ex-player I had clear views on ensuring competitive as well as financial competence was achieved. I was supported by Les Gray (Hamilton) and Ann Budge (Hearts) who were joint chair holders. I'd known Les from my days as a director at Hamilton Accies and he was a guy whom I trusted implicitly. I'd got to know Ann through conversations over the years and again I found her a committed and intelligent woman who was a credit to the game in Scotland.

After a week, I decided to put forward a proposal to the group. Les suggested that before I presented, I should spend some time with Ann to go through it. I had a couple of one-to-one video calls with Ann and she aligned with both the football and financial aspects which was encouraging. She did though believe that it should be a temporary reconstruction. I disagreed as, in my opinion, it had to be a long-term solution as the consequences of reverting back after a year or so would mean a big percentage of Premiership clubs could potentially be relegated. Knowing the landscape of self-preservation that existed I thought that wouldn't fly.

This was my proposal:

| PREMIERSHIP | CHAMPIONSHIP | LEAGUE ONE |
|---|---|---|
| 14 TEAMS | 14 TEAMS | 14 TEAMS |
| CELTIC | DUNDEE | CLYDE |
| RANGERS | AYR UNITED | PETERHEAD |
| MOTHERWELL | ARBROATH | FORFAR |
| ABERDEEN | DUNFERMLINE | STRANRAER |
| LIVINGSTON | MORTON | COVE RANGERS |
| HIBERNIAN | ALLOA | EDINBURGH CITY |
| ST JOHNSTONE | QUEEN OF THE SOUTH | ELGIN CITY |
| KILMARNOCK | PARTICK | COWDENBEATH |
| ST MIRREN | RAITH ROVERS | QUEENS PARK |
| ROSS COUNTY | FALKIRK | STIRLING ALBION |
| HAMILTON | AIRDRIE | ANNAN |
| HEARTS | MONTROSE | STENHOUSEMUIR |
| DUNDEE UNITED | EAST FIFE | ALBION ROVERS |
| INVERNESS CALEDONIAN THISTLE | DUMBARTON | BRECHIN CITY |

In the Premiership, each team would play each other home and away – 26 games – before splitting into top six and bottom eight.

For the top six, ten further games would be played – five at home, five away – giving a total of 36 games. This proposal would also address one of the perennial issues with the current split after 33 games, that of teams playing an uneven amount of home and away games The bottom eight teams would play a further 14 games – seven at home and seven away. That would give a total of 40 games played over the season and the two additional home games would bring in additional revenue.

At the end of 40 games, the team that finishes bottom is relegated, with the team second from bottom playing the winner of the Championship play-offs in a one-off fixture. This would be played at Hampden as part of *The Play-Off Weekend*, an event that I felt would create huge interest, large crowds and more revenue for the Scottish game.

I had a similar concept for the Championship. Each team would play each other home and away – 26 games – then split as per the Premiership.

The team that finished top of the top six would earn automatic promotion, while the other five would take part in the play-offs. These would again be one-off fixtures, with the team finishing sixth facing the fifth-place team at a neutral venue, then the winner playing the fourth-placed team and so on. The overall winner would face the team that had finished second bottom of the Premiership as part of that revenue-generating *Play-Off Weekend*.

TV coverage of those play-off fixtures would provide another revenue stream too. There would also be cash flow into the teams whose ground was used as the neutral venue.

After the bottom eight teams had completed their 40 games, the team finishing bottom would be demoted to League One. Meanwhile, the team finishing second bottom would go into the play-offs.

The newly constructed League One would also follow a similar model to the Championship.

The main advantages for the Premiership teams under this new model were things like fewer games for the top six – 36 compared to 38. This would allow more focus on European football, two additional home games for the bottom eight teams, and no imbalance in home and away fixtures post-split. Hearts would also retain their Premiership status.

In the Championship, Inverness Caledonian Thistle and Dundee United would be promoted, while Partick Thistle would stay up. Revenue streams would also be created through the play-off structure, and with all teams likely to have something to play for until the season reached a conclusion, that should boost attendances too.

And for the combined League One and League Two, Falkirk would be promoted with Raith Rovers, while Airdrie, Montrose, East Fife and Dumbarton would also join the Championship. The additional games and play-off structure would offer scope for more money to come into the clubs and there would be the opportunity to play at Hampden should they reach the Play-Off Final.

But for this to work, it had to be in place for a period of time before a review was carried out. I suggested a minimum of five years, as that would allow clubs to plan investment, strategy, and finances.

The idea of a new play-off structure would be beneficial too. In the first instance, travelling expenses would be reduced as the two-leg play-offs were being abolished. The SFA would also generate income from the showpiece Play-Off Weekend, which would also be likely to attract TV coverage by Sky and offer opportunities for sponsorship.

But above all else, this proposal for reconstruction would preserve some integrity for the game, as teams that were currently occupying the relegation places but still in with a chance of staying up, wouldn't go down.

There would be a couple of clubs disadvantaged as Brora Rangers and Kelty Hearts wouldn't have an opportunity to join the league ladder, but I thought that they could be compensated for that with financial support coming from pre-season friendlies against teams from the Premiership and Championship.

In general, my proposal was well received. But Les Gray said that while the 14-14-14 had support, he had also included a 14-10-10-10 proposal. He also rejected the play off proposal as the Premiership teams wanted to retain the current play off structure. Les reckoned that if agreed, we could try and move towards it in the next few seasons.

*****

Les had created his own proposal which he put to the Premiership clubs: *Why the Premier Division should agree to an expanded format of 14 teams.*

In the paper, Les, who advised that he had written the paper in his capacity as Chairman of a Premiership club and not as a co-chair of the Reconstruction Task Force, provided an update for the Premiership clubs on the progress that the task force had made regarding options to restructure the leagues. The advantages and disadvantages of what he thought the two main options were – my 14-14-14 and the alternative 14-10-10-10 were presented, but there was now a third option up for discussion being worked on by Ann Budge. Coming to a consensus on this was already looking like being a long and drawn-out affair.

It was also clear that most member clubs had openly stated that they felt bringing the season to a close and still retaining relegation was unfair. This would have introduced further financial hardship for a few clubs and given what we were all going through at that moment, it was unjust.

But Les had an idea to help 'right this wrong'. Promotion would be permitted, but no team would be relegated. That, therefore, meant that some form of adjustment to the league structure had to be proposed and considered. It was for that reason that Les was asked and agreed to work with a Task Force to explore options, as he wanted to maintain the integrity of the game during what was fast becoming an emergency.

Debates and arguments raged over a wide range of subjects related to reconstruction. But as they started to escalate, Les felt that it was prudent to intervene and get all to refocus on what was, in his view, the original objective. Clarification from the Premiership clubs that when the vote for an enlarged top division was conducted, fairness would prevail. For that vote to pass, 11 out of 12 top flight clubs had to agree, so if that wasn't going to happen then Les surmised that clubs were all wasting their time.

He stated at that point that he wholeheartedly agreed with many of the salient points raised at the previous meeting, that the circumstances were far from ideal – you shouldn't be pushing for significant, long-term structural changes when you are in the middle of a crisis – and clubs should have been given at least a season to consider the full impact of reconstruction. And making a snap judgement would likely see clubs heavily influenced by their own position.

We didn't even know at that moment how long the pandemic would impact upon our lives or indeed the effect that it would have on the next football season. There were so many unanswered questions, and the survival of some clubs was at stake too. But desperate times call for desperate measures, which meant that we had to be flexible in our approach.

Les had two key questions that needed to be answered:

1. Is it right that some clubs should be unfairly penalised because of the Covid-19 pandemic?

2. In this exceptional situation, should we take the opportunity offered by expanding the Premiership to avoid relegation

altogether for this season and thereby mitigate any unfairness?

Most of the clubs had already answered 'no' to the first question. Les believed that the answer to the second had to be 'yes' if we didn't want to become mired in a situation that questioned integrity and penalised other clubs through no fault of their own.

"It was a time for pragmatism", Les said. A temporary fix was needed, ideally for two seasons, while the worries around the pandemic were addressed or alleviated. Clubs also had to commit to conducting a full review of the game to determine what the best structure was for what could be a potential rebuild of Scottish football.

By season 2021/22, Les reckoned that we would have a better understanding of which clubs had 'weathered the storm', the impact that the pandemic had shown on the football landscape across Europe, and any changes that had to be introduced to any broadcasting agreements.

If we did all of the above and implemented the following steps, Les was certain that no club would be disproportionately disadvantaged due to the global pandemic, all clubs would have the best chance of survival, and we would improve the Scottish football product for the supporters. They are the lifeblood of every single club, but Les knew that once things returned to some semblance of normality, clubs would need them more than ever before.

The steps required were:

**Step 1**: The Premiership clubs agree to expand to a 14-team league for two seasons.

**Step 2**: The lower divisions agree on their preferred structure for two seasons. Based on recent meetings, this was likely to see a move to two divisions rather than three, comprising either a 14/14 or 14/16 structure. The main attraction of these options was the move away from playing all teams four times, something that has been shown to have a detrimental impact on attendances as it's not popular with the fans.

**Step 3**: Discuss the option of no promotions/relegations for next season to help clubs have some stability and certainty during these difficult times.

**Step 4**: Seek agreement from clubs to authorise the Executive to find a way to fund these changes from what would otherwise be parachute payments. Initial feedback from Iain Blair, SPFL

Director of Operations, suggested that this wasn't possible. If that was proven to be the case, other distribution models were available.

By taking this pragmatic step-by-step approach, we would eliminate the divisions that we tended to get due to different league priorities and limit the usual arguments around distribution of finances. Les also believed that the broadcasters should not see this temporary change as disadvantageous to them. If anything, it was more attractive, with more tasty games on the calendar, particularly derby matches.

Les concluded by saying that this would be viewed as a positive step. The member clubs would have shown solidarity and led from the front in what were uncertain and worrying times. And there would be some positivity for the fans too, which would boost post-pandemic attendance figures.

Les's proposal was discussed by the Premiership clubs on 5 May 2020. It had been mooted that the leagues would re-start in August, albeit behind closed doors, so it was imperative that we had a decision to plan the way forward.

*****

Later on in the month, Ann Budge sent the third option, a comprehensive and compelling document to all clubs outlining the current position across Scottish football as a whole. Therein, there were proposals to ensure that the game survived. Ann once again suggested a temporary two-year solution, but I continued to be of the opinion that this would create a problem for teams in the top division when 14 clubs suddenly had to be reduced back to 12.

Much has been said about the curtailment of the league season in 2019/20 due to Covid-19 with a number of matches still to be played. While it is now clear that there was no realistic workable alternative to bringing the campaign to a conclusion, the introduction of a 14-10-10-10 League structure for season 2020/21 would have addressed any perceived unfairness and ensured that Hearts, Partick Thistle, and Stranraer were not demoted.

Reconstruction would also see the teams occupying second place in the Championship, League One, and League Two – Inverness Caledonian Thistle, Falkirk, and Edinburgh City – promoted. And following the cancellation of the Pyramid Play-

Offs, a team from the Highland and Lowland League would enter League Two.

Over the next couple of weeks, several reports detailing the thoughts of clubs were leaked. Opinion on reconstruction was split. Unsurprisingly, the main issue centred around finance. For example, clubs in the Championship would have viewed games against Hearts as being potentially lucrative, and the same could be said for teams in League One when it came to the prospect of facing Partick Thistle. Had some of the perceived 'smaller' clubs occupied the relegation places I'm sure that reconstruction would have happened.

In the end, reconstruction was talked down in the media by the lower league sides and a vote on the proposals was destined not to take place. In my opinion, that was a travesty and proved once again that the voting set up allows an agenda of self-interest to perpetuate, while encouraging a short-sighted and short-term outlook.

There was indeed no vote in respect of Ann Budge's proposals, and after a hiatus, Hearts and Partick Thistle both took legal action. They weren't successful, though, and Hearts, Partick Thistle, and Stranraer were relegated.

*****

I had first encountered the self-interest agenda in 2008. I was CEO of Dundee, a Championship club at the time, and I worked primarily with Ronnie Macdonald of Hamilton, and Geoff Brown at St Johnstone, to research the feasibility of creating an SPFL 2 for the Championship.

At that time there were two league bodies governing Scottish football. Since 1998, The Premier League had been run by the Scottish Professional League (SPL), an organisation set up as part of a breakaway from the Scottish Football League (SFL).

In our opinion there were full time professional clubs in Scotland whose survival was in jeopardy due to the disparity in the financial distribution model. The teams in the SPL had enough prize money to sustain full time football, whilst the teams under the SFL had only enough prize money to sustain part time football.

Our study concluded that a larger SPL would encourage more sponsorship opportunities and associated revenue due to increased attendances. We started our work at the beginning of the season when the spectre of relegation or the promise of promotion wouldn't influence the agenda. We had 100 per cent support of the Championship clubs and we were initially given an amber light of encouragement from the SPL too.

But just when we eventually had everything lined up to put the proposal to a vote, teams within the Championship who were in the bottom half of the league, and teams in the upper echelons who looked as if they might be in with a chance of promotion, suddenly changed their position. This was a potential deal-breaker. We proceeded to vote, but we knew that the idea had to have the full support of the Championship clubs before the proposal was formally presented to the SPL.

I remember on the day of the vote sitting between two club representatives, who had pledged their support at a morning briefing. But as the vote took place, I saw both put an X in the 'no' box to vote against the proposal. I asked them both why they had done this and was told that as their respective clubs were near the bottom of the league, they had decided it would be too much of a risk to leave the SFL.

I was astounded and it gave the SPL a way out. If the Championships clubs couldn't agree amongst themselves, then we had no chance of making it work. The proposal hit the buffers, but it resurfaced some five years later when the Scottish Professional Football League was formed to take on the sole running of the leagues in Scotland with the SFL amalgamating with the SPL.

With re-construction off the table in the summer of 2020, the SPFL arranged for the return of football, albeit behind closed doors. In a statement, the SPFL stated that the season would commence on the weekend of 1 August with the Premiership. But the lower league campaigns were to be truncated. For example, the Championship was played over 27 games, with the first round of fixtures scheduled for the weekend of 17 October.

*****

There was another change too, the introduction of virtual season tickets. Thanks to the generous support of Sky, clubs could stream their games live which allowed them to generate revenue from these purchases and also from sponsorship.

This was hugely positive but there was no 'off the shelf' product to call upon. It was a new concept to SPFL and SFA, so they couldn't offer much support. But Sky stepped in once again to assist when they agreed to allow Premiership sides to stream their footage with the exception of live games.

For the Championship, the SPFL had negotiated a deal with the Israeli company Pixellot to install, free of charge, remote cameras in stadia. Like Sky, Pixellot saw the bigger picture and said that the footage could also be used by clubs as part of their streaming offering.

I carried out some research on Pixellot, and called their Chief Engineer, a supportive guy called Andy Calvert who was based in England. The Pixellot camera system was primarily built for indoor sports like basketball where in the confined court space, it could follow the ball to an extent that people watching the footage would believe that there was a full production team in attendance. Andy explained that there was also a latency of up to one minute where footage streamed on to the internet had a delay on live action.

At the time I wondered how this would be received by betting companies where someone could plant a person in the ground and relay a goal, prior to it appearing on screen. I never asked the question, though. I was keener on determining whether this was a feasible option.

In the end we trialled it for free at one of our pre-season friendly games. This threw up another issue in that people viewing were passing on the feed to mates and via social media. When games had to be paid for this would not work. In addition, due to the latency, you could not provide commentary.

When I was CEO at Dundee, I worked with some talented guys to launch live streaming via Dee TV for overseas fans. I didn't get involved in the technical aspects at the time, but I knew that there were people out there who could deliver live streaming and commentary.

I'd got to know a very talented IT guy called Alan Lorimer who had sorted a lot of the internet issues at the club. His company, Broadband Solutions, had some very talented employees, as well as Alan, and I asked to meet him to discuss alternative streaming options.

I firmly believed that if we provided a high-quality product, then not only could we satisfy season ticket viewers, who in essence were paying the same price as a full price season ticket to watch remotely, we could also attract opposition supporters too. With Covid now rampaging all over the world and restrictions tightening, this would allow supporters to safely watch a game at home, whilst not risking exposure to the virus.

Several video conferencing meetings took place and Alan provided a platform that ticked all the boxes. We had initial teething problems on access for a period during the first match, which was resolved, and we then went on to produce a professional production.

I also wanted to enhance the offering with commentary. The latency I spoke about earlier was still prevalent on our production, but Alan and his team created a software solution which aligned the commentary to the footage before streaming.

In respect of commentary, I approached Gerry McDade. Gerry had a great track record of creating professional media output for the club; we both agreed that there was only one man we wanted to do the co-commentary, the very likeable Morton legend, Andy Ritchie.

We also had to ensure that each season ticket holder and each 'walk up' had a unique viewing code, this ensured that they couldn't share with others which would have denied the club much needed income. And once again, Alan's genius created a software programme to ensure that this happened.

Logistically this was a big project to deliver, but we were all proud of what we achieved. Streaming revenue was never going to eclipse normal match day revenue, but it did add several thousand into the coffers for each home game.

Other clubs chose to use the Pixellot system and my initial fears were justified. At a fixture between Inverness and Ayr United in the early weeks of the season, the Pixellot camera mistook an assistant referee's bald head for the ball! It continually broke off from the action to follow that rather than the ball!

Football was back in business. But with news of a pending takeover of the club by a fans' group called Morton Club Together, I decided to leave. I took up an offer to work in finance as Managing Director with ZLX. This turned out to be a very positive change of direction and another opportunity to reinvent myself.

When my father started his career as an engineer, it was very rare to change your vocation, you had a job for life. But life has moved on. Life skills, experience, personal standards, and work ethic, allied with the ability to fully understand and utilise transferable skills, mean that you don't need to spend your working life in the same role. You should enjoy and maximise each and every opportunity that comes your way, and since joining Arsenal over half a century ago, I am happy with how things have panned out for me.

When I made the move to ZLX, little did I know that my accident would make my tenure a brief one. I was able to bring in additional turnover for the business, due to my introduction of new revenue streams, but I resigned as Managing Director in November 2022. When you are faced with a straight choice of health or work, the former wins every time, so after my fall, work was sidelined, my recovery had to be my prime focus.

CHAPTER 10
# IN THE END

*November 2022*
I'D BEEN FEELING tired and lethargic for a few weeks but had managed to get back to the gym to try and shift some of the 'timber' I'd gathered following months of inactivity and lack of exercise. I'd been used to training hard and keeping trim since I was 16, so I decided that the time was right to step up the level of gym work.

I decided to push the stepper exercise machine to the top level of resistance. As I got halfway through the programme, I suddenly felt a pressure in the left side of my chest and started to become breathless. At that point, the 'never beaten' mindset that had served me well during my career kicked in. I should have stopped but carried on regardless. But at the end of the exercise, I was struggling and knew that I had a problem.

The following week I had a pre-planned hospital appointment to test my heart function as an ECG had previously found an irregular heartbeat rhythm. The plan was to monitor my heart on a treadmill. Monitors plastered at various locations on my chest would record how my heart performed under stress.

Prior to the treadmill exercise a nurse scanned my heart with an ultrasound machine. When he was finished, he told me to wait until he spoke to the cardiologist. Just 10 minutes later he returned and told me that the ultrasound had detected an irregular electrical problem and the cardiologist had cancelled the test. I'd be informed in the next week or two of a new appointment date.

My visits to the gym came to an abrupt halt. I knew something was wrong with my heart and I wasn't prepared to risk things any further. And four weeks later that decision appeared to be correct.

I was in my office analysing financial data when I started to feel the same pain in my chest as I'd had on the exercise machine at the gym. I also started to get breathless despite the fact that I wasn't over-exerting myself.

I considered phoning NHS 24, or calling an ambulance, but decided the best course of action was to drive to Inverclyde Royal Hospital as the medical staff working there knew my story. As I left the office, the pain and breathing issue subsided. I felt confident to drive myself to the hospital, so I called my wife. Upon arrival, I went to A&E. I advised the receptionist of my situation and 15 minutes later, I was in a cubicle having an ECG and bloods taken for analysis.

The evidence suggested that I'd had a mild heart attack as my blood test had shown enzymes which are released into the bloodstream following an attack. I was subsequently admitted for further tests. In the end, I spent 10 days in the Inverclyde Royal Hospital, before being transferred to the Golden Jubilee in Glasgow, which specialised in heart conditions.

Ironically, my cousin, Murdo MacLeod, who had enjoyed a splendid career with Dumbarton, Celtic, Borussia Dortmund and Hibs, had just been discharged following a long recovery from a heart valve replacement.

Murdo had a pig's heart valve fitted 10 years earlier and had entered the hospital for a routine replacement. But due to endocarditis, a life-threatening inflammation of the heart's inner lining, doctors were forced to put him on a ventilator to save his life. Over three months later, Murdo was allowed home to recover. During his time in hospital, I was in regular contact with his wife, Mhairi, and eventually Murdo was well enough to communicate with me directly.

In the Golden Jubilee I met several nurses and staff who'd worked on Murdo and I felt that fate had played her hand once again.

During my time in the Golden Jubilee, I had an angiogram which determined that my heart attack was due to an electrical problem called arrythmia, but my arteries were clear. This condition could be cured by either medicine or the fitting of a pacemaker.

This electrical issue is becoming more and more prevalent in players of my generation. We all pushed our hearts to the extreme on countless occasions, so I count myself extremely lucky that this was picked up as part of the process following my fall in February, and through the diligence and care of someone who will forever be referred to as 'the brain doctor'. She is an incredible and caring doctor and a credit to the

NHS. I will always be grateful for her support. I would dearly love to name her, but she has asked to remain anonymous.

It was back to that old adage: everything happens for a reason. Had I not tumbled down those stairs, this irregularity in my heart may never have been identified. It was a problem that a player whom I played against while in the reserve team at Arsenal, and who later joined Rangers, also had. His name was Ray Wilkins.

Ray sadly died of heart failure after a fall. I spent some time in his company when we were both young players at Chelsea and Arsenal respectively. A team mate and friend of mine, John Davis, had a brother who was at Chelsea, and that's how I crossed paths with Ray. And before I signed for Arsenal, I had a couple of trial games at Chelsea and came up against Ray. We were both trialists and he was an exceptional player and a lovely guy. Another who was taken far too soon.

There have been many studies in the USA around arrythmia in current and past NFL players. One study identified that former players were five times more likely than the general population to have arrythmia disorders, such as atrial fibrillation later in life. In addition, former NFL players were 10 times more likely to need to have a pacemaker fitted when compared to a control group.

As part of my rehabilitation at the Golden Jubilee I will be taking part in a research study to identify new ways to protect the heart and to identify the relationship between the heart and the brain. Hopefully my contribution will be of some assistance. I openly discussed my condition with fellow ex-players; one, an ex-team mate over a decade younger than me, told me that he had been having symptoms and his doctor had told him he had arrythmia and that they would need to keep an eye on him.

When I was in hospital, I decided to look after my health. Prior to my hospital admission, I had not been enjoying work due to some internal differences at management level. Whilst in hospital it had been suggested that I return to work as soon as I was released. But I declined. With the concerns of my family at the centre, I decided that for the sake of my own health and recovery, I needed to take some time out over Christmas and New Year to get back to full fitness. As a result, I resigned as a director and employee of ZLX.

It probably wasn't the best financial decision that I've ever made, but it was time for me to take some responsibility. I had been given a sign, and I firmly believed that someone was looking after me. It was time to pay them back and to give some recognition to them. And while this was challenging for me – it broke the habit of a lifetime – I'm sure and steadfast that it'll prove to be the correct decision going forward.

Not working afforded me time to help out a former team-mate from my Dundee days, John McPhail. John had fallen down the stairs at home, but he hadn't been as fortunate as me. He ended up in a coma and when he emerged from it, he had brain damage and issues with his mobility. John was still in hospital, so I helped to arrange auctions and dinners to raise much needed funds to carry out building work to allow him to get home.

John was a centre-back, and after making his Dundee debut in a 3-0 defeat against Rangers at Ibrox in April 1976, he went on to play 84 times in dark blue. He was a real character and I recall a couple of special stories about him.

When I went to Dundee on loan from Arsenal, Gordon Strachan took me under his wing and made me feel welcome. He had a wicked sense of humour which he retained throughout his playing career and his time as a manager. He was also an exceptional player whose low centre of gravity made him unplayable at times. It was no surprise to me that he went on to have such a great career.

One thing that Gordon and I had in common was toe injuries. In professional football, injuries are inevitable, and in virtually every match that I played, I had opposition players stamping the studded heal of their boot into the front of mine. The pain was excruciating and to this day both my big toes are still black as a result of having those steel studs driven into my foot.

Gordon was also regularly stamped on as he patrolled the middle of the park. Indeed, the impact on his feet was so severe that he unfortunately had to have both his big toenails surgically removed. The thought of that operation makes me recoil as the pain must have been unbearable. In the end the wee man had to have his toes taped and padded up before each game. He was brave and talented in equal measure.

On the first day of my month-long loan, Gordon asked me if I played table tennis as there was a table in one of the Dens Park lounges. I said that I did and proudly boasted that I had played regularly on the table they had at Arsenal. Gordon took me deep into the bowels of the stadium after training and as we entered a lounge, I could hear the unmistakeable sounds of a table tennis ball being pinged back and forth.

Unbeknown to me a challenge beckoned. My boast of being a seasoned table tennis player saw Gordon match me up for an encounter with Dundee's top table tennis player, John McPhail. A fiver per game was the agreed stake.

I was handed a table tennis paddle and soon I was staring down the table at a handsome big fellow flashing a welcoming smile. John was nicknamed 'Lazlo', and I knew that I was in for a thrashing when John gripped his paddle with a backward Japanese grip. John was a magnificent player and he ran me ragged. I dashed back and forth and fought valiantly, but John won 21-17.

"Another fiver?" asked Strachan who was revelling in his role as promoter. My pride was dented, but although the odds were stacked against me, I was a fighter who never threw in the towel. The gauntlet was thrown down, but Lazlo pipped me again, 21-16 this time.

But my grit and determination, two traits that served me well in my football and business career, came to the fore again. John and I played two more games and I ended up going home £20 lighter in my pocket. I later found out that this was a regular occurrence at Dens Park, Strachan would set the encounter up, McPhail would win and the duo would split the winnings.

When I signed permanently for Dundee, John, Gordon, and I were inseparable on and off the park. John knew when to mix it, but he had a touch of class too, and he could pass the ball very well from the back. He also wore his shorts as high as he could.

John and I also had another thing in common, our affection for Rangers. John's hero was another sophisticated and elegant centre-back, Ronnie Mackinnon. When I told him Ronnie and his twin brother Donnie, were relatives of mine, we became even closer.

Big John liked his cars too and one day I asked him where he got them from. "From a friend of mine called Willie Douglas," said John. "He got me my [Toyota] Celica, do you want me to ask him what he's got in stock?"

I should have learned my lesson after the ping pong pounding, but I said, "Yes that would be great, Lazlo." The following week, Lazlo took me to Willie's garage after training. A red Fiat 124 Sport sat resplendent on the forecourt.

"Have a test drive," shouted Willie, "its only done 60,000 miles."

I walked around the car and, on the side, away from view there was a huge hole in the metalwork above the rear wheel. "Don't worry about that, Davie, I'll get a bit of Cataloy on it, and it'll be good as new. £600 and the car is yours."

I returned the next week with Lazlo to collect the car, but the following week, the windscreen wipers stopped working. I asked Lazlo to speak to Willie to see if he could rectify the problem and the next day Lazlo arrived at training carrying a large bin bag.

John informed me that Willie was on the lookout for a new motor to drive the wipers, but in the meantime, he had a temporary fix. John handed me the bin bag, but I was confused when I opened the bag and found a knife and six large baking potatoes.

"What's this, Lazlo?" I asked with a perplexed look on my face.

At that point, John replied, "Willie said until he finds the motor you've to carry the bag with you and if it rains, you've to pull in, cut a potato in half and rub it on the windscreen. The juice of the tattie will clear the windscreen of rain. Trust me, Willie's a genius."

A week later, in mid-November, we were due to play an away game against Dumbarton at Boghead. I decided to travel home to Renfrew after training on the Friday, as that would allow me to have a lie in before the game. But as I left Dens Park, the rain started to cascade down. I pulled into a layby on the Kingsway and went to the boot to retrieve the bin bag with the 'magic' potatoes.

As the rain came down in torrents, I cut a potato in half and rubbed it over the windscreen. The oily sap from the potato put a thin covering over the glass and the rain started to run down into the bonnet gutter. It seemed Willie was indeed a genius!

I got back behind the wheel and slowly pulled out onto what was now a busy southbound carriageway. But the view from the driver's position wasn't as good as I'd anticipated as the slimy film left by the residue from the potato made it difficult to navigate my position in the inside lane. I decided that I needed to exercise caution, so I slowed down to around 25 miles per hour.

Perhaps I hadn't applied the potato properly, so I decided to pitstop in Perth and phone Willie's garage. I parked the car, located a telephone box, dialled his number, and put 10p in the coin slot. When Willie answered, his Dundee drawl was unmistakeable.

"Hello, Willie," I said. "It's Davie."

"Aye, Davie, what can I do for ye?" replied Willie.

I told Willie about my potato predicament.

"Huv ye wiped the windae first, Davie?" asked Willie.

"No, Willie, I just put it on," I replied.

"That's yir problem, Davie," said Willie. "Yiv put the sap on top of grease so it's no wonder ye canny see. Have you got a cloth in yir boot?" I did, so I asked Willie what to do next. There was an audible sigh on the other end of the line.

Willie told me to pull into the bus station and drive the car into a covered bus bay to get out of the rain. I had then to spend 10 minutes clearing and drying the window and then cut another potato. When I was sure the window was clean, I had to rub the potato up, down and across the window and then give it five minutes before driving. At that point, the phone went dead as Willie hung up.

I knew the bus station was beside the railway station as I'd seen it on the occasions that I'd travelled up to Dundee by train. But as I drove into the concourse, I heard a shrill blast on a whistle and saw a bus inspector make a beeline towards me.

He stood in front of the car and gestured for me to stop. I stopped and got out of the car.

"Yi canny bring a motor into the bus station, son, it's buses only," he shouted above the racket of the rain. But then he recognised me.

"You're Davie Mackinnon that plays with the Dees!" he exclaimed. "How do you think we'll do tomorrow? My names Jimmy and I'm a Dee through and through. I live in Fintry," he added proudly.

Although this was only my fifth year as a professional footballer, I knew that being a footballer could open up many doors with fans. I was delighted that I'd met a Dundee supporter in the midst of the territory belonging to our near neighbours and rivals, St Johnstone.

I explained my predicament to Jimmy and he thought for a moment before answering. "Follow me and drive into the building on the right, Davie, my mate Geordie's the head mechanic and he'll see what he can do. He's a mad Dundee supporter too, so you'll be in good hands."

I got back into the car and slowly followed Jimmy as he walked with his hands outstretched as if he was a shepherd protecting his flock. As he reached the open door of the building, he stepped to one side and ushered me in. I pulled the car inside the doors, switched off the engine and jumped out into the large, floodlit room.

Jimmy moved towards a short man dressed in blue overalls.

I assumed this must be Geordie. The pair huddled together and eventually Jimmy walked over and introduced me to Geordie and assured me that I'd soon be back on the road to Renfrew.

"Ah Davie," said Geordie thrusting his greasy hand into mine. "I saw you score the winner against East Fife last month, you're doing well, son."

"Thanks, Geordie, I'm loving it," I replied.

"Right," said Geordie, "Jimmy's told me about the potato. Is your car guy Willie Douglas that owns Bridgefoot Services?"

"He is, Geordie," I answered with a smile as I was starting to feel that I was in good hands.

"I live near him in Strathmartine," said Geordie. "He's a good man is Willie. We go back a long way and I taught him that trick. But the windscreen needs to be prepared before it works."

At that Geordie went over to his bench and pulled out a bottle. "This is rubbing alcohol," he said as he flicked off the screw cap. "I mix this with filtered water in this spray bottle."

He soon had the two ingredients together inside the spray bottle and started to shake the bottle like he was making a cocktail. He then wiped the last remnants of potato from the window, sprayed the mixture onto the windscreen and started moving the fluid around, cleaning the window.

After 10 minutes he stopped rubbing and pulled out a clean cloth from his overalls and wiped the window until it screeched.

"That's it ready for the potato, Davie," he said. He turned towards the door and handed me the spray bottle. "You do the same as I did if you need to use the potato again, Davie."

"I'll do it now," I said, but there was no need. I looked outside, the rain had stopped and the sky was bathed in blue!

I thanked Jimmy and Geordie for their kindness and said that I'd leave them two complimentary tickets for our next home game against Hamilton the following week.

In all my time in football, I have met some incredible people. Fans are the lifeblood of our game and at times, they deserve to be treated better. Jimmy and Geordie were typical of the wonderful treatment that players receive from supporters. In my day players were closer to their fanbase, but there is a growing disconnect now. That's a real shame. The fans deserve to have that engagement and the players would feel better for the experience too.

I left Perth with the sun shining and arrived at my mother's home in Renfrew an hour and a half later. We went on to draw against Dumbarton 0-0, but my two knights in shining armour had a positive day at Dens the following week, when goals from Billy Williamson, Jim Shirra, and Eric Sinclair, gave us a comprehensive 3-0 victory against Hamilton Academical in front of a crowd of 6,686.

A few years later, I played against Lazlo when Kilmarnock faced Sunderland in a pre-season friendly at Rugby Park, six weeks after my spot kick against Cowdenbeath had earned Kilmarnock promotion.

Lazlo, who had left Dundee in February 1979 and enjoyed successful stints at Sheffield United and Bristol City, was now with the Wearsiders, and was in the team for the pre-season game. As fate would have it, the game stood at 1-1 when Kilmarnock were awarded a penalty. Still brimming with confidence after despatching the crucial promotion penalty, I grabbed the ball and placed it on the spot. Tommy Gemmell's mantra came to the forefront again and I struck the ball as hard as I could. It flew unerringly into the postage stamp corner to win us the game.

As I gathered the ball to walk back to the half-way line, I passed Lazlo. "Tommy Gemmell?" he asked. It transpired that John had also made use of the same penalty kick strategy during his career and scored numerous penalties. Fate can be a funny thing!

As 2023 dawned, it had been nearly a year since the almost fatal fall that ironically saved my life. I resolve that this year will be a better one.

The research study that I'm involved with has yet another top doctor involved. And as we work together, I continue to marvel at the work done by our NHS. I won't hear anyone say anything negative about it and as a nation we should be grateful that we have such conscientious and talented medical staff.

My MRI has determined that my electrical heart issue called arrhythmia requires attention. I do some digging and find that the medical definition of arrhythmia is an irregular heartbeat that occurs when the electrical signals that coordinate the beats of the heart don't work properly. The faulty signalling causes the heart to either beat too fast (tachycardia), too slow (bradycardia) or irregularly.

In my case my heart generally beats too slowly but occasionally irregularly. For one of the tests, I wore a heart monitor for three days, including during the night when I was asleep. The monitor recorded a low of 42 beats per minute which rose to 167 beats per minute.

The doctor said that I may have had the condition for a long time, perhaps even since birth. For a guy who played 20 years as a professional and pushed myself to the physical limit during pre-season and over the course of countless campaigns at home and in Europe, I never once had my heart evaluated or monitored during my career. In that respect, I count myself lucky to have survived while others haven't been so fortunate.

Since my fall, I have been convinced that someone was looking after me, and this was further reinforced by another strange episode. The night before my visit to analyse the results of the MRI, my wife and I went to bed as normal around 10 p.m.

At 3 a.m. we were woken up by the TV coming on and illuminating the room. As I sat up, I felt my heart racing and a powerful pain pushing down on my chest. I had been given a GTN spray for such an occasion and immediately sprayed it under my tongue. Within 10 minutes the pain eased and I felt comfortable enough to try and go back to sleep. I tried to settle down but the TV coming on was still at the forefront of my mind.

I thought I must have rolled over and hit a button on the remote control. To reassure myself that was what had happened, I put the light back on and attempted to locate the remote. But it wasn't in my bed, it was sitting on the dressing table a few feet away. I guess I'll never know how it happened, but I was thankful that it did.

On 31 January 2023, I met with a cardiologist. He was very thorough in his assessment and concluded that the MRI scan that I had in December suggested that my heart issue may not be arrythmia, but a rare condition called sarcoidosis that causes scarring on organs in the body. My scans had identified scarring in the heart muscles. The general condition for this is labelled cardiomyopathy.

The good news was that if this was the cause of my heart issues, then specific drug treatment could sort it quickly. In order to confirm this, I needed another scan called a CT-PET scan which gives detailed pictures of each area of the body to see if any of my other organs had been affected.

My health had been deteriorating in the weeks prior to the scan, so the doctor had prescribed more heart medication. The dip in my health had an impact on my mental health and well-being too, so getting the news that the end was in sight and that they may have a course of action to help cure the issue was uplifting. As I write this, I am becoming more confident that I will get back to good health and that my energy levels will return to what they once were.

When I was in hospital a nurse from another ward took the time to come and see me. She had the same heart issues as I have and she said once that she had treatment, she was able to run 10k on a regular basis. I laughed, as it didn't matter how much energy I regained, five operations on my knees meant my days pounding the pavements and parks as a runner were long gone.

I was grateful that this nurse had taken time to come and share the positive experience of her recovery. The year since my fall has been a rollercoaster ride of emotions and challenges, but I have been humbled by the support that I've had from my wife, family, friends, people I didn't even know, and the great people who work for the NHS. We live in a world where at times there is a lot of ill-feeling, but there are some very kind people out there. Their supportive words and actions have played a key role in lifting my flagging spirits at various points of my recovery.

My wife has always been incredibly supportive but in this recovery period she has been a rock. My fall had caused my brain to almost shut down, and as it reset, she has had to deal with the changes in my personality. But she has never wavered and was always there by my side, raising my spirits on a daily basis.

I also have a special word for Satty Singh, a gentleman who has hosted and entertained several US presidents, as well as a host of celebrities in his Glasgow restaurant, Mr Singh's India. In the last few years, he has re-established his Sikh faith and has regularly said prayers for my recovery, even doing so at the Golden Temple in the Punjab. He has also given me an insight into Karma. I have always been aware of people who have bad Karma, and those who have good Karma. Satty lives his life looking to give positive Karma to everything that he does and is an inspiration and an example of how to treat people the right way. His support also provided a welcome boost to my spirits as I travelled along the bumpy road to recovery.

Throughout that period, I have taken great comfort and solace in the fact that everything happens for a reason. Reflecting now on some of the negative experiences that have cropped up during my life, I know that they needed to happen to allow me to plot my way along the pathway that I have chosen. And I know too that, more often than not, a negative experience will invariably be followed by a positive one.

Life isn't easy. We all have to endure hard challenges at times and there are several occasions when it appears that there is no way out. But these challenges are thrown our way to help shape us; I have found that developing a mindset that troubled times will soon get better allows us to draw incredible strength.

Writing this book has proved cathartic. It has allowed me to revisit and reflect on my life, my football career, and my life in business, while helping to exorcise some demons too. I'm not fully recovered yet, but I'm a lot further into the journey than I thought I would be at various junctures since my fall.

Putting pen to paper and taking time to contemplate my life has brought to the fore several things that everyone reading this might seek to take on board:

Life is precious and is for living.

Things happen for a reason and whilst it may not be clear at the time, it will show itself eventually.

Think positively, even if the challenges that you face seem insurmountable.

Good times will follow bad times.

Look after the people that matter to you and support you.

Ditch the people who use you for their own ends and only contact you when they think you can open a door.

Don't beat yourself up and learn to love and respect your self.

Never give up.

Reflect and relive your memories and achievements and look back regularly at how far you've come on life's journey.

If you need to change career, do so with confidence as experience and life skills are transferable.

Believe that someone is looking after you.

Enjoy and cherish life and embrace whatever it throws your way.

Thanks to my medication, I can now walk longer distances and go back to the gym, but at 67 years of age, I don't know how long I have left on God's green earth. But as I continue to recover from my head and heart issues, I'll remain positive and use the time that I have left to bring happiness to those around me. Who knows, I might even get the trainers back on and try a 10k!

# EPILOGUE

*June 2023*

IT IS NOW 16 months since my accident. I'm continuing my recovery but haven't yet found out what the root cause of my heart issue is. It's been a year since it was discovered that all wasn't well with my heart, but today I finally get the answers that I have been looking for.

This morning I received a letter from the Clinical Genetics department at the Queen Elizabeth University Hospital. Contained inside the envelope were the results of DNA testing carried out three months ago. The tests have determined that I have an inherited gene variant, MYH7, which is likely to explain my irregular heart function. I have now been diagnosed as having cardiomyopathy.

The official explanation is:

*Mutations in the MYH7 gene are a common cause of familial hypertrophic cardiomyopathy, accounting for up to 35 percent of all cases. This condition is characterized by thickening (hypertrophy) of the cardiac muscle. HCM (Familial hypertrophic cardiomyopathy) is one of the leading causes of sudden death in adolescents and athletes.*

As I read the letter, I feel strangely relieved. The treatment I will now undergo should see me return to some sort of semblance of normality. The support that I received throughout from the medical professionals has been superb, and I will be eternally grateful for that.

Although I count myself very fortunate that I now have a diagnosis, unanswered questions continue to swill around my head and dominate my thoughts:

*When did this start affecting my heart?*

*Was I lucky to survive the strain and pressure that my football career put on my heart?*

*Why, in 20 years as a player, did I not have one medical test for heart functionality?*

*How many current players out there are walking a tightrope every time they train or play?*

*How many former players are unaware that they may have this timebomb in their DNA?*

*What can we do to get compulsory heart screening back to the front of the agenda?*

As far back as January 2008, the *Glasgow Herald* reported under the headline 'SFA wants to bring in compulsory heart tests for players.'

Following the sudden and tragic death of former Scotland international and Motherwell captain Phil O'Donnell, who died after collapsing during Saturday's Clydesdale Bank Premier League game against Dundee United, it was understood that the 35-year-old is likely to have suffered a little-known heart condition known as hypertrophic cardiomyopathy – a genetic disorder where the heart muscle thickens, making it harder for it to work. Experts say it is the leading killer of young athletes in the US. A post-mortem examination revealed O'Donnell suffered left ventricular failure of the heart.

The SFA's medical consultant, Professor Stewart Hillis, added that he wanted Scotland to follow Italy's lead in making annual heart checks compulsory. It would mean all footballers would be subject to a yearly echocardiogram - a test in which ultrasound is used to examine the heart. This would be discussed at a meeting of the SFA medical committee next month.

I knew Stewart Hillis well. He was a dedicated and supportive man but he sadly died in 2014 without his desire for compulsory heart checks to be implemented. I'm also fortunate to know his successor Dr John Maclean, having worked with him on my journey from player to executive. John has the same empathetic and skillful qualities as Professor Hillis and his support will be a key driver in getting this back on the agenda. Dr John now runs the Hampden sports clinic, which encourages, among other services, Scotland's football clubs to have their players screened for potential heart issues. Whilst many take advantage of the service to protect their players' welfare, there are others that don't, mainly down to cost or lack of knowledge of the issue. A funded compulsory service has to be the objective and I'm delighted that Dr John has indicated he would get involved in the discussion.

I have also discovered that a charity called CRY, (Cardiac Risk in the Young) is doing sterling work throughout the UK in providing free heart testing for young adults between the ages of 14 to 35. Since their inception in 1995, they have tested around 300,000 young adults with 1 in 300 identified as having heart issues.

I spoke earlier about the National Football League (NFL) monitoring programme of current and ex-players. The FA in England has indicated that all players up to the age of 25 will be screened regularly. These screenings are to reduce the risk of sudden cardiac arrest. This has come about after research conducted by a team of expert cardiologists identified that sudden cardiac death in elite footballers is much higher than anticipated. The study group screened over 11,000 young footballers over a 20-year period. They completed a health questionnaire and took part in a physical examination to assess if they had any visible abnormalities in their heart. The study showed:

Eight individuals died due to a sudden cardiac arrest during exercise. None of these players had symptoms. This incidence is considerably higher than previous estimates of sudden cardiac death in athletes. Importantly, of these eight players, six had shown normal ECG's and echocardiograms at their screening aged 16.

The major cause of sudden cardiac death in this study was cardiomyopathy, which is an abnormality of heart muscle. Before an Academy player signs a professional contract at the age of 16, they must undergo mandatory heart screening test. But the results of this study have prompted the FA to mandate that additional screening should be performed at the ages of 18, 20 and 25 to monitor heart health as players mature. The study's other main findings were:

One in 226 players were found to have heart disorders associated with sudden cardiac death. Reassuringly, almost three quarters of them have been able to resume their playing career following clinical assessment and/or corrective surgery.

One in 50 players had other heart abnormalities detected that required ongoing monitoring.

But whilst this screening programme is commendable, there appears to be no plans to screen players beyond 25 years of age, and certainly no plans to screen former players. And although the Scottish FA have the best of intentions in rolling out something similar, my experience as a club executive makes me think that this testing is not going to be across the board.

I discovered that I had cardiomyopathy as a result of DNA

clinical genetics testing, which identified the alteration in a gene called MYH7. Without that test, I would never have known that I had this potentially fatal condition.

This is a problem and further discussions are essential. This testing needs to take place across the board and funding needs to be made available. I am one of the lucky ones, who through the diligence and support of a team of NHS doctors, has had the necessary investigative testing carried out before the condition ended my life.

But there are a number of former players going about their daily business who potentially have cardiomyopathy that hasn't been detected. Without treatment, they may die. That's unsatisfactory and needs to be addressed urgently.

Since my diagnosis, I have spoken to several influential sources; doctors, football associations, media, and government officials. I believe that by bringing this group together, we can work on a strategic plan to develop a screening process to ensure this situation is finally addressed. This is my quest.

I have also spoken to an ex-player who has just undergone pacemaker surgery to sort a diagnosis on Arrhythmia. He is a key mover within a UEFA agency and he wants to assist in sorting. As word spreads this will increase awareness and allow us to ensure screening is in place.

I've been fortunate to have experienced many memorable victories during my career as a professional footballer. But if my book can spread the word about this condition and stimulate action that will save the lives of others in the profession, then those will all pale into insignificance. That would be the best result ever!

There is one further potential crazy outcome that has identified itself as a result of my desire to find out more about my background and ancestry. I'm sure at many times we've all asked ourselves, where did I come from and what DNA line makes me the person I am? With that in my mind, aligned to my mortality question, I decided to research my ancestry through an online research platform. Whilst I won't be dining out on it's findings or contacting King Charles for some land just yet, it has thrown up a direct lineage from my dad's mother, born Helen Davidson, to King James 1st of Scotland. My gran's sister was the gran of my cousin Murdo Macleod, and he suggested we engage a genealogist to confirm or dispel. Now there's a future story. . .

# Acknowledgments

During my life, I've been very fortunate to have had the support of many people. This was never more important than during the long recovery from my accident; and many stepped up to the mark. I would not be here to tell the story if it wasn't for the support I received.

My wonderful wife, who daily acted as a nurse to tend to my wounds, raised my spirits and mental health, and gave me love and motivation in my recovery process. I could not have got through it without her. She is an incredible woman, and I am blessed to have her in my life.

I have a great family and four wonderful children whom I'm extremely proud of. Kirsty, Eilidh, John and Robbie each played their own unique part in my recovery and my loving thanks go to them.

We in this country are very fortunate to have the support of an incredibly hard-working National Health Service, and I witnessed first-hand the compassionate and professional way they go about their business. From the paramedics who initially attended to me and ensured I reached hospital with a chance, to the sixteen doctors and nurses at Edinburgh Royal Infirmary who saved my life, I am indebted.

On the path to recovery, I was hugely fortunate to have the support of many eminent doctors in neuroscience, cardiology, and psychology, each one analysing and dissecting each test and putting in place a recovery solution. Each one though happy to have helped but professionally requesting anonymity. Thanks to all of you.

In writing this book, I was able to call on someone I met whist contributing to his book *Rangers FC in the 1980s - The Players Stories*. Alistair Aird has become a friend and his concise and highly professional editing of this book has brought it to another level. Thanks Alistair.

Thanks to the following people for providing my career stats: Andy Kelly (www.thearsenalhistory.com), The Dee Archive, William Sheridan (The Thistle Archive), John Henderson (Airdrie FC Historian), and John Livingston (Kilmarnock).

Great thanks must also go to the sponsors of this book, good business and football people:

Stuart Blyth, owner of onlydo.online, whose management company supports businesses through courses aligned to the principles of football management and strategy. A football guy who has combined his love of the game with developing a very successful business strategy.

Neil Duncan, the Chief Operating Officer of Clearwater waste management services, is a man I have only recently been introduced to.

During my long career both on and off the park, I have been able to quickly establish the credibility of people I am introduced to.

On introduction to Neil I quickly established that not only is he a personable and engrossing individual, but he also shares the same principles of business management as I do in respect and inclusion.

I am delighted that Neil has chosen to support me with the book, and I look forward to developing a long partnership with him and Clearwater.

Stevie Marlow of ubsolutions.co.uk, the experts in HMRC innovation capture. I've known Stevie for over 30 years, and he is a football man who is a great commercial supporter of Glasgow Rangers FC.

From my football career, I have mentioned many people in the book, but I would like to highlight them again: The late Alan Ball for giving me direction. Pat Rice for his empathy in helping a young player to understand the art of defending. The late Jackie Husband for saving my career. And Ranger's greatest ever player John Greig for his kind words in the foreword and for having the desire to sign me all those years ago.

I'd like to thank my publishers, Morgan Lawrence: Mathew Mann, Barrie Pierpoint, Lois Hide, Lee Clark, Peter Andrews, Harry Worgan and Lorne Gardner.

Finally, I'd like to thank the supporters of all the clubs I have been fortunate enough to have represented.

# Thank you to my Sponsors

This book is only possible because of the generous support from my sponsors.

# Urban Business Solutions

Spanning more than thirty years, our friendship began when David was a footballer with Partick Thistle before moving onto Glasgow Rangers.

On and off the pitch, David is loyal, dedicated, and passionate. These characteristics stood him in good stead when undertaking the challenge of segueing into a new, and what has become, successful career in commerce following his retirement from professional football. In acknowledgement of such achievements in the business world over the years, I am pleased to have worked closely with David over the last 5 years.

With these attributes, David is an asset to any company and Long may our professional endeavours and friendship continue. David MacKinnon, a good human being, a loyal friend, and an author worth a read.

UBS offers a range of specialist services from tax relief to green energy infrastructure capital to UK businesses. Services are tailored to meet individual business needs by maximising investment opportunities whilst ensuring financial relief.

Find out more at www.ubsolutions.co.uk

Director Steven Marlow
steven@ubsolutions.co.uk
07498 921083

URBAN BUSINESS SOLUTIONS

# onlydo.online

I'd crossed paths with David at various events, but I only really got to know him after the Covid pandemic, and I'm delighted to be sponsoring *Slide Tackles and Boardroom Battles*.

I remember David as a footballer because of his single mindedness and resilience; skills that helped him to switch careers when his playing days were over. David and I think very much alike when it comes to building teams and so we are collaborating on a number of interesting projects.

David's fascinating story is one of overcoming challenges. All businesses have challenges; the key to success is about solving them. At onlydo.online, the challenge we solve is helping business put the right people in the right roles.

As football fans, we all know which players we'd pick in each position. We all know who we'd sign and who we'd sell. But when it comes to business, when it comes to our employees, we aren't as clear as to what we want them to do and how we can help them to achieve it.

As the head coach would say, "Big man, just put the ball into the back of the net."

We all know that for that to happen, the 'big man' needs to receive the ball in the right place in a way that he can score.

That's where onlydo.online come in. We help companies build successful, productive teams as if you are the head coach.

Building your business and your team doesn't happen by accident. You need a strategy and a framework to get you there – just like the head coach of your favourite sports team.

But remember, "Only do what only you can do."

Stuart Blyth
Building Dream Teams for Businesses

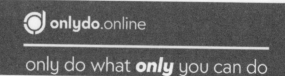

# DAVID MACKINNON

# Clearwater

www.clearwaterltd.com

# Youth statistics

| | Appearances | Goals |
|---|---|---|
| **Arsenal** <br> 1972—1976 | 152 | 5 |
| **Total** | 152 | 5 |

# Senior statistics

| | Appearances | Goals |
|---|---|---|
| **Dundee** <br> 1976—1978 | 56 | 4 |
| **Partick Thistle** <br> 1978—1982 | 143 | 0 |
| **Rangers** <br> 1982—1986 | 177 | 4 |
| **Airdrieonians** <br> 1986—1989 | 112 | 3 |
| **Kilmarnock** <br> 1989—1991 | 68 | 3 |
| **Forfar** <br> 1991—1992 | 30 | 1 |
| **Total** | 586 | 15 |

# Honours

| | | |
|---|---|---|
| Rangers | League Cup Winners | 1984 & 1985 |
| Kilmarnock | Division 2 Promotion | 1991 |

David won one cap for the Scottish League. This came against the Irish League at Windsor Park in Belfast on 18 March 1980. The Scottish League won 4-2.

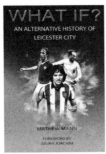

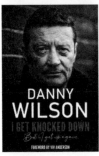

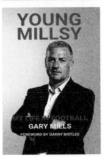
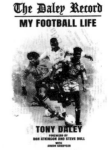